ALL *for* ONE

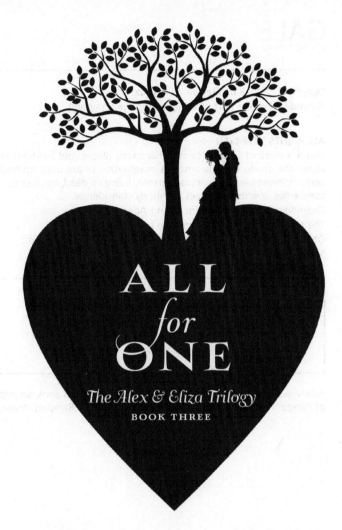

ALL
for
ONE

The Alex & Eliza Trilogy

BOOK THREE

MELISSA DE LA CRUZ

THORNDIKE PRESS

A part of Gale, a Cengage Company

LIBRARY OF CONGRESS CIP DATA ON FILE.
CATALOGUING IN PUBLICATION FOR THIS BOOK
IS AVAILABLE FROM THE LIBRARY OF CONGRESS

ISBN-13: 978-1-4328-7223-6 (hardcover alk. paper)

Published in 2020 by arrangement with G. P. Putnam's Sons, an imprint of Penguin Publishing Group, a division of Penguin Random House, LLC

Printed in Mexico
Print Number: 01   Print Year: 2020

For Mike and Mattie, always
And for Jen Besser, who believed from the beginning

Answer to the Inquiry Why I Sighed

Before no mortal ever knew
A love like mine so tender, true
Completely wretched — you away,
And but half blessed e'en while you stay.

If present love . . . face
Deny you to my fond embrace
No joy unmixed my bosom warms
But when my angel's in my arms.

— Poem from Alexander Hamilton
to Elizabeth Schuyler,
found in a locket she wore
around her neck until she died

■ ■ ■ ■

PART ONE: SYBARITES AND NEOPHYTES

■ ■ ■ ■

1
HER BROTHER'S KEEPER

New York Harbor
New York, New York
June 1785

To passersby, they must have looked like any other young couple enjoying the bright sun and cool breezes of a June day in New York City. Broadway was crowded with similarly affectionate pairs, arm in arm, or holding hands, or even giving in to the urge to steal a kiss, regardless of who was watching. City Hall Park was in full bloom, and the only odor that could push through the heavenly fragrance of lilac was the salt of New York Harbor, less than a quarter mile away. But unbeknownst to their fellow *flâneurs,* Alexander and Eliza Hamilton were engaged in that most high-stakes of marital negotiations: their social calendar.

"No, no," Eliza admonished Alex as gently she could. "We dine with the Van *Cortlandts* on the morrow. They are in town for just four days. We are seeing the Van *Wycks* on Thursday."

From the corner of her eye, Eliza saw Alex's brow furrow beneath his hat, a narrow-brimmed midnight-blue tricorne that brought out the red in his hair and the twinkle in his pale blue eyes. "But I thought we were dining with John and Sarah on Thursday."

"No, the Jays are Friday," Eliza said as soothingly as possible, regarding him from beneath the brim of her own bonnet, which was a handsome chocolate brown trimmed with pink ribbon that accentuated the apples in her cheeks. She patted her husband's arm as though he were a little boy. For a man who had supervised the schedule of the commander in chief of the Continental army for five years, he had a notoriously hard time remembering whom he was going to have dinner with three days out.

"Friday?" Alex repeated, as though she'd just told him Congress had voted to return the United States to British

12

rule. "Then when are we seeing the Morrises?"

"Do you mean Gouverneur, or Helena Morris that is now Rutherford?" Eliza responded. "We're having Gouverneur and his latest *belle du jour,* Miss Du Pont, to tea a week Saturday," she continued without waiting for her husband to answer, "and taking luncheon with John and Helena at their city residence after services on the Sabbath. Or, no," she corrected herself. "We are joining James Beekman at Mount Pleasant after church. The Rutherfords have had to push back their arrival until Monday, but we have tentative plans to join them for supper."

" 'Tentative plans'?" Alex laughed. "How on earth can such a schedule accommodate a tentative plan? My good wife, you manage our social calendar with more precision than General Washington arranged his parlays! If you were foreign minister to King George or King Louis, there would never be another war in Europe again!"

"As I recall," Eliza said, chuckling, "it was *you* who arranged General Washington's social calendar, which makes it that much more surprising that you cannot keep track of your own." She held up a string purse whose pink ribbon matched her bonnet. "If it makes you feel better, I have everything written down in a little diary I keep with me at all times."

"When I was General Washington's aide, I didn't *have* a social calendar," Alex said, laughing. "All my time was spent racing after him. It is your own fault, my darling," he continued, squeezing Eliza's silk-clad arm with a kid-gloved hand. "You are as impressive a hostess as you are a guest. Everyone wants you in their salon, and if they're not soliciting your presence at their table, then they're begging for a spot at ours."

Eliza blushed prettily at the compliment and allowed a few steps to pass before she answered. Catching a glimpse of herself in a shop window, however, she couldn't help but think that Alex might be right. He in Prussian-blue wool, she in dark rose silk with pink and chocolate accents — they were the picture of urbane, young New York society, and she noticed more than one set of eyes glancing at them both approvingly and enviously.

"Oh, pshaw!" she said at length. "I am naught but the wife of a war hero, who just happens to be the most capable attorney in New York City. If people court my presence, it is only so they can be closer to you." At that, she squeezed his arm to let him know that none could come closer than her.

"Did you just 'pshaw' me, Mrs. Hamilton?"

"I believe I did, Mr. Hamilton."

"That's Colonel Hamilton to you."

Eliza pretended to be shocked. "Of all the cheek —"

Alex soothed her with a kiss. "The only cheek that I'm interested in is the one my lips are pressed against," he murmured.

"Just be sure you don't neglect the other one," Eliza said, touching the opposite side of her face. "It will get jealous."

Alex dutifully leaned across his wife to give her a second kiss, then threw in one on the lips for good measure, and they continued on their way down Broadway. Eliza went on informing him of their social schedule, as Alex shook his head in disbelief at the number of bowls of creamed spinach he would be expected to consume in the next three weeks.

Such was the price of being the most popular couple in town.

Since the smashing going-away party Eliza had thrown for Angelica and John Church last winter, where everyone who was anyone in New York and New Jersey society had been present, the Hamiltons' hall table had been littered with calling cards. To accommodate all the requests, Eliza began hosting Thursday night dinners and Friday night salons, which quickly became the most coveted invitation in town. She was adept at mixing lawyers with painters, businessmen with artists, so the conversation was always knowledgeable and varied, and everyone left feeling like they'd learned a little bit more about how the world functioned, from the workaday business of brewing one's own ale to the exalted labor of forming a new country from the ground up.

For if Eliza provided the culture, Alex provided the politics. His brilliant and compassionate legal defense of Caroline Childress, the widow of a British soldier who'd fought against Continental troops in the War for Independence, not only had made him the most sought-after lawyer in town — the man who could win the unwinnable case — but also led to repeated calls for him to enter politics at the highest level. Several people approached him to run against New York's corpulent, corrupt governor, George Clinton, while others suggested something at the national level — senator, or perhaps foreign minister, should Congress decide to create an executive office. He might even be prime minister or president or whatever title they would bestow on the new leader of the country.

The Hamiltons' combined success had made them the It Couple in New York City. With Eliza's family relations to the Van Rensselaers, Livingstons, Schuylers, and the rest of the New World gentry, and Alex's military and legal connections to General Washington and other heroes of the revolution, there wasn't a soul in

New York who didn't want to meet them, whether to bask in their glory or ride on their coattails. But right now the Hamiltons were on their way to meet someone who meant more to them then all the towheaded Dutchmen and high-collared Anglicans you could stuff in a parlor.

As they turned a corner, the vista opened before them, revealing the clear southern sky over New York Harbor, whose sparkling waters were dotted with masts and brightly colored flags waving in the soft breeze.

"Papa's letter said that Johnny was nervous about the journey down," Eliza said, sounding a bit anxious herself. "It's been such a stormy spring, and apparently he gets seasick, even on a riverboat. Although," she continued, "I must say, *my* stomach feels rather restless this morning. I think Rowena's eggs were a bit underdone at breakfast."

"I found them delicious as always. I think you are just missing your Jenny or Martha, or whatever you called her."

"We just called her Cook," Eliza said.

"No doubt. To a child, she must have

seemed the source of all food, and no eggs, regardless of how well they are scrambled, can possibly taste as good as the ones your Cook made you for the first eighteen years of your life."

Eliza knew Alex had a point, but still, Rowena's omelet had seemed a little runny to her. Rather than linger on breakfast, she tried to focus on her excitement at being reunited with her brother, who was to start at Columbia in a few weeks. Everyone in her family was proud of the university's new name, no longer saddled with the British monarch's title as King's College. Since he was the eldest son, great things were expected of Johnny, and as her parents' representatives here in New York, Eliza understood it was her job to see that he was kept in line. Johnny was also the first child after the sisterly triumvirate of Angelica, Eliza, and Peggy — the first to survive, at any rate — some nine years her junior. Though she was grown now, and he nearly so, she still couldn't help but think of him as the baby she and Angelica and Peggy had fussed over for the first three years of his life, until Philip Jr. came along. They had coddled their brother and made a pet of him, and she knew that he wouldn't stand for runny eggs.

"You will admit that Rowena has been very distracted since Simon went away," she said now. "I do wonder if it was the right decision."

Rowena's son, Simon, had been in training as their footman, but from the start the energetic eleven-year-old showed no aptitude for it. He was an outdoorsy child, preferring bare feet to shod and loose cotton or linen to fitted wool. When, on an errand to the Beekman estate, Mount Pleasant, five miles north of the city, he had gamely assisted the chauffeur in delivering a mare whose foal was breach, Jonas Beekman was so impressed with his performance — both mare and foal pulled through swimmingly — that he offered Simon a job as a groom at a grown man's wages. Rowena had reluctantly agreed to let him go, but took it hard. Simon would have to go live at Mount Pleasant, and, since the death of her husband in the war, she would be all alone.

"The right decision for Rowena?" Alex

now asked pointedly. "Or for you?"

"Oh, don't tease me when my stomach is upset," Eliza said, but she had to admit that, like her mother, she firmly believed that happy servants made for a happy house, or, at any rate, that a house in which the staff was miserable would share in their pain. Fires would go out, dust would accumulate, the eggs would separate on the plate. And as the thought of them returned, her insides churned anew.

"Well, the nephew should be here next week," Alex said. "What's his name again?"

"Drayton," Eliza said. Drayton Pennington was the eldest child of one of Rowena's sisters. He was said to be a hale lad of seventeen, though Rowena had not seen him in nearly a decade: The Penningtons had moved to the Ohio Territory to avoid the war. They transformed a considerable bit of land into a farmstead, but it was still essentially wilderness, and Nigella, Rowena's sister, had written that Drayton seemed somehow "cut of an urban cloth." He knew his letters and read every book he could get his

21

hands on, was even better at math, and, owing to a dearth of sisters, was remarkably spry with needle and thread.

"Drayton and Johnny, both arriving within a week. Our household will be incredibly full."

"Not *too* full," Eliza said, patting her all too flat stomach.

"There, there, my dear," Alex said, squeezing his wife's arm tenderly. "It will come."

After Alex's momentous victory in court last year — and the settlement fee — the Hamiltons had at last felt ready to start a family of their own. But eight months of "carefully coordinated activity," as Eliza had referred to it in a recent letter to her mother, produced nothing in the way of nascent Hamiltons. In an earlier letter, Mrs. Schuyler asked why Eliza had not joined her two sisters in giving her a grandchild to spoil, and, in a rare moment of candor, pointed out that the activity in question was not without its own charms: "You and Alex should persevere, and take pleasure in the perseverance," she concluded. Eliza had thought the page in her hands would spontaneously combust when she read those words, but it was just her cheeks burning. And yet, her mother's disappointment did not compare to Eliza's greater one. Her wish for a child was much too painful at this point.

"Having Johnny here will be almost like having a child I suppose. Though he is nearly grown, Mama says that he is as headstrong as Cornelia, who is not even five," she told her husband.

Alex stifled a groan. "I hope he is ready for school. Columbia is fast becoming one of the best universities in the country — I heard enrollment will reach nearly twenty students this year, and they have brought on a fifth professor! It will be big change for a boy used to studying with his brothers and a tutor in the schoolroom."

"How hard can it be? They let *you* in," Eliza teased. "Although as I recall, you didn't stay around to graduate."

"Hmmm," Alex mused. "*I* seem to recall a little revolution getting in the way."

"Excuses, excuses."

Alex chuckled. "At any rate, I'm less

concerned about Johnny's ability to handle the classwork than the distractions of the city. New York is a far cry from Albany. There are theaters and parties and museums and visitors from a score of countries all vying for a young man's attention."

"And girls," Eliza said. "Don't forget the girls."

"And girls," Alex agreed. "But I trust the formidable Mrs. Schuyler will have imbued her eldest son with a firm sense of decorum and probity."

"Well, let's see," Eliza said. "Of her three eldest daughters, the first eloped with a man rumored to have fled debtor's prison — and possibly a wife — in England, the third was engaged for nearly a decade before she *finally* got her intended to commit to a wedding, and the second, ahem" — Eliza goosed her husband's arm — "ran away from her fiancé at the altar to marry a boy from the Indies with no name."

"I take exception to that statement," Alex pretended to protest. "The name Hamilton is one of great distinction. My grandfather is an earl or duke or laird or something in the old country."

"Well then, yours is the worst Scottish accent I have ever heard in my life," Eliza said with a giggle. "It's not even a good Caribbean accent, for that matter. And the very fact that you don't even know your grandfather's title calls into question your claims of aristocratic lineage. Correct me if I'm wrong, but you never even met your *father,* let alone your grandfather."

Eliza suddenly caught herself, worried that she'd gone too far, as she knew her husband was sensitive about his background. But Alex only laughed, if a bit cynically.

"And a good thing, too, lest I ended up following in that incorrigible man's footsteps." Shortly after Alex was born, his father had abandoned his mother and never reappeared in his young sons' lives, even after Rachel, Alex's mother, succumbed to yellow fever when he was eleven.

"Well," Eliza said soothingly. "You seem to have done pretty well on your own."

"On my own? No, my darling. Whatever I have and whatever I've accomplished, I owe half of it to you. Without your constancy and steadiness, I would be nowhere."

"Goodness," Eliza said, though she blushed with pride. "I'm not sure if you're describing a wife or a saddle pony upon which one might teach a child of five to canter. Oof!" she added as Alex pulled her into a bear hug and covered her face in butterfly kisses. "The corset's bad enough after Rowena's eggs. Don't squeeze so hard!"

The two continued their banter for the next hour as they made their roundabout way to the docks on the Hudson River. It was a glorious day at the beginning of summer, the sky as blue as Delft tiles and the mercury hovering in the mid-seventies. Horses' hooves and wagon wheels clattered over the rutted roads with the insistent jangle of commerce — it hadn't rained in nearly a week and the dirt was baked hard as bricks. The streets and sidewalks were alive with tradesmen and women hawking their wares, and servants and messengers hurrying about their masters' business. Wheat and corn from the fields of upper New York State, tin and pewter from Pennsylvania, cotton from the southern states, fragrant spices and sugar from the Caribbean and farther afield: With a population of thirty thousand, New York had surged past Boston and Philadelphia to become the young nation's largest city, and virtually anything you desired could be had there, and at any price, from the cheapest bits of dented, tarnished flatware to the most exquisite silks and china (these safely ensconced behind store windows, but still easily visible from the broad wooden sidewalks of lower Manhattan).

The sun had just passed its zenith when they emerged on the river just above New York Harbor. The Hudson was more than a mile wide here, an impressive, flat, gray highway upon which ran hundreds of boats, from the tiniest oared dinghies to ships of the line measuring nearly two hundred feet. The mail ship from Albany was a single-masted, heavy-bellied vessel that sat low in the water, and it took a few minutes before the Hamiltons were able to make it out amid the larger merchantmen at dock.

When they spied it, Eliza hurried forward. After dawdling and window-shopping through the city, she was suddenly impatient to see her brother. It had been a year since she'd seen anyone in the family, and two since she'd seen Johnny. Loosing her arm from Alex's elbow and taking his hand instead, she pulled him through the crowd, equally divided between stevedores and porters and other dockworkers, and people like her and Alex, there to greet an arriving loved one or see someone off.

"I can't believe he's really here!" she said excitedly. "I cannot wait to show him the sights! Bayard's Mount and Collect Pond and Federal Hall and Fraunces Tavern. Oh, I do hope he loves the city as much as I do and doesn't miss the country too much!"

"He need only hop on a horse and ride a half mile north of Chambers Street and he'll have all the country he wants. But I suspect he will take to the big city like a fish to water. Johnny has always been a worldly boy," Alex replied.

"You speak as if you know my brother better than I do!" Eliza said. "He is a delicate child! The noise and bustle may be too much for him!"

"A delicate child! As I recall, he took a shot at the British raiding party that came to kidnap your father in the last year of the war. I say New York should look out for *him,* and not the other way around."

"Well, I say *we* should look out for him right now. The pier is so crowded today, I don't know how we'll ever find him."

Alex took a moment to glance around. "I think I have an idea where he might be," he said then, and, taking Eliza's elbow, steered her off to the right.

Eliza peered ahead, but all she saw besides the dockworkers was a group of women crowded in on one another as closely as their bustled skirts and parasols would allow. The way they were huddled together, Eliza assumed they must be inspecting some exotic goods just off a merchantman from the Indies or Europe. *Maybe there'll be oranges!* she thought. Since Jane Beekman had introduced her to the unusual fruit last year, she couldn't get enough of them. Alex recalled them fondly from his youth in the Caribbean, although he said he preferred something he called a "banana." The way he described it made her think he was pulling her leg, but apparently they were quite delicious.

As it happened she was half right. The women, who ranged in age from sixteen to thirty and change, were indeed inspecting a new arrival fresh off the boat. But the merchandise they were haggling over turned out to be —

"John Bradstreet Schuyler!" she cried. Eliza's upset stomach fluttered again as the covey of women whirled around in unison, revealing the slim figure of Eliza's eldest brother, seated on an upended steamer trunk. His cheeks were so red that at first glance Eliza thought they were covered with lip rouge from multiple kisses, but it was just a blush. He sprang to his feet with a sheepish smile even as one of the girls said in an accusatory voice: "John? Why is this *woman* speaking to you?"

Eliza didn't like the way the girl said "this woman." It made her feel as though she were forty years old.

"Johnny," she said in her most commanding older-sister voice, "why is this *girl* speaking to *you*?"

Johnny stepped in, his arms out wide for a hug, but Eliza's look held him back.

Several of the women, sensing a familial authority in Eliza's demeanor, lowered their hackles slightly, though they were still clustered around Johnny as if he were a skittish kid goat and might bolt if they let down their guard. But the boldest one of the pack did not back down and turned to Eliza with her fists on her waist and her chin jutting.

Eliza summoned all the dignity her mother had instilled in her. "He's seventeen," she said serenely. "Maybe you should hunt for something a little closer to your own age."

The woman's jaw dropped open.

"And as for the rest of you, you are free to call on *John* in the proper time and place — which is not a busy dock on a weekday afternoon."

"And what is the 'proper time and place'?" said one of the girls, a rather pretty little thing, Eliza had to admit, though her hair looked a tad dirty beneath its powder, and her dress, which had never been fine, and might even be considered gaudy, was in need of patching.

"I'll leave that up to *John,*" Eliza said. "If you don't mind now, we need to get my brother home."

The girl was ready to ask for her address, but the look on Eliza's face stopped her.

"Come along, ladies," the girl said. "I'm sure the son of General Philip Schuyler won't be that hard to track down. Bye, *John,*" she said, all but throwing him a kiss, and then she and her companions tittered away.

"Check your pockets," Eliza told her brother when they were out of earshot. "Make sure you still have your coin purse."

"Oh, Eliza, please!" Johnny said. "I know they weren't exactly our set, but they were perfectly respectable. Don't be such a snob."

Alex chuckled. "Your sister is the farthest thing from a snob, as you well know. She married a poor man, as she reminded me not twenty minutes ago, and I'm sure would back you if you chose to give your heart to a penniless girl. Nevertheless, those delectable beauties, who just, ah, paid their respects to you, were not doing so merely because they found you a strapping specimen of young manhood."

Johnny looked a bit hurt, and Eliza softened toward her younger brother, of whom she had always been very fond. She was struck by the fact that little Johnny had had quite the growth spurt since the last time the Hamiltons saw him, and stood nearly six feet tall, lean and lanky. His wrists and ankles protruded slightly from his sleeves and pants, which only added to the perception that he was a boy who was not yet a man.

"What do you mean about those ladies?" John said at last, self-consciously pulling at his cuffs to cover the exposed bones of his wrists.

"Let's just say that their time is not exactly free," Eliza said.

John's brow furrowed. "I don't understand."

"Your sister means that if you wanted to continue your, ah, intercourse with them, a certain quid pro quo would have been expected."

"Quid pro quo? You mean . . . payment?" John seemed even more confused. "But payment for what?"

Alex turned to Eliza helplessly, but she only covered her smile with her gloved hand.

Then John's eyes went wide. He whirled toward the crowd of women, who were now descending on their next target in a flurry of silks and laces and titters. Their gloved fingers danced nimbly over the shoulders and arms of their new mark, as they had done on John's just a moment before.

"No! You mean they're —"

"Now, Johnny," Eliza cut him off. "There is no need to name names. Their situation is unfortunate, but we do not have to add indignity by saying it aloud."

"Wow!" John said, even as Alex flagged down a porter and directed him to have John's luggage sent to the Hamiltons' Wall Street home. "My first hour in the city and I've already been solicited! How exciting!"

"Welcome to New York," Eliza said, finally giving her brother that hug. "And I was serious before. Check your pockets and make sure they didn't steal your purse."

2
"Lovely Lasses Left"

Columbia College
New York, New York
June 1785

Since his practice had expanded, Alex moved his law office to a new building just around the block from the Hamiltons' home on the corner of Wall Street and Pine. As a consequence, he was happy to relinquish his study on the second floor to be his brother-in-law's bedroom. The Hamiltons still had another bedroom for guests, and should Alex need privacy he had only to nip out a five-minutes' walk to his own quarters. In fact, he was there, or deeper in the city, at least twelve hours a day, and sometimes more, so he hardly noticed the loss of the room at home, which had mostly become a catch-all for abandoned furniture, Eliza's old dresses, and extra crockery.

The following morning, Alex took his breakfast at home as usual, then went upstairs to give Eliza a kiss before heading to work. It was but eight o'clock when he prepared to leave — early for many people, though late for him. Late for Eliza, too, who usually breakfasted with him before he left, lest, as she said, she didn't "see his face in the daylight." She, Alex, and John had enjoyed a quiet evening at home the night before, but there had been much family news to catch up on, and the talk — and the wine — had flowed liberally until well after midnight, so no wonder she was tired. Johnny, too, was still abed, though as Alex recalled, he had never particularly been a morning person.

When he got upstairs, though, Alex found that Eliza was awake and looking rather wan. He smiled wryly at her as he kissed her forehead, which was warm, though not feverish. "Are you all right, darling?"

In answer, she whimpered a little. "My

stomach was feeling queasy again, as it is now."

Alex thought back to the evening before and remembered that Eliza had in fact picked at her food, declaring the leg of lamb not to Rowena's usual standards. Yet the leg of lamb had been succulently tender. Perhaps Eliza was truly ill.

He pulled a glove off and laid the back of his hand against Eliza's forehead. Warm, yes, but she was well covered by her nightdress, cap, and bedclothes, so that was hardly surprising. There was neither the telltale flush nor perspiration of a fever, and the brightness in Eliza's eyes was the flash of pique — an industrious woman, she hated to laze about — rather than delirium.

"Should I call the doctor? I hate the thought of you being sick."

For the first time that morning Eliza smiled and patted her husband's hand. "I think it's just something I ate. I really must speak to Rowena about taking more care at market. I don't know how you managed to eat so much of that lamb last night. Why, I wondered if it had been fresh when she bought it, it tasted so rank to me."

Alex held back his response. He had thought the lamb particularly savory, as had John, who wolfed down three servings to Alex's two, but instead of pressing the issue, he just said, "Well, let's be gentle with her. She is heartsick for Simon, and understaffed as well."

"That is the only reason why I didn't reprimand her last night, even if I thought I'd been poisoned."

Alex fought to keep a grin off his face. It wasn't like Eliza to be so dramatic, and he found himself enjoying it — he was usually the one whining in their household. "Drayton is due today or tomorrow, so things should settle down soon. But I'll have a brief word with Rowena before I go to work. Tell her to keep the 'poison' to a minimum."

Eliza peered at him to see if he were teasing, but then her face went even paler. "Oh no! I was meant to take Johnny to the Columbia campus to meet Brockholst Livingston!"

"Don't you worry, dear," Alex said quickly. "I shall take him. What time was the appointment?"

"Not till ten," Eliza said.

"Ten! It is half eight already, and Johnny is still asleep." Alex gave Eliza another quick kiss and hurried across the hall to Johnny's room. He knocked on the door but received no answer. He pushed it open and peered into the gloom — the room faced north and the velvet curtains were drawn as well. The sour smell of alcohol filled the room. Alex noted a three-quarters-empty bottle of wine on the table beside the bed. No glass was visible.

"Johnny," he said, "it is time to rise. You are due at Columbia in a little over an hour."

No words came from the prostrate figure, but a white hand reached out and pulled the pillow over his rumpled head.

"John!" Alex said more sharply. "Brockholst Livingston is expecting you promptly at ten. It wouldn't do to keep such an important man waiting."

"If cousin Brock was an important man," came a muffled voice from under the pillow, "he wouldn't work at a school. He'd run an estate like a real gentleman."

Alex was unaware that Brockholst Livingston was Johnny and Eliza's cousin, but all these old families of New York had intermarried so many times it was more than possible. Still, General Schuyler had entrusted Alex and Eliza to see his eldest son through college — and he was paying the school good money for the boy's tuition — and Alex was not going to fail his father-in-law.

He strode to the bed and yanked the pillow from Johnny's head. "Up. Now. Or I pour the contents of the washbasin over your head."

"The washbasin's empty," Johnny mumbled.

Alex glanced around the room. "But the chamber pot's not."

Johnny leapt from bed and began dressing.

While Johnny washed and dressed, Alex dashed off a half dozen missives to the clients he was supposed to meet that morning, pushing back their appointments to the morrow. "Simon!" he called as he finished the last of them. "I need you to deliver —"

He broke off when Rowena's sad face

appeared from the dining room, where she had been polishing the silver after breakfast.

"Simon is off at the Beekmans'," she said in a voice that could have been describing his death from a slow, wasting disease. "Perhaps I can be of service, Mr. Hamilton?"

"No, no," Alex said, "you are much too busy with your regular duties." He offered her a wan smile. "I know you miss him, but think how happy he must be in the open air."

Rowena did her best to smile back. "I received a letter from him yesterday — Miss Jane Beekman was nice enough to scribe it for him — that says he is in the saddle every day. It is like an Eden to him, but a mother can't help but miss her only child."

"Yes, well," Alex said, wanting to be understanding, but also not wanting to lose a hundred pounds in business, which, among other things, paid his grieving servant's salary, "perhaps you can visit him tomorrow. Eliza, Mr. Schuyler, and I can fend for ourselves, you know."

"Oh, I don't like the thought of someone else in my kitchen. I have things just so, you know."

"No need to worry about that. Mrs. Hamilton's many virtues do not extend to the culinary arts. We shall probably just take our meals at the Stork and Whistle."

The Stork and Whistle was an inn on Fulton Street, and the only establishment Rowena liked her master and mistress to patronize, because the woman who ran the kitchen was a friend of hers. "Oh, Glynis will be glad to have you! And thank you, Mr. Hamilton! I do so appreciate it!"

Rowena disappeared, and Alex ran upstairs to fetch Johnny. He was shocked to find him once again facedown on the bed, though at least he was fully clothed.

"John Bradstreet Schuyler!"

John sat up with a start, glancing nervously in the direction of his chamber pot. "What, what? Are the redcoats back? Point me to those lobsterbacks and I'll shoot the lot of 'em!"

Alex couldn't tell if Johnny had been

43

dreaming or if he was having him on. "If you don't mind," he said. "Pull a brush through that hair, grab your hat, and let us be off. Daylight's burning!"

"I find that the day gets on just fine whether I deign to notice it or not," Johnny said as he stumbled out of his bed, pulled his fingers through his unruly dark locks, and clapped a hat over them. "Lead on, General."

Bright sunlight greeted them as they walked out onto Wall Street, which was bustling with pedestrians, carriages, and men on horseback going about their business.

"Egads!" John said, pulling his hat lower over his eyes. "Are we in the south of New York or the south of Italy? My God, that sun is bright!"

"I find that the same sun shines on New York as shines on Albany," Alex couldn't resist saying. "Tell me, Johnny, is it possible that you are a little the worse for wear this morning?"

"I beg of you, please, call me John. No one called 'Johnny' can command the respect of his peers, let alone of the fairer sex."

Alex rolled his eyes even as a smile crept onto his face.

"Now, then," John continued. "If you are asking if I drank too much last night, the answer is of course not. I am no wastrel. If you are asking if I feel like the Revolutionary War is still being fought inside my head, though, then the answer is yes." He squinted in pain. "It is a naval battle, with lots of cannon and rough seas to boot."

Alex had to chuckle at the boy's ingenuity. "We did celebrate your arrival a little too heartily, I'm afraid. Do not think every evening is quite so festive in the Hamilton house."

"What? I loved it!" John said. "A couple nippers of sherry and I'll be good to go for another round."

Alex shook his head. He didn't remember little Johnny being quite so . . . boisterous when he was young. But then, he himself wasn't a rich man's son. When he was John's age he had already moved from Nevis to St. Croix and back again, been abandoned by his father, orphaned by his mother, and sponsored for a life-changing scholarship to the northern colonies by William Livingston, the governor of New Jersey. Though he knew little about the world back then, he understood that he was on his own, and that he and he alone would determine whether he succeeded or failed. John had better learn some discipline soon, Alex thought, or he would find himself back in Albany sooner than he realized.

Oh God, he thought, *I sound so old.*

Just then they passed a pair of girls walking the opposite direction. Servants likely, to judge from their simple gray garments. The pair were about John's age, and dressed lightly on account of the day's warmth, with only shawls and lace sleeves covering their shoulders. John all but stared as they walked past, then turned and watched as they walked away. "Somebody call a policeman, because they just stole my heart!"

"Ouch," Alex said. "That line hurts me more than your headache hurts you."

John laughed. "I've been told I come on a bit strong, but what can I say? I'm a lover of the ladies. Always have been."

"Always? You're seventeen. How much loving have you done?"

"I know Albany isn't exactly New York City, but we still have our fair share of misses. As I recall, you found your own in our neck of the woods." He patted Alex on the shoulder as though they were a pair of war veterans reminiscing about their days under fire. "Never you fear, brother, I'm well experienced."

"I'm less afraid of your *lack* of experience than its opposite. Do I need to be concerned here, John? I am entrusted with your protection, after all. It is hard for me to imagine just how . . . disappointed General Schuyler would be if I wrote him to say that you had to get married in a hurry."

"The only thing you need to worry about is the trail of broken hearts I plan on leaving in my wake. But don't you fret, Alex. No one's going to be throwing their noose around me before I'm ready."

Alex grunted.

"But seriously, how do you stand it?" John said, making eyes at another young woman across the street. "I mean, this city is a virtual banquet table of female delights."

"I'm not certain you've noticed but I am married to your sister. 'For all time.' "

"Right. But still. We're men, right? It's in our nature to —"

Alex pulled up short. "If you think I won't wash your mouth out with soap right here on the street, young man, you are sorely mistaken."

John's voice was guileless when he answered, but there was a wicked gleam to his eye. "You carry soap with you when you walk around?"

Alex took John's head in his hands and turned it to a shop window.

SOAP
ALL TYPES
INCL. LYE

"This is New York. You can get anything you want, anyplace you want it, anytime you want it. Including *lye,*" he added in a threatening tone.

John just stared at the sign for a moment, as though he were having trouble reading. Then he laughed. "Fine, fine. I was just teasing. I'm new here, remember? It's all a bit overwhelming."

John affected a naïve tone, but Alex suspected it was just an act to placate him. Still, anything to get the boy to stop talking about women as though they were side dishes. John was clearly a self-possessed boy, and a smart one, but he had a lot to learn if he was going to make it in New York. Alex wasn't sure if he was prepared to be the one to teach him, but if he didn't who would?

"It's but a few minutes more to the college," he said. "Come, let us hurry so we're not late."

After being closed for seven years due to the revolution and the occupation of New York City, the former King's College had reopened as Columbia College in the state of New York just last year. The story had it that when Mayor James Duane learned that DeWitt Clinton — the son of Revolutionary hero James Clinton and the nephew of Governor George Clinton — was going to university at the College of New Jersey in Princeton, he persuaded the university to reopen so that New York wouldn't lose one of its first citizens to a neighboring state. With help from the governor (who had appointed himself chancellor of the reopened school, a largely honorary position, though it came with a nice stipend, which Clinton, as governor, had awarded himself), the university's handsome Park Place campus was cleaned up, and the school opened its doors to nine students — the inaugural class of 1798, which included his nephew DeWitt. John Bradstreet Schuyler was to be part of the class of 1799, which had swelled to ten.

The campus was on a lovely bluff west of City Hall Park overlooking the Hudson River. Three acres of grass and trees, half wild after nearly a decade of neglect under British occupation, surrounded a single long, low building, nearly a city block long, a tall cupola rising out of its center like a domed vault.

John whistled as it came into view. "That is a big building," he said.

"Eventually, it is to be complemented by three more, forming a quadrangle," Alex said, pointing at the future buildings' locations.

"A quadrangle, you say?" John said. "Is that like a fancy rectangle?"

Alex started to explain the concept, then saw the look on John's face.

"You are so serious," the young man said. "We should take this act onstage. We'd make quite the comic duo."

"I do hope you'll curtail the jokes while we meet with Mr. Livingston. First impressions are rather important."

"Oh, I've met Brock a couple times. I think he was at Peggy's wedding, although who knows? There had to have been fifty Livingstons there, and I was well sauced."

Alex could hardly believe his ears. The Schuylers were such a reserved family, full of quiet probity. True, the elder girls had something of a mischievous streak about them, but it was all done in innocent fun. Whereas it appeared little Johnny Schuyler had grown up to become a positive Lothario.

Alex pulled up short on the path leading to the College Hall's front entrance and placed his hand on John's shoulder. In his head he'd imagined that he'd be looking down on the boy's face, but he was disconcerted to discover that his young brother-in-law was a good inch taller than him.

"Forgive me for speaking bluntly," he said. "But I must insist that that when we take our meeting with Treasurer Livingston you avoid any mention of inebriated evenings or, or romantic adventures. If you are unconcerned with your own reputation, at least think of your esteemed family's."

He made his voice as stern as he could. *There,* he told himself, *that should settle the boy down.*

John looked at him incredulously. Then, to Alex's shock, he doubled over in a fit of laughter so violent that Alex thought the boy was going to fall to the ground.

"Oh my Lord, you've been a lawyer too long!" John managed to spit out between laughs. " 'Curtail any mention'? 'Inebriated evenings'? Is this how you wooed my sister? I don't know how she controls herself."

Alex started to protest, but John put a hand up. "Alex. Please. I'm John Bradstreet Schuyler, eldest son of General

Philip Schuyler." He passed his hand down his body, pointing out the excellent cut and fabric of his suit as well as his lean but sturdy physiognomy and aristocratic face, with its strong jaw and elegantly narrow nose. Even his hair, so cavalierly combed, managed to look debonair.

John flashed a wide grin at Alex. "Henry Brockholst Livingston doesn't stand a chance against me."

"Wait," Alex said. "Treasurer Livingston's first name is Henry? As in the third son of Governor William Livingston of New Jersey?"

"You didn't know?" John once again doubled over in laughter. "That's hilarious!"

"He was already at school when I first arrived in the north and took up residence with the Livingstons. They always referred to him as Henry."

"Well, it's Brock now."

"Somehow I doubt he goes by —"

"Brock!" John interrupted. "Hello! Brock!" he yelled at a dark-robed figure trotting up the path.

The man turned. "Johnny boy! Is that you? Excellent! I was afraid I was late."

As he approached them, Alex saw that the man's wig was slightly askew on his head, his cheeks unshaven, and one of his collars on his shirt flapped above the top of his robe. All in all, he looked nearly as disheveled as John.

The two clapped each other in a hug. "Good to see you again!" Brockholst said. "I can't tell you how happy I was to learn that you'd opted for Columbia. Just between you and me, DeWitt Clinton can't hold his liquor. I need someone who knows how to have fun."

"Brocky, this is —" John began.

"Oh, I know this knave," Brockholst said with a leer. "Alexander Hamilton, who tried to woo my sister Susannah once upon a time. Or was it Catherine? Or was it both of them? Better lock up your sisters, John," he added with a wink.

"Too late," John said. "He already snagged Eliza."

"Another good one off the market," Brock said. "Never you fear, John, there are still plenty of lovely lasses left in the city for both of us."

" 'Lovely lasses left.' It sounds like the beginning of a beautiful story," said John. And, throwing their arms around each other, John and Brock sauntered breezily toward the building, heads close together in conspiratorial whispers.

Alex had no choice but to hurry after them.

3

A STRANGER IN THE HOUSE

The Hamilton Town House
New York, New York
June 1785

Meanwhile, back at 57 Wall Street, Eliza lingered in bed for much of the morning, catching up on her correspondence. For the past several months, she had been working to facilitate the placement of several orphans into good homes or churches. She saw her husband's face in every orphan and was determined that no child would be abandoned as he had been. She would have loved to take in each and every one of them into her own home, childless as they were, but decided it would unfair to choose just one or two to save personally, and so she devoted herself to all of them.

New York City lacked both a foundling

society and an orphanage, and too many poor children whose parents had been taken from them by disease or war ended up fending for themselves on the streets if someone didn't take them in. Eliza had only last week placed a six-year-old girl with a lovely family who ran a prosperous farm not far from the Beekmans, and now there was a sweet lad of just four whose mother, a fallen woman unable to identify the boy's father, had been taken away by the pox at the tender age of twenty-two.

As it happened, Eliza knew that Michael and Prudence Schlesinger, a young couple she had met in Trinity Church, had lost their own son to fever half a year ago. She did not think that Augustus, as the orphaned lad was grandly named, could ever take the place of their Joshua, but surely, she wrote to them, this was the Lord's way of helping them through their grief? The boy was currently staying in the church's rectory, and on her visit there she had him dip his hands in watercolor paint and impress his prints on a sheet of parchment, which she had sent to the Schlesingers. They were so tiny, so delicate — how could they fail to melt Pru's and Michael's hearts?

She was aware it was a stopgap plan. In a city as large as New York, Eliza knew there were far more foundlings and orphans than were being brought to her attention, and eventually a home would have to be built for them, so they could be fed and clothed and educated in comfort until they were placed with families of their own. But for now, if she could match young Gus with Pru and Michael, she would consider her morning not entirely wasted.

As a precaution — she didn't want to risk becoming more ill or infecting her friends — she sent her regrets to the Van Cortlandts, telling them that she wasn't feeling well and wasn't up to dinner that evening. (In Simon's absence, she had to send Rowena with the note, along with her letter to the Schlesingers, which didn't please her cook *at all.* An hour later came Joanna Van Cortlandt's gracious response: "I completely understand, my dear. Take a day in bed — I find it always helps!")

Eliza had procured a copy of *Moll Flan-*

ders by Daniel Defoe some weeks ago, the latest fancy, and began indolently cutting the pages open to read it, but soon gave the task up: the dusty paper tickled her nostrils, which somehow upset her stomach even more. She set the book aside and closed her eyes. To her surprise, she fell asleep again.

But Eliza was too used to activity to pass an entire day in bed, and thankfully, when she woke after noon she felt refreshed. Stirring herself, she arose, washed, dressed, and decided to take herself to market on Rowena's behalf (and also to avoid another batch of not-quite-right eggs or questionable lamb). Rowena was getting ready to head out when Eliza came into the kitchen and told her cook that she would do the shopping herself. Though Rowena protested that she always preferred to choose her ingredients herself, it was clear she was feeling overwhelmed without her son's aid and appreciated her mistress's offer.

"If you go the stall on the corner of Beaver and Broad, the man there will kill the chicken for you, so you don't have to do it yourself. If you tell him Rowena sent you, he might even pluck it for you."

"Oh, Rowena, you flirt!" Eliza teased. "I am perfectly capable of plucking a chicken."

Rowena practically guffawed. "You'll forgive me, Mrs. Hamilton. You are a hale lass for a gentlewoman, but you are barely capable of plucking out a wig, let alone a chicken."

"You slander me, Rowena," Eliza said, but she knew her cook was right.

Though she left the town house with a bounce in her step, two hours later she was back, sapped of energy. Eliza entered through the kitchen, dropped her baskets on a table, then made her way upstairs to the rear parlor and collapsed into its softest chair. There was a volume of Richardson on the side table — Alex was reading it — and she picked it up with the intention of peeking in, but when Alex came home around eight, he found her fast asleep in the chair with the book closed on her lap.

"Thanks for losing my page," he said with a grin. She had looked so serene when he walked in, he hadn't meant to rouse her. But the opportunity to tease his dear wife was just too irresistible.

"It's Richardson," Eliza said drowsily. "Every page is the same. Some poor maid is pretending to fend off the advances of her master, but secretly hoping the mistress will die so she can marry him and take her place. Just once I'd like to read a story where it is the man who is poor and is making love to a woman to try to get her property."

Alex laughed. "That would require a change in property laws, among other things. Thanks for spoiling the plot, too."

"Ever the lawyer," Eliza said, rolling her eyes. "How did Johnny fare today?"

"You mean John," Alex informed her. "He's asked us not to call him by his family nickname anymore. He's not here?"

"I don't think so?" Eliza said. "Unless he snuck in while I was sleeping. But if he did I'm sure he'd have drawn a mustache on my face or something equally as sophomoric."

"I left him at the college this morning. Somehow I failed to realize that Brockholst Livingston is also Henry Livingston, Governor Livingston's son."

"Yes, that's why I was originally going to meet with him instead of you. Brocky used to follow me around like a puppy when we were children. I figured I could dispose him favorably toward John."

"John seems to have that angle covered," Alex said. "I am not sure if we are sending him to school or merely to a fraternal organization."

"Hmm," Eliza said. "Should I be worried?"

"Oh, he's probably just running errands in anticipation of his classes. It's a new city and he doesn't know where everything is. I'm sure he'll be in shortly."

And just then the door opened and John came in, a sheepish smile on his wine-stained lips. When prompted for details of his day, he explained that he had stopped for a bite to eat at a charming inn and met a passel of "capital fellows" as well as "a few charming lassies." One thing led to another, and here he was, a few hours later than expected, though "none the worse for wear." He had supped at the inn, and if Alex and Eliza didn't mind, he was going to take himself straight to bed. Without waiting for an answer, he staggered up the steps. A few moments later, they heard the creak of bedsprings as he fell into bed, they could only assume still fully clothed.

"None the worse for wear?" Alex quipped. "We'll see if he's still singing the same tune in the morning!"

Though John slept in till half past ten, when he did finally wake, he was as energetic as a five-year-old. He wolfed down a few slices of hearty bread slathered with butter (as Rowena had already departed north to the Beekman farm to visit Simon), then announced he had to buy books for class, and vanished out the front door. Alex said he had a half day's work to catch up on because of yesterday's college visit, and headed out shortly after, leaving Eliza alone in the house. Her stomach was churning. Despite the fresh eggs she'd purchased yesterday, Rowena still managed to sour them before she headed out that morning. Or perhaps it was not Rowena's cooking at all that had turned her stomach? Perhaps — could it be? But after so much heartbreak, to even think the thought was to jinx it, and so Eliza banished it from her mind.

"Sod all," she said out loud. "This time I really am taking the day in bed."

It felt positively sinful to crawl back between the covers at eleven in the morning. Her mother was a firm believer that "idle hands make for the devil's work," but she believed even more strongly that an idle mind was a truly dangerous thing. Daydreaming was an invitation to free-thinking; novel-reading was even worse since it gave picture to heretofore un-imagined ways of life. To hear Mrs. Schuyler tell it, all of humanity had lived in sensible brick houses (though perhaps not quite as stately as her own) since Adam and Eve left the Garden, and the goals of any good housewife should be kept to seeing that the floors were waxed, the plate polished, the table surrounded by only the most desirable dinner guests, and the nursery stocked with a fresh infant every fourteen to eighteen months. Eliza had the shiny floors and shinier silver; her dining room rang with the voices of the men and women who were creating the United States of America out of the disparate and constantly squabbling thirteen colonies. Only the nursery remained starkly empty.

Eliza heated some water, made a pot of herbal tea, and brought it up to the bedroom, where she plumped the pillows so she could sit up comfortably. *Moll Flanders* sat on the bedside table expectantly, but she opened a drawer and pulled out a passel of letters instead. Intrigued as she was by the story waiting between the book's pages, she hadn't the energy to devote to such a strenuous pursuit and decided to focus what little strength she had on family matters.

Ever since her own brood had started to arrive, Angelica's stories of London were equal parts lords and ladies and soiled nappies; Peggy's letters from Rensselaerswyck had their own tales of infant joy: she and Stephen had welcomed daughter Catherine — named after both their mothers — just a few months ago. Eliza had meant to cheer herself by revisiting her deeply missed sisters, at least in prose, but all the stories of new toys and new dresses and first steps and first words left an ache in her heart that was more painful than her restive stomach.

Of course, these days she had been keeping herself busy with church and the orphans and arranging her and Alex's social calendar to benefit both his career and her charity work, but she had always expected that by now these activities would be arranged around her duties as a mother. Without that missing piece, her life seemed a bit hollow somehow.

"You're letting us down," she said, wagging her finger at her stomach, which rumbled in reply.

In truth, though, the inactivity felt like a necessary respite after the day-in, day-out hustle of the past year and a half. The Hamiltons barely had a moment to themselves since Alex's career had taken off, and if their social life was electrifying, it was also so all-consuming that Eliza hardly had time to realize just how tired she was. No wonder she hadn't been able to conceive. Her poor body needed energy, and it was all going to carrying her from luncheon to play to ball to bat mitzvah (a moving Jewish ceremony that Eliza's acquaintance Ruth Levy invited her to, to celebrate her daughter Sarah's coming of age), and back again, in an endless cycle of gaiety.

As she thought back to the joyously exhausting barrage of events, she basked anew in the quiet of her bedroom. One solitary day away from all that was just what she needed! To close her eyes and sleep with the warm sunlight on her face was simply heaven!

But only an hour later she was up again. Sleeping all day just wasn't in her. She was a Dutch *vrouw* to her core.

She decided to call on the Schlesingers to see if they had given her proposition any thought. Perhaps — oh, but this was mischievous! — she would stop by the rectory first and fetch little Gus to come with her. No one could resist the boy's plump cheeks and flashing eyes. She had half a mind to adopt him herself, even though she had promised herself not to choose favorites.

Eliza threw open a window and stuck her arm out. The day was as warm as it looked, and grabbing her lightest lace shawl more for decoration than for cover,

she raced down the stairs, already anticipating the smile on Gus's face when she
greeted him at the rectory. On second
thought, she decided she would just pop
in and say hi. It wouldn't be fair to take
him to the Schlesingers'. If they said no,
it would be too painful . . . for Gus and
for her. Even if he didn't understand
exactly what was happening, the sadness
would be palpable. Children pick up on
those kinds of things.

I must have a treat for him, she thought,
and so she continued down to the kitchen
to search for some cherries or grapes. The
faint smells of bread and meat and butter tickled her nose as she pushed open
the door —

"Oh!" a voice exclaimed.

"Oh!" Eliza echoed, startling at the
sight of a strange boy of about sixteen or
seventeen sitting on the lip of the butter
churn: "Who are you?!"

"E-e-excuse me!" the boy stammered.
"I thought Mrs. Wilcox was expecting me
but she —"

"Mrs. Wilcox? Rowena? How do you
know her? And why are you in my
kitchen?" Eliza demanded.

"As I said, I thought I was expected. I mean, I was sent for —"

"Sent for? By Rowena?" Suddenly it hit her. "Are you Drayton?"

The boy nodded his head vigorously, then, for good measure, bowed. "Yes, ma'am. Drayton Pennington, at your service."

"Oh!" Eliza said nervously. "Well, I must say, you gave me quite a start. I had completely forgotten you were coming. As has Rowena, apparently."

"I — I'm sorry, ma'am. I — I guess I can go home and try again some other time."

Eliza grinned at the good-natured boy. "As I recall, home is the Ohio Territory. It seems a rather far distance to go just because someone is not here to greet you."

"Indeed, yes, ma'am, I suppose it is. I, um, I guess I could go back to the river and wait where the boat left me. When — that is, do you know when Aunt Rowena will be back?"

"Not till the morrow, I'm afraid. We've sent her off to visit Simon in the hopes

69

that she'll stop mooning about."

"Simon!" Drayton's face brightened. "He was barely born when we left. I'm glad to hear he's doing well. He was a sickly child, you know."

"Well, he's healthy as a horse now, and riding them all the time, too, if the reports from Mount Pleasant are to be believed."

"Mount Pleasant, ma'am?"

"Never mind about that. Well, no, if you're here to become a footman, then you must learn who's who so you can greet them properly. Mount Pleasant is the estate of the Beekman family. The pater is Jonas and his wife is Catherine. James and Jane, their eldest son and daughter, are Mr. Hamilton's and my good friends."

"Jonas, Catherine, James, Jane," the boy repeated gamely, as though it were multiplication tables. "And pardon me for asking, but you *are* Mrs. Hamilton, yes?"

Eliza slapped her head. "How very rude of me. Here I am grilling and lecturing you, and I haven't even introduced myself." She took the last step into the kitchen and walked toward Drayton with her hand outstretched. The boy didn't exactly shrink into the wall, but he looked as if he wanted to. "I am indeed Eliza Hamilton," she said, taking his limp hand and squeezing it in hers. "I am very pleased to meet you. Mr. Hamilton and I are so grateful that you'll be joining us and Rowena."

"I, ah, thank you, ma'am. Mrs. Hamilton," Drayton said. When Eliza let go of his hand, he stood there for a moment, then bowed again. She supposed that he had never met a lady on the frontier.

"That's quite enough with the bowing," she said with a smile. "We run a proper house, but we're not royalty. We're all Americans now."

"Yes, ma'am," the boy said, though Eliza could see he was resisting the urge to bend forward yet again.

As she inspected him, she saw that he was a well-made boy, obviously used to heavy farmwork, but there was also a sensitivity about his eyes and mouth. She had worried that a farm lad was no more suited for the job of footman than Simon, but now she thought that perhaps Rowena's sister had chosen wisely. The boy was shy, but he was also curious and alert, which were fine traits to have in the city.

"Well," she said, "I have an errand to run, and you are no doubt tired from your long journey. The larder's through there, and beyond are the servants' bedrooms. Yours will be the second door on the right. Help yourself to some food and take rest as you desire. We've already purchased some fabric for your uniform, and we'll get you measured up on Monday."

"Uniform, ma'am?" Drayton said, as Eliza wrapped a couple of scones in a napkin for little Gus and put them into a small basket.

"Yes, your livery. Also, I don't know if you're a reader, but there is a nice selection of books in the parlor upstairs. Feel free to help yourself."

And, waving at the bewildered-looking boy, she headed out into the day. How funny to think that the big, awkward, but somehow self-possessed boy in her kitchen was once a little boy as tiny as Gus. A baby. Would there ever come a day when she would have to look up into her own son's eyes?

"God willing," she said aloud, then hurried on to the rectory before the Schlesingers'.

The errand was a qualified success. Pru and Michael were far from finished with their mourning for Joshua, but they were also full of love and lonely for a child. Both had married late — they were already in their thirties — and time was running out for them to start a family. They couldn't agree to adopting Gus sight unseen, but they said that if Eliza brought him to church on Sunday they would meet him with open hearts and open minds. Eliza returned home with a spring in her step.

That night she dreamed that her mother wrote her a letter. It was written on an elaborately folded, extremely heavy piece of parchment, and it took Eliza forever to open it without damaging the creamy linen. When, finally, she managed to get it open, she was surprised to see that the letter contained only a single line — but then, in the way that dreams do, the line blurred before her eyes, and the next thing she knew, she was awake in bed beside Alex, her cheeks streaming with tears.

But this was no melancholy dream — they were tears of joy. She had no memory of what had been in her mother's letter, but she knew it was glad tidings nonetheless.

4
THE BUSINESS OF FAITH

Trinity Church
New York, New York
June 1785

That Sunday, Colonel Alexander Hamilton (retired) had the honor of escorting his wife, Eliza Hamilton, née Schuyler, and her brother John Bradstreet Schuyler, Columbia College, class of 1789, to their reserved pew in Saint Paul's Chapel of Trinity Church, accompanied by the fresh-scrubbed form of Augustus Slater, Esquire, age three and one half, or as near as anyone could tell.

Trinity had been the center of New York's ecclesiastical community for nearly a century, and even though the main church, built all the way back in 1698, had burned down right before the war started (and had not been torched by the British, as Aaron Burr once claimed in court, in a blatant attempt to turn the jury against Alex's loyalist client), services continued in its small but stately ancillary chapel, Saint Paul's, located a pleasant ten-minute walk from the Hamiltons' home, on Broadway just below City Hall Park.

Alex recognized that the care of one's soul is no doubt an important activity, and one not to be taken lightly. He was always moved by Eliza's faith, especially the sweet tone of her voice as she sang the hymns. But he himself could not quite believe. It's not that he disbelieved in the Episcopalian god exactly, but he didn't see why that particular deity was any more compelling than the Catholic god, say, or the Lutheran or Dutch Reformed or Methodist, or even the god of the Mohammedans or the Jews. (After he was orphaned, he and his brother James had been denied membership in the Church of England because his mother and father hadn't been legally married, and, being denied a place at the parish school, he was instead educated by a Jewish tutor, whose actions had always seemed to him more *Christian,* in the charitable sense of that word, than the Anglican rectors who labeled him a bastard.)

For that matter, he questioned why the many gods of Africa and Hindustan and the Indies weren't more deserving — after all, why would an omnipotent god reveal himself to a few people in one part of the world and hide himself from everyone else? And so, he was inclined to live and let live.

It seemed self-evident to him, as it did to many of the men who had helped to found this new country — John Quincy Adams, Benjamin Franklin, Thomas Jefferson, James Madison, and General Washington being only the most prominent — that an awesome intelligence had created this world and ordered it in such a way that it could be understood by men, who would find happiness if they allowed reason to guide their minds rather than letting superstition cloud their hearts. But the world was a vast, and vastly complicated, creation; it seemed a little silly to Alex that a being who could conjure it out of the ether would be concerned with such trivial concerns as the garments one wore or the foods one ate or even the words with which you spoke to him — or her or it or whatever the proper pronoun might be.

Yet the solemnity and procession appealed to him as the rites did to Eliza, and the civic opportunities — though never labeled as such, lest one contravene Matthew 21 — were hard to ignore. For if going to church was first and foremost a religious activity, it was also, undeniably and indispensably, a social one. Trinity was a small church, Saint Paul's even smaller. With only a few hundred seats available, competition for entry ran high, and in the wake of overcrowding following the liberation of the city, the church had started subscribing its pews. This was ostensibly a fund-raising opportunity to help erect a new building at Trinity's original location farther down Broadway, but it served the much more immediate function of ensuring that the church's most elite congregants were never without a seat. The price for reserving a pew could run as high as thirty pounds a year, which was the salary of a good lady's maid. (Alex had pointed this out one morning as Eliza was complaining that it always took her twice as long to get ready without Dot, her maid at the Pastures: He told her that if she was willing to forgo church he would be only too happy to procure her a new one. Eliza didn't speak to him for the rest of the day.)

Say what you want about Eliza's drawing power as a hostess; no one could rake them in like God. The prim wooden pews — as unadorned and uncomfortable as they were expensive — were filled with all the Bayards, Beekmans, Cornells, Lawrences, Livingstons, Morrises, Murrays, de Peysters, Reades, Rhinelanders, Schermerhorns, Stuyvesants, Van Cortlandts, Van Rensselaers, and Wattses you could shake a stick at. The once-a-week function was the only time Alex looked at Aaron Burr, accompanied by his wife, Theodosia, their daughter, also Theodosia, and his wife's children from her first marriage, and didn't want to punch him in the face. (Even so, he couldn't stand that Burr had managed to secure a pew three full rows in front of Alex, and he often found himself daydreaming about swapping pews with his friend William Bayard, just so that Burr would have to stare at Alex's back for a change — not exactly pious thoughts, he knew, but it would be worse to lie to himself about it, wouldn't it?)

On this particular Sunday he was happy to again see his good friends John and Sarah Jay, who were in town from their farm up in Rye. The two husbands embraced warmly, as did the wives, and John and Sarah met young John Schuyler eagerly. Alex was relieved to see that the sober environment had for once curbed John's wandering gaze, although perhaps the lad was just hungover — he had not come home last night until nearly three in the morning. John shook hands with the Jays and then quietly took his seat in the Hamiltons' pew, looking for all the world like he was getting ready to go to sleep with his eyes open.

"And who is this handsome young fellow?" Sarah Jay asked, leaning over to inspect Gus, who clung to Eliza's hand but let his eyes roam all over the church, which he had already pronounced the grandest building he had ever been inside.

"This is Master Augustus," Eliza said, as though that explained everything.

Sarah smiled at her. "I can't help but feel you have some plan in mind that involves this sweet one's future."

"Who? Me?" Eliza said, the very voice of guilelessness. Like Gus, she too was inspecting the church, though her eyes were trained not on the high ceilings or stained-glass windows, but on the bright faces of the congregants coming in to worship. "If you'll excuse me a moment, I see Michael and Prudence Schlesinger. I'll just go say hello if that's all right. Come along, Gus."

Sarah smiled at Alex as Eliza led the three-year-old to be interviewed by his prospective parents. "Another one of her orphans?" she asked.

He nodded. "I've told her she needs to start a home for them. I daresay that she actually will one of these days. At least then they'll all be gathered in one place."

"Her benevolence is inspiring," Sarah said. "I do wonder, though, if she spends so much time caring for parentless children because she has none of her own." Sarah's face paled as the words left her mouth. "Oh dear. That came out wrong. I only meant —"

Alex laid a comforting hand on her wrist. "I know you meant no harm, Sarah. We pray that Providence will bless us with a child one of these days. But whether we have one or a dozen, I think that Eliza will always care for those less fortunate than herself. It is just her nature. She took in this orphan, after all."

Sarah looked puzzled for a moment. "Oh, you mean you!" She laughed nervously. "She is one of the kindest, most generous souls I have ever met."

"Speaking of generosity," John Jay said now, "would you mind joining me in the rector's office a moment? Reverend Provoost asked if I would bring you over when you arrived."

Alex tried to think of an excuse to say no, but despite his famed reputation for thinking on his feet, nothing came. "Of course," he said.

Alex knew what the meeting was about. His annual subscription fee was due. And it's not as though he wasn't earning any money. He had more clients than he could handle alone, and had taken on a partner, Richard Harrison, to help with the load. The overflowing receipts reflected his success. But as his income had grown, so had his expenses. Being wealthy wasn't just a matter of having money, after all. It was a matter of spending it, and hosting six or ten or forty people every week for dinner and drink ran to quite a tidy sum, as did hostess gifts for the many households that entertained him and Eliza, and theater tickets, and tailor's fees, and let's not forget taxes. But apparently God — who had, after all, made the world on a tight six-day schedule — liked to receive his rents promptly.

Reverend Provoost was a rosy-cheeked man in his early forties. Like Alex, he had been educated at King's College (the now-renamed Columbia). He came out from behind his desk as they entered his office and shook each man's hand warmly.

"I must congratulate you and Mrs. Hamilton on the matriculation of John

Schuyler. I am pleased to learn that our alma mater is continuing to attract boys from the finest families. New York needs a school to rival those of New Jersey and Connecticut and Massachusetts."

Alex didn't bother to point out that he had not actually finished his degree. "Indeed," he said.

"At any rate, discussing your brother-in-law is not why I asked you in this morning."

"Ah yes," Alex said. "You will forgive me. Today's date had entirely slipped my mind."

"Today's date?" Reverend Provoost said, looking genuinely confused.

Alex paused. Perhaps the rector hadn't called him in for his subscription after all. "Oh, nothing," he said in a nonchalant tone. "What can I do for you, Reverend Provoost?"

The reverend waved his hand at a pair of plump chairs, and Alex and John took their seats. The reverend sat down behind his desk.

So this is to be a business meeting, Alex thought. *On a Sunday. How interesting.*

84

"As you know," Reverend Provoost began, "the church has been raising money since the war ended to erect a new edifice to replace the one that burned down in 1775."

Then again, Alex thought, *maybe this is about my dues after all.*

"As of now, our primary fund-raising efforts are centered on our pew subscriptions, to which you and Mr. Jay so generously contribute, and a portion of the tithe. But most of the latter money goes to regular church upkeep, salaries for the lay staff, and our necessary charities, while the former, though much appreciated, will not raise enough to build a new church for nearly twenty-five years. Saint Paul's simply doesn't have enough pews to raise ample funds off their rent."

"You could raise the rent," John Jay suggested amiably.

Spoken like a rich man, Alex thought, suppressing a groan.

"Even if we doubled the rent," the reverend answered, and Alex did his best not to blanch, "it would still take more than a decade for us to raise the necessary funds. Assuming, of course, the congregation would even consent to such a steep increase."

"Oh, I'm sure they'd be only too happy to," John Jay said. "Trinity is the crown jewel of the New York diocese, after all. The people who worship here want to do so in an environment that is, shall we say, commensurate with their rank in society."

It was all Alex could do not to chuckle. *Only in America is one's church a status symbol. God bless us!*

"Your generosity is once again appreciated, Mr. Jay," Reverend Provoost said. "Nevertheless, the church feels it is within its means to erect a new building in a much more timely manner, and without putting undue financial strain on the congregation."

"Indeed?" Alex said. "Do tell."

"As you know, the church is in possession of fairly ample amounts of real estate throughout the city. Under normal circumstances, these holdings would provide substantial income. However, the church's charter, established by the crown a century ago, limits Trinity to an income of five thousand pounds per annum."

Jay nodded for the reverend to continue.

"It's not a great sum, once you consider the size of the church's holdings. Were we allowed to charge competitive rents or to sell off some of our holdings at market value, we could easily realize an income of twenty or even fifty times that amount."

Alex bit back a "Good God!" Considering his surroundings, he didn't think it would go over well. "That is a rather different figure," was all he said. His mouth felt dry, and he told himself to have a drink of water before the communion chalice came to him, lest he gulped it all down.

"Indeed it is. Not only would it let us commence work on a new church immediately, it would also allow us to greatly expand our charitable endeavors. Nation-building can be a rather callous endeavor, I'm afraid, and our city is clogged with people in need of homes, food, medicine, and education. If Trinity was allowed to earn its fair share of income from its holdings, we would be able to build shelters to feed and house the homeless, establish hospitals to care for the sick regardless of their ability to pay, and start schools that would be open to all."

Open to all Anglicans, Alex thought, though he didn't say it aloud. If the church did start building schools, he would make sure they were indeed open to all.

"We would even be able to erect the orphanage Mrs. Hamilton has been agitating for since she arrived in the city."

Alex smiled. "She is at this very moment attempting to find a home for Master Slater with the Schlesingers."

"A delightful child and a delightful couple. We have enjoyed having him running around the rectory, and will enjoy it even more when he's gone."

The three men shared a laugh at this.

"The Schlesingers and Gus are well matched, and well served by your wife." Reverend Provoost gave Alex a pointed look. "And you, sir? Will you serve your church?"

Alex sat up uncomfortably. "I would be honored to, Reverend. Only I am not quite sure what you want me to do."

Reverend Provoost looked surprised. "But you are the lawyer of last resort. The patron attorney of hopeless causes."

Alex wasn't sure if he was being mocked or not. Well, the rector probably wouldn't have called him into his office to make fun of him. "Thank you, Reverend, but I'm not sure this is a legal matter."

"But I tell you it is, sir!" The rector's voice grew quite firm. "We want you to break our charter with the state and allow us to control our own destiny!"

Alex adopted a stolid, expressionless look. "Are you saying that you want me to sue the state of New York in order to free the church from governmental oversight?"

"I am saying exactly that, sir. The church is supposed to *administer* charity. But under the terms of our current charter, we're practically a charity case ourselves."

Numbers whirred through Alex's his head. One hundred thousand pounds a year or more — maybe much more. The income was staggering. And the fee for brokering such a deal would be similarly astronomical.

"Well, yes," he said, struggling to keep his voice calm. "I would need to see the original charter."

The reverend nodded. "I assumed as much. I have had a copy made for you. Shall I have it delivered to your office on the morrow?"

Alex supposed it would be unseemly if he walked into Sunday services carrying a box full of legal documents. It was the Sabbath, after all. "That would be excellent," he said.

The three men stood up and shook hands.

"I knew you were the right man to help us," Reverend Provoost said, taking Alex's hand firmly in his, then continued to hold on. "You understand, of course, that we are not in a position to remunerate you for your services unless you are successful in your suit."

There's always a catch, Alex thought. "Of course, Reverend," he said, mustering as much brightness as he could. "I wouldn't feel comfortable taking money from God's coffers if I had failed to serve him well."

The rector smiled and patted Alex on the shoulder. "Very good then. If you have any questions, please don't hesitate to call on me."

Alex nodded. "I'm honored that you've placed your trust in me. I won't let you down."

He turned to follow John out of the office. But just as he was leaving, Reverend Provoost called after him: "Oh, and Mr. Hamilton?"

Alex ducked his head back in the door. "Yes, Reverend?" He could have sworn the rector's smile was teasing.

"I believe your pew subscription is up for renewal? I assume you and Mrs. Hamilton wish to retain it for another year? The chapel has grown so crowded," he added, almost mischievously. "We've had many inquiries after open seats."

Alex smiled weakly. "Of course, Reverend. I'll have a check delivered to you this week."

"Thank you so much, Mr. Hamilton.

I'll see you in the nave."

So close, Alex thought as he closed the door behind himself. *So close.*

Alex made his way back to the pew in relatively high spirits. He would be out thirty pounds, but the prospect of thousands loomed. As he moved down an aisle, he shook hands with his neighbors and acquaintances and work colleagues and even Aaron Burr, who he was pleased to see had lost even more of his hair. It seemed to have migrated from the top of his head to the bottom of his chin, where there was ever more room for it to sprout.

"A couple of years ago I had no children," Burr moaned, running a hand over his nearly bald pate. "Now I have six. How did that happen?"

Alex wanted to say something about chasing other men's wives — Theodosia had still been married to a British officer when Burr scandalously began courting her — but he held his tongue. He also refrained from finding an excuse to mention how he had defeated Burr five out of the last seven times they had faced off in court, or that he himself had just landed what might turn out to be the most lucrative case of his career. All he did was lean forward to chuck baby Theodosia beneath her plump chin.

"I see she's got a bit of her father in her," he said in a slightly mocking coo. "More than a bit even." Nodding serenely at Burr's confused face — the man wasn't sure whether he'd been insulted or not — Alex continued on to his pew.

As he arrived he saw that Gus was no longer with Eliza, but that a young girl was. She looked about seventeen, with fair, though not blond, hair, and dark, rather mournful eyes. John looked as though he were sleeping beside her.

Alex slipped in next to his wife. "Did you, ah, make a trade for Gus?" he whispered, even as the deacon came in and the congregation rose to its feet.

"In a manner of speaking," she said. "This is Emma Trask. She's going to be living with us now. But — more importantly —"

Alex had been staring in amazement at Miss Trask, but something in Eliza's voice made him turn to her. "Yes?" he asked with some trepidation. What was

5
Catherine Schuyler Is Never Wrong

Trinity Church and the Mercer Shop
New York, New York
June–July 1785

It had been in her dream. The letter from her mother — the letter that she had dreamed her mother sent her. The letter that had caused her to wake up with tears on her cheeks.

When she introduced Gus to Prudence Schlesinger, she saw Prudence's eyes fill with an ineffable mixture of sadness for her lost child and joy at the beaming face looking up at her. Gus's gaze held, on the one hand, absolutely no expectations, and on the other, complete trust. As Eliza looked between his face and Pru's, the single line of cribbed, slightly blotchy script in her dream — for all her natural elegance, her mother's handwriting looked like a five-year-old's — popped into view:

It would please me greatly if you named your son after your father, General Philip Schuyler.

Just then, Eliza's mouth dropped open in a gasp. Gus looked up at her as though she were about to pull a candy from her pocket. Pru stared at her with a confused, wondrous smile for a moment, and then her eyes fell to Gus's face for a longer moment before she looked back up at Eliza and nodded.

Eliza knew the dream's letter was telling the truth and explained the cause of her lethargy and morning sickness. She would have to plan a visit to the doctor to confirm this happy news posthaste of course. Besides, only Catherine Schuyler — even in a dream — would feel the need to remind her daughter of her father's name and rank. Such was the matriarch's formality, even with her own children. To outsiders, this formality might appear cold, but Eliza knew it was just her mother's love of ritual and order — to her, the words *General Philip Schuy-*

ler were filled with thirty years of marriage, with two houses they had built together and filled with eight living children and seven lost in infancy, with a Dutch heritage that came out in little words like *schatje* ("sweetheart") and *hartje* ("my love"), an English spine that found form in a love of courtly etiquette, and an American soul that expressed itself in an uncompromising belief in liberty and individuality. And now, through the magic of dreams, she had delivered the most blessed news of all to Eliza:

She was going to have a child! A boy! Philip Hamilton.

Eliza took a moment to collect herself, then knelt down beside Gus.

"Gus," she said, smoothing the boy's hair away from his wide, unlined forehead. "Do you like Mrs. Schlesinger's dress?"

"It's violet," Gus said. He stared at the dress for an instant, then reached out a hand to touch it tentatively. "It's soft."

Eliza nodded. "And do you like lambs? Mr. and Mrs. Schlesinger have a new lamb on their farm."

"Oh yes!" Gus said. "I like lamb! It's so tasty!"

Eliza chuckled, looking up at Prudence.

"How would you like to go and see the lamb on Mrs. Schlesinger's farm after the service is over?"

Gus stared pensively at Pru's face for a long moment, then turned back to Eliza with a doubting expression. "Will you be coming, Mrs. Hamilton?"

"Not directly after church, but I'll be able to stop over later in the week if that's all right?"

Gus pouted, but it was more a pout of consideration than consternation.

"Can you come Wednesday?" he said at last.

Eliza nodded. "I will come Wednesday right after luncheon. How's that sound?"

Another pout as Gus mulled this plan. Then he nodded. "All right."

Eliza kissed Gus on the forehead and told him to eat all his vegetables but especially the green ones, which would only be in season for a few more months, then transferred his hand from hers to Pru's.

"I would tell you to take care of him," Eliza said, "but I can see from your face that it is he who will be taking care of you."

"He is a blessing," Pru nodded. "But —"

Eliza was starting to go, but stopped. "Yes?"

Pru turned and indicated a girl sitting in their pew. She was sixteen or seventeen, with straight, straw-colored hair that had been pulled up into the soberest of buns. She held her hymnal in her hand, and one finger lightly chased the Chi-Rho embossed on the cover over and over.

"This is my cousin, my second actually, Emily. Emma, her family calls her. Or, rather, called her."

Eliza's hand had strayed to her stomach, and she stroked it as delicately as Emma was stroking the monogram of the Lord on the hymnal cover. It was as flat as it had ever been — well, almost — but still, she imagined it swelling beneath her with new life. She had known her condition all along, had felt it deep within her, but had been too worried about being wrong, too nervous to believe that her dearest wish had come true, to admit it to herself.

"Oh!" she said, suddenly realizing what Pru was saying. "She has lost her parents?"

Pru nodded. "Her mother went before the war, and her father this past winter, both from influenza. Emma has been living with us, but with the addition of a new child I'm afraid we will have neither the space nor the means to provide for both adequately — a farmer's income isn't quite that of a lawyer's, I'm afraid. She is a sweet girl, quiet and well-behaved, an accomplished pianist, a lovely singer, and remarkably adept with a paintbrush. She is even" — Pru laughed lightly — "a skilled archeress. I have heard you speak of your lack of a lady's maid, and I thought . . ." Her voice trailed off. "And perhaps when you have children of your own, she could serve as a . . ." Again her voice faded away.

"Of course," Eliza heard herself saying, before she could think too long on it or worry about what Alex would say. "We may well have need of her before too long."

A moment later she was walking back to her pew, Emma following meekly behind.

Eliza shook her head in wonder at her own audacity. But the revelation from her dream had filled her with such compassion for all of humankind that there was no way she could have said no. And there was something about Emma. An air of gentle, studious seriousness. Exactly the kind of qualities one wanted in a governess. Even so, her impulsiveness shocked her.

What have I done?

Eliza had expected Alex to tell her that she would have to send Emma back, like a lame horse or a bolt of silk that's been gnawed by moths, but to her surprise he all but embraced the quiet girl on the street outside Saint Paul's after services were over and they finally had a chance to talk.

"It's fate," he said, beaming. "Now that you are pregnant — oh my heavens — you *are* pregnant, I didn't dream you said this, did I?"

"I am pregnant," Eliza said, only half believing it herself. "I need to see the doctor, but I am quite sure." She ran through the math in her head. Her courses were normally as regular as clockwork, but she could not remember it coming the last two months. For a woman who was practically obsessed with having a child, it was a stunning oversight. But her eyes had been on the far end of the experience — the child itself — and the whole carrying-it-in-her-womb phase remained rather tentative in her imagination.

"Well then, I mean obviously, you'll be taking to your bed and you must have someone to attend to you, to bring you food and build your fire and of course to do your shopping —"

Eliza burst out laughing. "Good heavens, husband, I'm pregnant, I haven't been run over by a carriage. My confinement is still months away!"

"Of course, of course," Alex stammered, eyes gleaming with a mixture of fear and exultation. "But still. I insist that you take it easy. This is your first child, after all. We do not know how your physiog— I mean physiolo— I mean — oh gracious — how you will react! Some women find it quite onerous, I, uh, have heard tell."

"I could do without the nausea," Eliza admitted, "and I have been quite tired of late. But we have far too much going on for me to simply retreat into my chamber like a cloistered nun. Especially with John here, and Drayton to train, and now Emma — my goodness, it's as though we have a whole new house!"

She nodded at her brother, who had slipped his arm through Emma's as they walked down Broadway toward Wall Street. Emma was nodding shyly at something John was saying, her bonnet pulled low over her forehead, while John was gesturing grandly with his free arm, as if he had grown up in New York and was now sharing the sights of his home-town with a new arrival. Eliza was struck by how natural the pairing seemed. The shy, serious girl; the gregarious, brash boy. They fit together like a pair of puzzle pieces.

"Look at that! The two have made

friends already!" said Eliza.

From the corner of her eye, she saw Alex frown.

"Alexander Hamilton!" She lowered her voice. "The Schlesingers are not as blessed as we are, but they are still gentlefolk. I hope you don't think Emma is beneath my brother's station!"

A snort burst from Alex's lips. "In truth, dear wife, no thought could be further from my mind."

Something in Alex's tone rubbed Eliza the wrong way. "What are you talking about?"

"It is probably just the excesses of youth," he said in a guarded voice, "but I can't help but notice that since his arrival here, your brother has been wont to play the roué."

Eliza didn't know if she was more shocked or amused. Johnny! A lady's man! It seemed only yesterday that he had been in short pants!

"Good heavens, Alex, he's only been here for several days. That seems an awfully short time in which to establish himself as a roué!"

Alex patted his wife's arm in apology. "Of course, I do not mean to say he has completely given himself over to debauchery or that his reputation is ruined. It is just that he seems to have developed some rather, ah, epicurean tastes."

"Epicurean! Roué! One needs a dictionary just to keep up with your insults of my family! If you mean to say that my brother is indulging in too much rich food and wine, just say so."

"Well, that is what 'epicurean' means."

"Oh! So in addition to your brother-in-law being an epicurean, your wife is a philistine!" she said jokingly. Well, mostly jokingly.

"Eliza, darling, please, I didn't mean to —"

"I know you didn't, because if you did you would be sleeping in the guest room tonight — or, rather, on the couch, since the guest room is now Emma's!" Eliza pinched his arm playfully. (Well, mostly playfully.) "My brother, like all eldest sons, but especially those with a trio of older sisters, was certainly always a bit of a coddled child, and it will take him some time to realize that the world will not at-

105

tend to his every whim as indulgently as did his father and mother and sisters."

She glanced again at John and Emma, who had reached the edge of the boardwalk. John offered Emma his hand as she stepped onto the street. She smiled shyly and accepted it gratefully. Again Eliza was struck by how easily and naturally they seemed to go together, and a wild idea filled her mind.

"Perhaps that is why Emma was sent to us," she ventured. "Perhaps John will never have to endure living without a woman's care. He can go straight from his mother's house to his wife's."

"His wife's!" Alex exclaimed. "Now who's being premature! Do you even know her last name?"

Eliza blushed, acknowledging the rashness of her matchmaking.

"Tatchall," she said. "Or, no, Trask. All right, perhaps I am anticipating. They say that being with child can excite a woman's constitution in that way."

Alex pulled up short at the words *with child.* He turned to face Eliza and took both of her hands in his. "You're sure, my darling?"

She nodded tremulously. "If my calculations are correct, our son will be born in November."

"A son!" Alex exclaimed. "You are certain?"

"My mother told me in a dream. Catherine Schuyler is never wrong about these things."

"Oh, Eliza, you are remarkable! I am so happy!" he exclaimed, wrapping her in his arms.

The following week was filled with one shopping expedition after another as Eliza, usually with Emma's help, though sometimes with Rowena's or Drayton's, stocked the house with all the things it needed for its new occupants. The two years the Hamiltons had lived in New York were the city's first since its liberation from seven years of British rule, and it had changed dramatically in that time. When Alex and Eliza first moved in, two out of three storefronts sat empty, and the stores that had managed to remain open were awash with goods that had been seized from or abandoned by the fleeing British, who had themselves seized most of their booty when they took the city in 1776.

The city had basically been one big thrift store, with the contents of entire houses up for sale, usually for pennies on the pound. The cash-strapped young couple had furnished a good portion of their first house this way, but such bargain shopping was a thing of the past. New York was a boomtown now, the financial center of the country, and the major trading port of the northern states, quickly relegating Philadelphia and Boston to the status of satellite cities. The flood of new arrivals made it a seller's paradise. The overstuffed secondhand stores had transformed into elegant specialty establishments, with this one offering furniture, that one china, the next silver and pewter. Certainly the variety had increased and the quality, too. But so had the prices, as Eliza was discovering. She was fingering a swatch of exquisitely embroidered silk that John had brought to her in the same mercer's shop where she and Alex had bought their first set of china. It was her brother's hope that it could be transformed into a bed sham and curtains for his bedroom.

"Alex would have me tried for treason if I purchased this," Eliza said. "It's seven pounds fifty! That's more than we paid for the bed!"

"Well, we can replace the bed later," John teased. "For now we'll just drape it in ten yards of this."

"Ten yards!" Eliza said, pretending to swoon. "My God, John! Father has extravagant tastes, but you put him to shame. Where on earth did you develop such a fondness for luxury?"

"What do you mean, where? In my parents' house, surrounded by my parents' riches. Their décor may be more sober than my own taste, but don't let the subdued hues fool you: Father's and Mother's tastes are anything but cheap. It costs a lot of money to look that drably sumptuous."

"Yes, but Father and Mother have their own income, whereas you are a ward of your middle sister, who, unlike her older and younger siblings, did not have the foresight to marry a business tycoon like John Church or the heir to the largest fortune in the North like Stephen Van Rensselaer."

"Yes, you married the genius," John teased. "A genius at everything but making money."

Eliza bristled at any criticism of her love. "Alex's earnings are more than respectable, thank you very much. But we are a young family, and still establishing ourselves. The outlay is considerable."

"Well, I can't think of anything that would establish you more than this silk," John cooed.

Eliza let her hand trail across the sumptuous fabric one more time, then shook her head. "I'm sorry, John, I have to say no. We are not shopping for your bedroom today. We're shopping for the nursery."

"Bah, babies!" John spat, though his eyes were twinkling. "I need a second robe for school, and not one made from scratchy wool carded from some mangy ten-year-old ewe. Don't worry," he added, as he headed over to a pile of sumptuous inky black worsted that gleamed nearly as much as silk, "I'll pay for it out of my allowance."

Eliza shook her head at her brother. Though she loved him dearly, not least because he was the namesake of a dear little child that had died shortly after his first birthday — the third Schuyler infant to die in a row — she was starting to wonder if Alex's assessment of him after church last Sunday wasn't grounded in reality. In the past week, John had been out every night till long after she and Alex had fallen asleep. He ate in seedy inns and alehouses, and Rowena had reported that half his handkerchiefs were indelibly stained with lip paint. Even worse, though classes had begun, she had yet to see him crack a book or put pen to paper.

As a girl who had been denied a formal education, she found it hard to believe anyone could take the privilege of college so cavalierly. If he weren't so damned charming, she would have liked to give him a good swift kick and tell him to get his act together. But as it was, she was more than a little concerned, though she had confidence he would settle down once the novelty of being out of his parents' house wore off.

Just then Emma came up to her. "Perhaps this will do, Mrs. Hamilton?" she said, proffering a bolt of white fabric.

Eliza smiled at her new ward and took the fabric from her. It was so soft that she had to lay it against her cheek. "Oh, this is lovely. Baby will feel as though he's being swaddled in ermine."

"It needs a little lace at the border, but Cousin Schlesinger says I have a fair hand for the work," Emma said.

"A fair hand!" Eliza scoffed. "Somewhere in Europe there's a cloister full of nuns who are seething with jealousy at the delicacy and intricacy of your lace! It is remarkable!"

Emma smiled meekly, although the word *meekly* is redundant, as the girl did everything with the utmost humility. "My mother taught me when I was little," she said quietly. "She supplemented my father's income with lacework and embroidery for the ladies of New Haven."

The girl's face clouded over at the mention of her parents, as it always did. Though her father had been gone a year and more and her mother for a full decade, it was clear she still felt their loss acutely.

"I have no doubt she would be extraordinarily proud to see how her lessons have taken," Eliza said. "I hope I can pick up a few pointers from you. Your lace is as delicate as snowflakes, while my own tends to look rather . . . melted."

"I'm sure it is as beautiful as you are, Mrs. Hamilton. Shall I have the mercer cut ten yards of this?"

"Better make it fifteen," Eliza said. "The fabric is so lovely we'll do sheets and bunting for the bassinet as well."

"Oh, how grand! I have an idea for an embroidery border for the bassinet. It will require some indigo yarn?"

"Buy as much as you think you'll need," Eliza said, and Emma hurried off.

If John had been a source of consternation to Eliza, Emma had been an unexpected comfort. Eliza didn't think she'd ever met a girl as unaffectedly grateful as Pru Schlesinger's unfortunate cousin. As Eliza soon learned, Emma had lost her mother at the tender age of seven. Earlier that year, her elder brother had died of consumption and the same flu that swept away her mother also took her younger sister with it. There had been one more sibling, a brother just two years old when his mother was taken, a sickly child who every year seemed on the verge of death until finally he was taken home when he was nine.

But the hardest burden of all was the girl's father. Dennis Trask had, according to Pru, been overly fond of drink and the sort of louche activities that are known to accompany that vice: gambling, loose women, and, apparently, violence, which sometimes found its victims in those nearest to him — and least able to fight back. Pru had written to Eliza in "strictest confidence," saying that she did not like to tell tales about the departed, but that it was in Emma's best interest that Eliza understand her background, so that she might avoid causing the girl unnecessary pain by asking the sorts of questions that one might normally ask about a lost loved one. And despite her father's many failings, Emma had indeed loved him. She had devoted her life to caring for him and her younger brother, and almost took their deaths as a failing on her part.

"All this by way of saying," Pru had wound up her letter, "that as Emma reaches marrying age, I hope that you will help her exercise caution in the suitors she entertains. The girl's greatest virtue — her empathy — is also her greatest fault, for she seems driven to save those who would not save themselves. After seeing her childhood stolen by my wayward brother, my one wish is that my niece be partnered with a steady man — one who will care for her, as a man should — rather than a selfish one, who would demand, shall we say, undue succor from his helpmeet."

Eliza had taken Pru's letter almost as a challenge. After all, why shouldn't she help her new maid to find an appropriate husband? Eliza's circle brought her into contact with the upper crust of New York society. Emma was a poor girl, but comely, and the Trask name, coupled as it was to the Schlesingers', was still solid. Dennis had raised his family in the relative obscurity of Concord, Massachusetts, so word of his degradation had not reached New York City, and Prudence was such a solid member of society that it could only add to Emma's attractiveness as a prospect. Eliza knew of hundreds of second or third sons from well-off families who would gladly accept a poor daughter-in-law of good breeding and better habits.

She glanced over and saw Emma pull a bolt of dark cloth from John's hands and replace it with another from the shelf. John's face lit up; clearly Emma had given him a fabric of superior quality to the one he had picked out, too.

"And it even costs less!" she heard her brother exclaim. "Miss Trask, you are remarkable!"

Yes, Emma would make someone a good wife. And she thought she might already know who that someone could be.

"John, Emma," she said once they were back on the street. "I am thinking of having a little party in a few weeks — maybe a month to do it properly — to celebrate the new additions to our household. Although my confinement is still some time away, I feel as though I have to get all my entertaining in now before I retreat into seclusion. What do you think?"

As usual when they were out together, John had taken Emma's arm and served as her escort. If at first she had seemed somehow shy about John's gallantry, now she took it in course, and even looked up at him to allow him to speak first.

"What do I think about you going into seclusion?" her brother said. "Or what do I think about a party? Because I think the idea that a woman must hide her pregnant body is a little silly myself, although I suppose it saves some money on dress fabric."

Emma blushed a little at this outré comment, though a smile also flickered at the edges of her mouth.

"Oh, John, you're incorrigible!" Eliza laughed, although if she were being honest, she agreed with him. Her mother had spent almost a quarter of her adult life above stairs when company was over, lest someone not of the family catch a glimpse of her in the motherly way — as if they had not seen exactly the same thing in their own homes! "I meant the party, and you know it."

"Well, if Peg's and Angie's stories are to believed, my rather boring middle sister somehow throws the most exciting parties in New York City, so I think my answer is obvious: Let's pop some corks!" said John.

"And you, Emma? You would be the party's second guest of honor. Have you any thoughts on the matter?"

She was pleased to see Emma glance at John before answering, as though he might speak for her. Her deference was a sure sign of their growing connection.

"Oh, Mrs. Hamilton," Emma said with genuine modesty, "there is no need to honor me. I am a housemaid in all but name, and more than content to fulfill that role."

"Nonsense," Eliza said. "You are a Trask, and a niece of Prudence Schlesinger, and as such fit to dine at any table that plays host to my wayward brother."

"Hey!" John protested. "Who are you calling wayward?"

Emma looked timidly up at John's face.

"I hardly think I deserve such an honor."

John smiled down at Emma. It was a wry smile to be sure, but charming as well, and Emma lowered her eyes demurely.

"Allow me to tell you something about my sister, Miss Trask," John said. "Although Eliza has this way of phrasing things so that it sounds as though she's asking you a question, the truth is she's simply telling you how things are going to be. In my experience, it's always best to just smile and nod, and allow her to move your arms and legs about as though a marionette. Because in the end that's what's going to happen anyway."

"Why, John Bradstreet Schuyler!" Eliza laughed. "You make me sound a positive battle-ax!"

"Trust me," John said to Emma, ignoring his sister. "If she hadn't been born a lady, I'm pretty sure she'd have ended up as a muleteer or drill sergeant. She may wear silk and powder, but underneath she's all steel."

"Who are you accusing of wearing powder?" Eliza said. "My complexion is wondrously fair!"

"It seems I have no choice then but to accept," Emma said — meekly, of course. She stole another shy glimpse at John, and Eliza could see she was trying not to smile.

"Perfect!" Eliza said. Then, in a leading voice, she added: "You know what a party means, don't you?"

Emma could only shrug.

"We have to shop for dress fabric!"

"And that's my cue," John groaned. "I'm going to meet some of the lads from school." He bowed to Emma and winked at Eliza. "Don't wait up."

■ ■ ■ ■

PART TWO:
FOOTMEN AND
GENTLEWOMEN

■ ■ ■ ■

6
PATERFAMILIAS PANIC

The Law Offices of Alexander Hamilton, Esq.

New York, New York

July 1785

The news that Eliza was expecting their first child had a curious effect on Alex. At first he was elated. Over the moon. He literally couldn't wipe the smile from his face. He would smear his hand over his lips, and when it came away they would still be curled in an upward-facing curve, like a bowl set out to catch a fresh spring rain. Eliza teased him that he had the same goofy smile on his face that Thomas Jefferson was wont to sport after he'd drunk a cup or two of his famed poppy tea.

As a fatherless child, all Alex had ever wanted was to shower paternal love on a family in a way that had never been shown to him. Since he'd met Eliza, his dreams had been filled with children. He wanted a huge family, as big as William and Susannah Livingston's, as big as Philip and Catherine Schuyler's. Bigger even. Like the biblical Jacob, he would have a dozen children — a score — and he would pour love and kisses and presents and prestige down upon them, and spawn a family lineage to rival those great American dynasties. The Hamilton name would live on in his descendants for countless generations and enable this country that he had helped found to reach its greatest potential.

"I feel like Abraham himself," Alex told Eliza as he covered her face, her hands, her belly with kisses that evening.

"You're being silly," Eliza said, although the truth was she felt a little like Sarah.

"I'm just so happy," he told her.

And then he panicked.

Alex went to bed that first night with his wife in his arms and a smile on his face, and he woke in a sweat from a terrible dream in which a group of faceless creditors — is there an uglier word in the English language! — broke down his door and turned him and Eliza and their son (his name was going to be Philip, Eliza had already told him) out of their house, transforming them at a stroke from one of New York's first families into a just another gang of sooty-faced beggars. Alex was a rational man. He didn't put much stock in dreams. But Eliza told him that her pregnancy had been revealed to her while she was sleeping, so if he rejected the omen of his own fantasy, wasn't he forced to reject hers as well?

But that's not how it works, he told himself. Sometimes such visions are gifts from Providence, informing us of the future, and sometimes they're just manifestations of our own fears. Alex's own childhood had been rocked by bad luck and worse behavior. His father had absconded, his mother had drifted from man to man until she succumbed to illness at a young age, he and his beloved brother, James, had been torn apart and sent to live in separate homes. It was only natural that he would be nervous about starting a family of his own.

Why even Eliza's childhood, which could seem idyllic, was marked by tragedy! Her mother had given birth to fifteen children, but seven of them had died as infants or toddlers. And so, yes, what if his and Eliza's baby died? What if Eliza died? What if *he* died? What if the tide of public opinion turned against him, and instead of a brilliant lawyer who could win the most hopeless cases he came to be regarded as just another amoral conman, a man who would say or do anything to defeat his opponents?

And what of his political ambitions? They had been placed in suspension for the past couple of years as he worked to establish himself financially, but he had always believed that his true destiny was not to be just another well-heeled lawyer, but a civil servant — a civic leader. But all of that would be over before it began. He would be forced to forgo all his prestigious clients for a blundering procession of grifters and graspers seeking to use the law to defraud law-abiding citizens and businesses and even the government out of their hard-earned money. If he managed to get his name on a ballot, voters would scratch it off. The people who actually won elections would refuse to appoint him to even the lowliest clerkship. He would be a joke.

It was as if all the promise of his early life and career had been revealed to be a treacherous lure, a piece of meat sitting in a pair of concealed iron jaws that would snap shut the minute he reached for it. How could he have ever been so stupid as to think that a nameless boy from a tiny little island in the Caribbean — not Cuba or Puerto Rico or Saint-Domingue or Jamaica or one of the other colonial jewels, but poor pathetic Nevis! — could talk his way into power in a new country? How could he have ever been so brazen as to believe he could join the upper echelons of society? What a fool he was!

"Oh, Alex, you're being a bit dramatic, don't you think?" Eliza laughed the next morning over tea, when he confessed his anxieties and recalled his dream. "Calm down, for heaven's sake. I'm the one who's growing a baby in her belly, after all."

127

Alex couldn't calm down, but he could do what he always did when he found himself overwhelmed by ephemeral fears: He threw himself into his work.

Since his dramatic success with Caroline Childress last year, he had acquired dozens of new clients in similar straits: one-time Tory supporters who had pledged allegiance to the United States after independence was won rather than return to a country on the other side of the Atlantic that most of them had never seen. But their new country, or at least their new government, had not always returned their amiability, and in many states — especially New York, under its rapacious blond buffoon of a governor, George Clinton — the retaliation had been especially punitive.

Because the new nation did not yet have a supreme court with the ability to set legal precedents, each and every case had to be tried individually. One after another, aggrieved farmers and landlords and merchants and tradesmen and tradeswomen came to Alex asking only to be allowed to hold on to what had always been theirs, and one after another

Alex pled their cause for them, forcing the government of New York to live up to the words with which Mr. Jefferson had begun the Declaration of Independence, and to allow its citizens to claim their unalienable rights to life and liberty and the pursuit of happiness. And one after another he won.

The damages ranged from a few dozen pounds to many hundreds, and Alex spent as many as fourteen hours a day writing brief after brief to earn his ten percent of the takings. To speed his task, he hired a trio of clerks with the colorful names of Nippers, Turkey, and Bartleby, and with their help he was able to double his output (though his profits increased rather more modestly, because of course the new employees did not work for free, and the larger office he was forced to take on was an additional expense).

Alex loved the work, but he couldn't help but feel it was a bit of a distraction from his true calling, which was politics. He had been elated when he won a seat as New York's representative to the Congress of the Confederation back in '82, but he resigned in disgust after less than a year in office. In the absence of a strong central government, the Congress was like a dysfunctional family of thirteen feuding siblings all fighting for their parents' inheritance.

Everyone was more concerned with getting something for themselves than in choosing the course that would make the whole family stronger. Alex had spoken with a few other political leaders about the need for a new Constitution that would truly unite the thirteen states. Several of them had agreed with him, including the brilliant James Madison, but as yet their plans had not proceeded, not least because Alex was too busy with his law practice to devote much energy to politics.

If he was ever going to make an impact on the national stage — let alone establish himself as the true paterfamilias of a large and powerful clan — he would need to shift away from these small-time cases, or at least augment them with more lucrative work. And so, once he had set his clerks on course, he turned his attention to the charter Reverend Provoost had showed him just minutes before

Eliza shared her own momentous news. It was a fascinating legal question to be sure, but to Alex it was also a life raft: his big chance to ensure his financial stability and turn his mind to the kinds of great questions that would ensure his place in history.

As Alex studied the document, he found the church's charter was admirably concise and frighteningly clear, and why shouldn't it be? Since Henry VIII created the Church of England in the 1530s, the British government had had two and a half centuries to perfect its management of that nation's ecclesiastical affairs. The kernel of the document was that, as a "religious rather than fiduciary concern," the church was directed to run its affairs for "the enrichment of the community" rather than itself, and as such could not "use, lease, grant, demise, alien, bargain, sell, and dispose of" properties "exceeding the yearly value of £5,000." From what Alex could see, the church had been pulling in nearly twice that amount for the past three decades, with the exception of the war years, and had only managed to come in under the £5,000 mark by dint of some rather creative accounting: In 1784, it had shown net income of £4,999.98, which was cutting things about as fine as you could. Alex saw ways in which he could manipulate the numbers still further and perhaps eke out another £200 or £300. For example, the church had not deducted the cost of the wheat it purchased to make its communion wafers, perhaps not wanting to admit that the Heavenly Host had earthly origins. Ditto the wine used for sacrament. But these would hardly make a dent in the church's financial woes and, more to the point, verged on dishonest manipulation of both the law and mathematics, if not religious doctrine itself, which ran contrary to Alex's deepest principles, not to mention the church's. Try as he might, Alex could see no loophole that didn't flirt with crass opportunism or outright criminality.

In desperation, he asked Reverend Provoost if he could see a complete accounting of the church's holdings. The rector seemed to have anticipated this request, for within two hours of Alex's sending a messenger over, three porters arrived bearing nineteen large wooden crates of musty documents going back nearly a century. The pile took up nearly half of Alex's private office, filling the room with the smell of sour, yeasty mold; but until someone invented a way to turn paper into ether, there was nothing else to do but dive in. Alex threw open the windows, letting in the warm summer air, pried the lid off the first crate, and set to work.

It took him the better part of the month of July to begin to make heads or tails of things. From a filing standpoint, at any rate, the church certainly wasn't run like a business. There was no discernible order to the documents that Alex could make out, and he would peruse one twenty-page tract thoroughly only to wade a few inches deeper and discover another that superseded the one he'd just studied so thoroughly. After a week of this, he realized he was going to have to sort and classify the thousands of files before he could actually review them, a task that took over a week. With each dusty, unpaid minute, Alex was painfully aware that his chances of actually making any money off this case were growing as dim as the filthy, worm-eaten papers he was sorting.

But in for a penny in for a pound (or five thousand, as the case may be): Alex's fingers turned darker than a ditchdigger's and he was coughing like a coal miner, but eventually he had what he thought was a fairly clear grasp of the situation. Shortly after its charter in 1697, the church had acquired large tracts of land on the island of Manhattan, including a two-hundred-acre grant by Queen Anne in 1705. Most of that land had been empty at the time, its rocky, rolling soil heavily forested, and had been let to area farmers to clear, level, and till.

But as the city grew, a good portion of the farmland was developed for urban use and now housed a variety of businesses whose rents, in order to artificially lower the parish's income, were kept at a fraction of market rates, if not waived entirely. Dozens of buildings on church property stood empty and decrepit because the church was forbidden to rent them due to the income limitation, nor could it afford to maintain them because of a shortage of funds. Similarly, more than half of its remaining pasturage lay fallow, or was farmed by squatters who had no legal right to the land but recognized that Trinity would do little to drive them away. The church even owned the land on which Columbia's College Hall had been built, for which it received a mere fifty pounds a year in rent. That was hardly more than Alex paid for one pew in the church. It was absurd.

And punitive as well. The more Alex researched the matter, the more it appeared that Trinity's income restriction had been imposed on it because the mother church back in England didn't want a "mere colonial" parish growing too powerful. So it hobbled Trinity's finances, and whenever the New World church found itself in straitened circumstances, the mother church back in England provided the money from its own deep coffers, which, connected directly to the crown's treasury, weren't restricted in the way Trinity's were. And yet it was all perfectly legal. Furthermore, since the church and New York State had agreed to maintain the charter in the wake of independence — Governor Clinton was unwavering in the matter — there was not even the claim of bad faith upon which to challenge it.

It took Alex nearly a month to work this out. A month of exhausting fourteen- and sixteen-hour days, and for no pay as well. A month of lost income, and meanwhile two new mouths to feed in the form of John and Emma, and a footman's salary for Drayton and a nursery to be appointed — and in a manner suitable to the Schuylers' expectations to boot.

By the end of the month, Alex's panic had returned, and doubled. He glanced around the stacks and stacks of brown moldy paper that made his office look like the inside of a termite's nest.

What on earth have I gotten myself into?

Just then there was a knock on the door.

"Enter," Alex called, adding *sotto voce:* "And please save me from myself."

The door opened and Nippers stuck his whiskered, sallow face in.

"A lady to see you, Mr. Hamilton."

"Please tell me it's my wife." Alex needed to see Eliza's smiling face right now, needed to hear her tell him that everything would be all right.

"I could tell you that, sir, but then you would fire me for lying."

Alex grunted out a little laugh. "Nippers, you should take that show on the road; you'd make a fortune."

"More than you're paying me, no doubt," Nippers said.

Another groan from Alex. "Please, send in my visitor."

Nippers disappeared. A moment later a female form, rather smaller and less hirsute than Nippers's, appeared in his place, standing hesitantly at the edge of the room. She was in her early twenties, with a slight figure and auburn hair peeking out of a simple, pleated bonnet that shaded a delicate, pensive face, rather heavily powdered for the afternoon. She was wearing a sober workaday dress in midnight blue, and Alex was almost relieved: If he had to fight off yet another love-starved Revolutionary War widow, he didn't know what he would do with himself.

"Please, do come in, if you can make

your way through the mess, Miss, ah —"

"Missus," said the woman. "Reynolds. Maria Reynolds."

A married woman, Alex thought. *I'm safe.*

He didn't know how wrong he was.

7
A LADY AND A GENTLEMAN

The Hamilton Town House
New York, New York
July 1785

Eliza knew only the briefest details about Alex's new case. When he had first set up shop she had followed his work eagerly, and prided herself on the legal knowledge she absorbed both from her husband and from the massive tomes he left around the house. But running a household is as demanding a job as any attorney's, and Eliza had her own interests as well, not the least of which was the plight of the hundreds of orphans who had lost their fathers to the war and their mothers to societal neglect. And now she had her pregnancy, too.

The truth was, though, the work of appointing a nursery went surprisingly quickly. The furniture was bought or ordered, the fabric purchased. In four or five months they would move John into Columbia College quarters, after which they would paint and paper the room for baby Philip. Until then, there were just quiet hours with Emma spent knitting, sewing, and embroidering: swaddling clothes and nappies, christening gowns and bedsheets, booties, blankets, beanies.

And while all this was happening there was the miracle of her body, which was not just hers anymore, but shared space with the new life taking form within her womb. The changes were minuscule, yet Eliza could feel them every day. First, there was a general swelling. It wasn't like gaining a few pounds after a week of dietary excess. It was more like she was becoming bigger, more powerful, like a Titaness preparing to bring a Zeus or Poseidon into the world. After the initial lethargy and stomach discomfort, she found herself ravenously hungry and full of energy. As a little girl, she had marveled at the mares on the Pastures, who, minutes after foaling, were back on their feet and keeping a wary eye on their newborn, ready to defend it from any threat. She had seen deer and sows and even chickens display the same zeal, and once she had even seen a wolf charge a pack of her father's hunting dogs and drive them away from her pup single-handedly. Eliza felt like that: fierce, wild, braver than she had ever been. The anxiety around conception was already a distant memory. She was suffused with calm — which left her free to concentrate on other things. Like her new charges, Emma, John, and Drayton.

Eliza knew before the voice came from the other side of the door that it was Drayton. In the past month she had come to recognize his unique knock, which, though quite firm, was some-how . . . polite, as if he wanted to make sure you knew that he didn't want to disturb you, but also didn't want you *not* to hear him, lest you miss whatever information he was conveying.

"Come in, Drayton," she called.

Drayton's door opening was similarly forceful yet controlled. Unlike Loewes, the footman at the Pastures, who was wont to nudge the door open with his hip, Drayton never risked banging the door against the wall by such a maneuver. He always kept one hand on the knob and walked through the door as though he were setting a puzzle piece in place; if he was delivering a large tray, he would have set it down on the hallway credenza, and retrieved it after. On this occasion, however, he held only a small salver, on which, presumably, sat a letter or calling card.

"This came —" Drayton's voice caught in his throat. "Oh, pardon me, Mrs. Hamilton. I didn't realize that Emma, that is, Miss Trask, was attending to your toilette."

For a boy raised in the wilds of Ohio, Drayton had acquired an extraordinarily courtly manner, although his French accent was an approximation at best. Eliza had to fight back a giggle at his pronunciation of *toilette,* which sounded like "wallet" with a "t" in front of it. Even Emma, standing behind Eliza but visible in the mirror over her vanity table, couldn't quite suppress her smile.

Her own eyes were staring out of a face

that was only half made up, the powder applied but no color as yet painted onto lips or cheeks or eyes, so that she seemed a ghostly visage in the lamplight. Above her, Emma's face was a vision of youthful purity, free of paint or powder, her hair worn in simple braids that coiled around her head like a tiara. Emma's eyes flickered to Drayton, then quickly shifted back to the top of Eliza's head. For a girl who had helped raise her brother and taken care of her father, she was remarkably skittish around boys.

Eliza found Drayton's eyes in the mirror now. "I hope I'm not shattering any illusions about the nature of female beauty. I'm afraid that there is more than a little artifice to it." She glanced at the tray in Drayton's hand. "Please tell me that's not from Mr. Hamilton."

Drayton's mouth opened, then closed. "I, I —" he stuttered. Then, in a voice that sounded almost defeated, as if he hated to disappoint his mistress: "Yes, ma'am."

Eliza sighed. "If you don't mind, Emma?"

"Of course, Mrs. Hamilton." Emma

stepped across the room to Drayton. There was a little awkwardness as Drayton held the salver out to her, then pulled it back and instead handed it to Emma, perhaps thinking it inappropriate to proffer a letter to Emma in the same manner as he would the mistress.

"Thank you, Drayton," Emma said pertly, and curtsied.

Even in the lamplight Eliza could see Drayton's blush.

"Y-you're welcome, Miss Trask. Mrs. Hamilton," he threw in, backing from the room like a courtier.

"Oh, Drayton, I was just teasing," said Emma gently.

Drayton turned even redder as he closed the door.

"Be kind to him," said Eliza. "The Penningtons come from good stock, even if they did decide to set out for the frontier like pioneers. Rowena herself always says that her sister was much more interested in decorum than she is, and no doubt she inculcated those values in her son. He is perhaps trying too hard, but we should attribute that to an eagerness to do his job well, rather than an affectation to a station not his own."

"You mean, like me?"

Eliza whirled around on her stool, nearly getting a brush in her eye. "Emma! Whatever do you mean?"

Emma resumed her work, keeping her eyes fastened on her brush rather than Eliza's. Her voice was modest, bordering on self-deprecating. "I mean that, while I appreciate your invitation to tonight's soiree, Mrs. Hamilton, I do not think it appropriate for a servant to mix with gentlefolk as though there were no difference in their stations."

Eliza sat back, then took Emma's hand in hers. "But you're not a servant, Emma. You're more like a, a houseguest who helps out, as it were."

Emma smiled wryly, her hand limp in Eliza's. "That is kind of you to say, Mrs. Hamilton, and I hope you know how very grateful I am to you and Mr. Hamilton for taking in a strange girl of somewhat dubious origins. Nevertheless, it is you who sits in the curule and I who applies the paint." She twirled her brush in her fingers, though she didn't pull her hand free.

Eliza smiled warmly. "No servant would know the word *curule*," she said.

"Servants can read, Mrs. Hamilton. Why, just the other day I saw Drayton curled up beside the kitchen stove, engrossed in a volume of *Don Quixote.* 'The Smollett translation,' he told me, as nice as you please."

"Well, it is far superior to the Ormsby," Eliza said.

Emma shook her head in bewilderment. "Which only proves my point, that servants like me and Drayton can have a certain amount of discernment. Yet it doesn't change our class. Now, please turn, or we shall never finish."

Eliza turned obligingly, and Emma resumed work on her maquillage. Like her husband, Eliza had signed on to the idea that in the new America class was nothing more than an indication of income, not values or, even worse, social station. On some level she knew that it was easy for her to think this, being wealthy and well-educated herself. She knew, too, that it was more an ideal than an actuality, since the amount of money one's parents possessed determined so much about one's opportunities. If you were born poor there was a good likelihood that you would remain poor, no matter how hard you worked, not least because you would be working in the fields or at the hearth from an early age, and not learning the kinds of skills that would lead to more remunerative opportunities. But even if it was only a goal, Eliza still felt it important keep it in mind, lest the United States end up reproducing the hidebound ways of the Europeans.

"Well," she said now, "and will you still be a servant if you become my sister?"

Emma had to step away to laugh, lest she splatter Eliza. "Oh, Mrs. Hamilton, please! Do not tease me so, or you will leave this room looking like a child's drawing of a lady."

"Who is teasing? I have seen the way John dotes on you. Why should that not blossom into romance?"

Eliza's words only prompted more laughter from Emma. "Mr. Schuyler? Flirt with *me*? He certainly enjoys teasing me even more than you do, but he is hardly interested, I assure you."

"Oh, Emma Trask, you adorable naïf. What do think teasing is? It is but a boy's subterfuge for affections he is not yet ready to give voice to. With a little encouragement from you, John will surely speak his mind."

Emma stepped back a bit. "Oh, Mrs. Hamilton, I could not flirt with your brother. I would feel . . . *forward.*" She pronounced the word in the softest tone, yet one would think Eliza had asked her to pose nude for some French painter recreating a Roman bacchanal.

"My dear," she said gently, "you are much too polite and modest to ever be forward."

Eliza looked for some sign on the girl's face that she was interested in her brother, yet Emma's visage was as serious as it was when she weighed a roll of fabric in her hands. Well, the girl certainly did love sewing.

Still, Eliza thought she heard just the tiniest bit of steel in Emma's voice, which she found almost refreshing. The girl was so afraid of giving offense that she could sometimes come across as a bit of a wet blanket.

And why shouldn't Emma be interested in John and John in Emma? They would make an excellent match! Emma's modesty and thrift was just the antidote to her brother's carousing. She would settle him and he would raise her station, proving that the newly formed United States was truly the land of equality. Their love would be patriotic, Eliza decided, and she was determined to do everything in her power to encourage the suit.

She was about to say something on that topic, but Emma spoke first. "Mr. Hamilton's note still awaits your attention," she said quickly, and, pointedly handing it to her, resumed work on Eliza's face.

Yes, the note. Eliza hadn't forgotten about it. She just had no desire to open it, since she was pretty sure she knew what it said. Sighing, she broke the seal and unfolded it.

Darling Eliza,
    The Gunn case has been moved up from Monday to today. I will be late

at court but should be home before 9. 10 at the latest.

Love, A.

Eliza didn't remember which was the Gunn case. Another of Alex's beleaguered loyalists, no doubt, from whom he would realize a ten- or twenty-pound payment when all was said and done. Sometimes Eliza wished that Alex had never won the Childress case. His office was constantly full of sad-faced petitioners hoping to recover their home or job or pony, and would it be permissible for Alex to collect his fee from the settlement rather than in advance? Perhaps he would accept a nice suckling pig or a clutch of eggs in lieu of coin? Alex was certainly making money, but not "hand over fist," as they said, and she wondered if it was worth the endless days at the office and at court.

But if she didn't like his busy schedule, she had certainly grown accustomed to it, and forty-five minutes later, when Emma had gone off to her room to change into what she called her "party frock," Eliza headed downstairs to make sure everything was in order and to prepare to greet her guests on her own — again.

As soon as she got downstairs, however, she realized she wouldn't be on her own tonight. "Well, well, you don't look half bad," said John.

He was sitting on the yellow sofa in the living room, his white-stockinged ankles crossed on the lacquered top of a low table before it.

"First, dear brother, thank you for the compliment, as it were. Second, if you don't remove your filthy shoes from my table, I will be forced to have Drayton remove them for you."

"Filthy?" John laughed as he sat up and moved his feet to the floor. "Why, these shoes have never touched pavement. I only wear them to at-home parties."

Eliza had to admit that the shoes did look pretty immaculate. They were powder-blue silk with gold and silver embroidery, matching his suit. That suit, Eliza saw as John stood up, was of a rather affected European courtly cut, with exaggerated cuffs that reached nearly to the crook of his elbow and lapels that folded open all the way to his shoulders and a veritable Niagara Falls of lace spilling down from his throat. Eliza still remembered when John was loath to don naught but coarse woolen breeches and linen tunics. This foppish apparition in front of her was something entirely new. It was not unhandsome, albeit in a ridiculous way. It just wasn't the John who used to throw snowballs at her.

My little brother is growing up, she thought. *And turning into a dandy.*

"That is a . . . shiny suit," Eliza said.

"Thank you — I think," John replied. "I assumed you would be wearing one of your 'handsome' dresses in burgundy or ruby or emerald or some similarly dark jewel. I thought I'd stand out."

Eliza laughed. She was in fact wearing a burgundy dress, although it was lightened by a pale green bodice — uncorsetted, of course, so as not to squeeze the baby. (This might have been her favorite part of being pregnant — no corsets for months and months and months!) The bodice was, however, heavily embroidered with a dark thread, so the effect

152

was not exactly bright.

"This is a lovely dress," she protested.

"Indeed," John said. "I can see Mama wearing it." Eliza gasped as John continued: "You're lucky you're so beautiful, sister. You can get away with a sober dress. And of course you're married — and 'with child,' as they say — so it doesn't really matter," he added with a wink.

"And you're lucky you're my brother, or my husband would surely be calling you out for speaking to his wife in such a manner."

"Just as long as it's not swords," John said. "This jacket must weigh twenty pounds. It is all I can do to lift my glass to my lips. Speaking of which —" He turned to a cabinet on which a decanter of amber liquid sat next to an array of crystal goblets.

"Do not dare, John! That is the last of Stephen's honey wine. It is for our guests."

"Never fear, I just want a glass." John grabbed a goblet and pulled open the door to the cabinet, revealing a plain bottle filled with a dark brown, slightly sinister-looking liquid.

"This is brewed by a man over on Vesey Street," he explained as he opened it. "It doesn't have a name, but the fellows at Columbia call it Rite of Passage, since every freshman has to drink a bottle of it on his first day at school." He smiled proudly as he poured a healthy dose of the evil-looking medicine into his glass. "I'm the only one who was able to do it, and I finished James Frantz's and Frederick McAdams's bottles as well."

"God save us," Eliza said. "I can smell it from here. You must have the constitution of an ox."

"It has nothing to do with constitution," John said, downing his shot in one gulp. "And everything to do with practice, practice, practice." He topped off his glass and proffered the bottle to Eliza. "Want to try?"

"No thank you," Eliza said, waving her hand in front of her nose. "If you applied yourself half as much to your studies as you do to your carousing, you would be top of your class."

"I'm already top of my class. Professor

Lewis called my paper on *Paradise Lost* 'commendable, if unconventional.' "

"Let me guess," Eliza said, "you took Satan's side?"

"But he has all the best lines! 'Farewell happy Fields / Where Joy forever dwells: hail horrors, hail / Infernal world'! How can you not root for someone who says that?"

Before Eliza could answer, John turned to someone behind her and brightened considerably. "And who have we here?

Eliza looked up to see Emma coming down the stairs, sporting a sunny dress complemented by a richly embroidered arabesque in an array of pale greens and blues. The dress had been Eliza's, though she had never worn it in public. Its brightness made her feel as though someone were shining a lantern on her whenever she walked into a room, but it complemented her fair hair and ivory complexion perfectly. In its original form, the dress had had open shoulders, but when Emma had taken it in — the girl was slimmer than Eliza had been even before she got pregnant, and a little shorter as well — she had used the removed fabric to make a pair of delicately pleated shoulders. She had also sewn a double layer of lace into the top of the bodice, making it on the whole a more modest garment than it had been when it belonged to Eliza, but still stunning. It seemed to Eliza that she had recoiled her braids on her head. If before they had looked like a tiara, now they reminded Eliza of a halo. They emphasized the girlish innocence of her face, but not without sophistication.

"I would whistle," John said now, "but I'm afraid my sister would turn me out, and then I would be deprived of the sight of your radiant form."

Emma's pale cheeks turned bright red, which was all too obvious as she hadn't applied any powder to her face. She said that it was too difficult to do on one's own, but Eliza suspected that she simply found it too artful. Emma would rather be scorned than thought the seductress.

In any event, Eliza knew that Emma was just being too humble. John was most certainly interested.

"I-I'll just check on Rowena in the kitchen," Emma said to Eliza, without acknowledging John's flirtations.

"Nonsense!" Eliza said. "Do I ask my guests to supervise the cook? My mother would fly down from Albany and drag me back home by my ear! I'll check on Rowena. John, why don't you pour Emma a glass of Stephen's honey wine?"

"Don't mind if I do," John agreed as Eliza skipped through the door to the kitchen stairs.

As soon as she'd closed the door behind her, though, she immediately turned and crouched down so she could spy through the keyhole. She was thankful yet again she wasn't wearing a corset: She would have never been able to sink low enough to see through the tiny aperture.

"It's really not necessary," Emma was saying. "I almost never drink spirits."

"Be that as it may, the mistress has commanded you to drink honey wine, and so honey wine you shall drink."

"Just a drop," Emma said uncomfortably as John filled a goblet nearly to the brim. "That's much too much!"

"That's for me," John said with a laugh, pouring a second, smaller measure. "This is for you."

Emma chuckled, and when she spoke again, Eliza thought she could hear a trace of the girl who had wrung the necks of chickens on a farm outside of Concorde. "Oh, is that so?" challenged Emma.

There's the spunk, Eliza thought. *Show him who's boss!*

Just then there was a sound behind her.

"Mrs. Hamilton?" Drayton said from the lower stairs. "Are you hurt?"

Eliza stood up quickly, pressing a finger to her lips.

"Mr. Schuyler and Miss Trask are alone in the front salon."

Drayton frowned in confusion. "Are they . . . that is, do they have need of anything?" He was carrying the soup tureen, and he turned to place it on a table beside him but stopped himself. Perhaps he thought setting it down without permission was a dereliction of his duty.

"They need naught but what nature has already gifted them. That, and perhaps a bit of liquid courage."

Drayton continued to regard her with confusion. Then his eyes went wide, and he started so much he nearly dropped the tureen. "Oh! Yes! Well, should I . . . ? That is, I mean, well . . . what *should* I do?"

"Drayton, boy!" came Rowena's voice from deeper in the kitchen. "I told you to take that tureen up to the dining room and come back down for the mutton. Hurry it up now!"

Drayton looked back and forth between cook and mistress. Rowena, sensing that someone was on the stairs, came into view.

"Mrs. Hamilton? What on earth are you doing crouching there like a pickpocket?"

"Shh," Eliza said. "I'm keeping the way clear so that Cupid has a clear aim with his arrow."

Rowena frowned. "You'll pardon me for the impertinence, ma'am, but have you hit your head? You're not making any sense."

"Miss Trask and Mr. Schuyler are in the salon," Drayton said now. Eliza noticed that a sweat had broken out on his forehead and his arms were quivering slightly. Eliza had once tried to lift the tureen when it was full and had barely been able to budge it. Drayton had been holding it for several minutes.

"Put that down before you drop it," Rowena said, and Drayton set the tureen on the table with a relieved sigh. "And I understood what Mrs. Hamilton was saying, there being no one else in the house as yet. I just wondered if she'd gone daft."

"Rowena!"

"Apologies, Mrs. Hamilton," said Rowena, sounding not at all contrite. "But Emma, Miss Trask, that is, and Mr. Schuyler are not cut from the same cloth. She is a simple girl, in manner as much as in money, and Mr. Schuyler is, shall we say, a certain type of gentleman who requires a certain type of lady."

"Careful, Rowena. I will tolerate a little of your cheek directed toward me, but I will not have you speak ill of my brother."

"I do not mean to speak ill of him, ma'am. He is young and full of sauce, and why shouldn't he be? He is a Schuyler and a rather gifted intellect from what I hear. He should have his fun. But his type is not Miss Trask's. She would do much better with a boy like Drayton here, than with a boy like Mr. Schuyler."

It seemed to Eliza that Drayton's face resembled a turnip he was blushing so hard, but Eliza had not time to soothe her footman.

"Oh, come now, Rowena. Don't be so hidebound. Why shouldn't Emma improve her station by marrying a Schuyler? No offense, Drayton."

"None taken, ma'am," the footman answered, his face now as red as one of Rowena's tomato sauces. He was staring at the floor as though he wished it would open up and swallow him.

"This is not about station, Mrs. Hamilton. It is about temperament. Miss Trask is a quiet soul, Mr. Schuyler a raucous one. She wants a man who will read poetry to her, not drag her to one ball after another until the heels are danced off her shoes. They are ill-matched," said Rowena in a matter-of-fact tone.

Eliza frowned. Rowena had given the matter a bit too much thought entirely, and Eliza was about to say so when there came a peal of laughter from the front salon, so loud that Rowena and Drayton heard it in the basement kitchen.

"Ill-matched, you say?" Eliza said with a smile. "Opposites attract, *I* say." She nodded to the footman. "I think it is safe to bring the tureen up now. Love is a like a good soup," she added to her cook. "It needs to simmer, not boil."

Rowena rolled her eyes. "All respect, Mrs. Hamilton, but the day I take a cooking lesson from you is the day I go looking for another line of work. Hurry it up, boy," she added, swatting Drayton with a kitchen towel. "It may be a leg of lamb, but that don't mean it's going to scamper itself up the stairs on its own."

8

MRS. MARIA REYNOLDS WALKS INTO HIS LIFE

Ruston's Ale House and Inn
New York, New York
July 1785

Alex stared out the window of the carriage, barely seeing the buildings and pedestrians that passed by. His briefcase sat on his lap as he kneaded the leather so violently it was starting to crack beneath his fingers. His sweating palms had stained the leather with dark, ugly, accusatory smears.

Why did I lie to her? he berated himself. *What possessed me?*

It was such a bad lie, too. The Gunn case was still set for Monday. Should Eliza read the legal notices in the paper next week — which she unfailingly did, clipping out any mention of her husband's name — and take the time to do the math, she would realize that the case had not, in fact, been moved up to the date of their party.

He turned and looked at the pale female face sitting on the carriage seat beside him.

Stupid, stupid, stupid.

Why didn't he just tell his wife he was helping a woman in distress? What would have been so wrong about that? Eliza would have been glad to hear he was helping someone in need of it, to be sure.

So why did he lie to his wife?

Earlier that afternoon, Maria Reynolds had walked into Alex's office hesitantly. Alex was used to nervous clients, and by now he was good at categorizing them into types. There were those who were nervous because they didn't have the money to pay him up front, and they were hoping they could work out a deal. Others hesitated because the idea of interacting with the legal system unnerved them, as if it would suddenly emerge that they had committed some grievous crime that they were heretofore unaware of. Still others had, in fact, done something wrong, and were wondering if Alex would help them anyway, and if they could get away with it.

But Maria Reynolds was different. She wasn't nervous. She was afraid, but whether it was of him or someone else Alex didn't know.

"I apologize for the mess," he said when the silence had gone on too long. "I just took on a new client, and they saw fit to deliver every piece of paper that has ever crossed their threshold."

A smile flickered over Maria's lips at Alex's joke, then quickly faded. Well, he had to admit, it wasn't a particularly great joke.

"Please, have a seat."

Maria sat in the one chair that wasn't piled high with paper. She was silent for a moment, and then she pulled the chair closer to Alex's desk — as close as it could come and still allow her to sit in it — and then she sat back again, and yet she still remained silent.

Alex offered his warmest smile. "How may I help you today, Mrs. Reynolds?"

A strange mixture of emotions flickered

over Maria's face. Fear, sadness, resolve, guilt. Her lips quivered. Her mouth opened, then closed again. And then, without a sound, she began to cry.

"My dear Mrs. Reynolds!" Alex said. He burst from his chair and hurried around the desk, pulling his handkerchief from his pocket. He fell to his knee in front of her and pressed the handkerchief into her hand. "Whatever is the matter?"

"I'm so sorry, Mr. Hamilton," Maria blubbered as she dabbed at her eyes with Alex's handkerchief. "I had not thought I would react so. I thought I had inured myself to it all. I — I'm so embarrassed."

"There is nothing to be embarrassed about. In my line of work, I see clients cry all the time."

"Yes, but *I* do not cry," Maria said reproachfully, though Alex couldn't tell if she was reproaching him or herself. "In my position, I cannot afford to cry, or I would never have survived what I did."

Alex nodded sympathetically.

"Well, you are here now, and I give you my word as a gentleman as well as a lawyer that I will do everything in my power to make sure whatever is grieving you can never hurt you again."

Maria nodded without speaking. After a moment, she turned and looked at the open door. Alex jumped up and waded through the boxes to pull it closed. When he returned, he pulled the stack of papers off the second chair and sat facing her.

"Please, Mrs. Reynolds. Unburden yourself."

Maria sat without speaking for another long moment, though the occasional silent sob still wracked her body. Then she raised Alex's handkerchief to her cheek. Alex thought she was going to dry her tears but instead she began wiping at the powder on her left cheek. At first Alex didn't understand. But then the dark shadow of a bruise came into view.

Alex's widening eyes served as Maria's mirror, and she stopped wiping.

"You see now the nature of my problem," she said in a voice that was at once defiant and ashamed, defeated and determined.

Once again Alex was on his knees before her, and this time he pressed her tiny hands between his. "Oh, you poor, poor creature!"

He had seen a woman in distress like this before.

His mother.

In the carriage, beneath his gaze, Maria gathered herself to speak. "I really did not mean to put you to such trouble," she said in a contrite voice. "Only I do not know how I could possibly return to my — to my husband's home."

"Put it out of your mind," Alex said soothingly. "I am only happy that I have the means with which to help you."

"I am in your debt."

"You owe me nothing."

"Except your fee, of course," Maria said with a small smile.

"There will be time enough to talk of legal matters later. Our first priority is to make sure that you are safe and out of reach of that brute."

The carriage pulled up short, and Alex looked out the window. A cheerful sign proclaimed RUSTON'S ALES in crisp black letters on a bright yellow background.

Below that, a smaller sign advertised ROOMS TO LET. They had arrived.

Maria looked at the inn dubiously. "You are sure this is a discreet establishment?"

"I know the proprietress," Alex said as he handed the driver a couple of coins. "She can be trusted absolutely."

"Proprietress?" Maria sounded defeated. Then, pulling her bonnet more firmly around her face, she allowed Alex to help her from the carriage.

Alex led her in by the side entrance, which opened on a narrow hallway instead of directly into the ale room. He directed Maria to wait for him and stepped into the main dining room, in which perhaps a dozen people were eating at tables or drinking at the bar. He should have told Eliza the truth of why he was late in coming home, and yet something had stopped him. Mostly, he did not feel like explaining the whole sordid tale, and Maria was in immediate danger, of course, but was there something else?

"Mr. Hamilton!" one of the barmaids said. "We have not seen you here in quite some time! May I fetch you a pint, or perhaps some of cook's Yorkshire pudding? I know how much you love it."

"Good evening, Sally. I may well be ordering some food in a bit, but for now I wonder if I could ask you to escort me to Mrs. Childress's office."

"But of course, sir. Right this way." Sally turned toward the front stairs.

"If you don't mind," Alex said. "Perhaps we could take the back way."

"Oh ho, top secret stuff!" Sally chuckled. "Of course, of course." She walked into the back hall, pulling up short when she saw Maria. She seemed about to say something, then looked back at Alex. Her eyes went wide.

"This is Mrs. —"

"Smith," Maria said quickly. "Mary Smith." She kept her face down and mostly shadowed by her wide-brimmed bonnet. Alex could imagine how it might look like she was trying to conceal her identity — which, in a way, she was — but he knew she was more likely concerned about concealing the tell-tale bruise on her cheek.

"Mrs. Smith will be staying here for a while. I trust that I can rely on you to see to it that she's comfortable."

Sally looked confused, if not suspicious, but just nodded. "Of course, sir. Let me take you to Mrs. Childress."

She led them up two flights of stairs and knocked on a door on the third-floor landing before easing it open.

"Mrs. Childress?" she called into the apartment beyond. "It's Mr. Hamilton here to see you."

"Oh, how nice!" a voice called from within. "Do please bring him in."

"This way, sir, ma'am," Sally said, and led them into the apartment.

Caroline sat at her desk in an office that was larger and more comfortable than Alex's, being furnished with a marble-topped desk at one end and a deep couch flanked by a pair of equally cozy chairs on the other. Since the last time he had seen her, she had traded in her widow's black for a sober but not quite so dreary midnight-blue dress. It was also a good bit smarter than her previous dresses, her finances having rebounded significantly since Alex won her case against the state of New York. Her face was clearer, too, free of the worry that had clouded her for so many years through the war, and made all the more radiant by the genuine smile of joy with which she greeted Alex.

"Mr. Hamilton, what a treat! I was just thinking to drop you a line to see —"

Caroline's voice broke off as she saw Maria.

"This is Mrs. Mary Smith," Alex said. "She is a client of mine. I was hoping that I might be able to rent one of your rooms for her use for the next few weeks."

"It shouldn't be a problem," Caroline said cautiously, clearly sensing that more was going on than just a simple room rental. "Just let me check my books. Sally, bring a pint for Mr. Hamilton and Mrs. Smith, and plates as well."

"Yes, ma'am," Sally said, and hurried back down the hall. A moment later, the door could be heard latching behind her.

Caroline, meanwhile, had flipped open a large, leather-bound ledger and begun to scan its lined surface. She looked up a moment later.

"Room three is available. It has a lovely southern exposure and a small sitting area in addition to the bedstead. If you're going to be staying with us for a while, Mrs. Smith, you'll find it quite comfortable."

Alex turned to Maria, whose eyes never left the floor. When she didn't speak, he answered for her. "Thank you, Mrs. Childress. It sounds perfect."

Caroline stared at Maria a moment longer, then shrugged. "All right, then. I'll have Sally bring your bags up."

Maria's head snapped up, a distressed look on her face. "Oh, I haven't any bags. I haven't —" Her voice broke. "I haven't anything at all."

Caroline looked at Maria for a moment, then turned to Alex. He shrugged but didn't say anything.

"Well then, in that case I'll just see you to your room and have Sally bring your food there."

She led them back outside and down one flight of stairs, to a large room that did indeed sport a lovely, sunny pair of windows facing Water Street and the harbor beyond. Though the water wasn't visible because of the buildings across the street, it was still palpable in the quality of the air and the light, which shimmered and gave the room a liquid quality of its own, as if it were inside a fishbowl. The room was furnished with a wide wooden bedstead covered in a handsome multicolored quilt, a plain but sturdy dresser, a large stuffed chair, and a handsome if somewhat spindly wooden rocker. An oval rag rug, as brightly patterned as the quilt, covered the floorboards.

A small sound escaped Maria's mouth, a sigh of release, surrender even, as if she had been holding something in since she walked into Alex's office two hours before. Although the likelier truth, Alex thought, was that she had been holding her breath for far longer.

"This will do very well," he said to Caroline. "Allow me to help Mrs. Smith to settle in, and then I will be return to you to arrange for payment."

"Oh, there's no need for that, Mr. Hamilton," Caroline said. "I owe you far more than this room is worth."

"And you already paid me in full."

When Caroline looked ready to protest again, he spoke firmly. "I insist on paying you the going rate for Mrs. Smith's room; it is a matter of principle."

Once again Caroline scrutinized Maria, as if looking for something unsavory about her. Once again she shrugged.

"As you wish, Mr. Hamilton. Sally will be back with your food shortly. I will be in my office upstairs." And, handing him the key to the room, she turned and made her way back upstairs.

Alex closed the door behind her, then turned to Maria and presented the key to her. Maria took it as though it were a strange object she had heard about but never beheld, a magic wand, a religious relic.

"Consider this the first step toward your liberation," he said in a gentle voice.

Maria looked up from the key and regarded the room as if it, too, were some kind of magician's trick.

"I cannot quite believe it is possible. Am I really here? I feel as though at any minute I will hear his voice, summoning me, calling me to —" Her voice broke off as she pressed a hand to her mouth.

"There, there," Alex said, taking her to the chair and easing her down. The only other chair being the rocker, which seemed somehow too feminine a seat from which to conduct business, he knelt down before her as he had in his office. "I know it is extraordinarily painful for you to think of it, let alone speak of it. Yet you must. In order for me to help you, I need to know the . . . the nature of your situation. And I am afraid that when it comes to trial, opposing counsel will ask you these same questions, but in a far less gentle manner."

"Trial?" Fear filled Maria's voice and eyes. "What do you mean, trial?"

Alex patted her knee. "The only way you will ever be free of your oppressor is if you and Mr. Reynolds divorce."

"Divorce! But I — I couldn't. Mr. Reynolds would never —"

"Mr. Reynolds's wishes do not matter here. The court can sever the bonds of matrimony even if he doesn't want to."

"But I would be a divorced woman! My name would be ruined!"

"You would be a *free* woman. And names can be saved — or changed," Alex added with a little smile. "Mrs. Smith."

Maria sat silently for a long moment. At last she stirred herself. She looked at Alex, bewildered, as if she had forgotten he was there, or forgotten she was.

"It just doesn't seem possible. I have been betrothed to Mr. Reynolds since I was sixteen. This misery — this affliction — has been a part of my life for so long. It is hard to imagine that one could just walk away. I feel as though I am the one who is breaking the law."

"Neither the court nor the church wants you to persist in a union in which your protector is in fact your tormentor. We can take steps to do this as quietly as possible, but if Mr. Reynolds chooses to fight us, he will find that it is his reputation that will be destroyed, not yours. Society has no sympathy for brutes like him."

Another long silence from Maria. "It has been so long," she said, shaking her head. "Seven years. A third of my life."

"And many, many good years still ahead."

She turned and looked him the eye for the first time since they had entered the room. "You promise?"

Alex held her gaze, setting his face in a mask of determination. "I promise."

He couldn't save his mother, but he could save her, and he would.

9
FLIRTATIONS AND FANCIES

The Hamilton Town House
New York, New York
July 1785

"Mr. and Mrs. John and Sarah Jay!" Drayton announced from the living room doorway. The footman, resplendent in new blue livery trimmed with gold at the collar and cuffs — and looking, Eliza couldn't help noticing, similar to John's new suit — stood aside to let an elegantly dressed young couple enter the room. The expression on their faces was half confused, half amused. John Jay paused as if awaiting further fanfare, then bowed low to the room, to Sarah's obvious mortification. He kissed his wife, then immediately went off to a circle of men clustered around Gouverneur Morris and his brother-in-law, John Rutherford.

Sarah Jay scanned the room until her eyes met Eliza's.

"Eliza Hamilton!" she called as she pushed her way through the crowd with the kind of rudeness that only a patrician can pull off. Her father was the governor of New Jersey, after all. She had a whole state at her beck and call. "I heard a rumor and — yes, it's true!" she exclaimed, all but jumping in the air as she pointed at Eliza's not particularly different stomach, then threw her arms around her friend. "Oh, my darling, I am so very happy for you!"

Eliza felt her cheeks were going to burst from smiling so much. This was her twentieth congratulations tonight, and her twentieth hug. The men embraced her gently, as if her condition implied a new fragility, but these dainty women, powdered, wigged, and corseted within an inch of their lives, wrapped surprisingly strong arms around her torso and clutched her as if they were trying to squeeze the baby out six months before it was due.

"Alex and I are unbelievably happy," Eliza said when she could breathe again.

"We were starting to wonder if it was ever going to happen." Just a few weeks ago, the doctor confirmed it as well — everything was in order, and she would be a mother very soon.

"Oh, I always knew you and Alex would be blessed with children. God would not have made you such a warm, loving person only to deprive you of the gift of motherhood. I tell you right now, I am setting aside Ann and William as potential mates for whatever comes out of you." Ann and William were her and John's youngest.

"It will be a boy," Eliza said in all seriousness. "His name will be Philip."

"Lovely!" Sarah said, without questioning the source of Eliza's surety. "Ann it is then. I'll start getting her ready now. Oh," she interrupted herself, "thank you," she said to Drayton, who had appeared at her side with a tray of glasses filled with amber liquid. "This is some of Mr. Van Rensselaer's honey wine, yes? Do see that Mr. Jay gets some of this. He has been talking about it ever since he received your invitation."

"Already done, madam," Drayton said

in a voice that would have seemed supercilious had it not been so clearly deferential.

"Oh, well, there's a good chap! Find me in about, oh, nine minutes, and I'm sure I'll take a top off," said Sarah.

Drayton nodded and backed away with a serene expression on his face, as if Sarah had given him a profound reason to go on living. Sarah watched him walk away for a moment before turning back to Eliza.

"So, your new footman," she said, a little smile on her face.

Eliza shrugged helplessly. "Yes," she said, knowing just what her friend was referring to. "I found a guide to protocol in the courts of Louis Quatorze among his books. It explains a lot."

"Really?" Sarah said. "That's almost . . . admirable. Odd, and perhaps a little off-putting, but sweet in its way."

"I was joking actually," Eliza said. "But he does have a fondness for a certain kind of chivalrous novel of the type Cervantes made fun of in *Don Quixote.* Men who are stripping off their coats and laying them on puddles for women to walk on, when the ladies could have just as easily walked around them, that sort of thing."

"I think Señor Cervantes might have rethought his position if he met . . ."

"Drayton. Drayton Pennington."

Sarah raised an eyebrow. They turned to watch him across the room, where he was refilling the emptied glasses of a cluster of young male guests including John Schuyler and DeWitt Clinton, John's school friend, and the nephew of the governor of New York. The college boys were making Drayton's job difficult by sliding their glasses back and forth, either because they were too drunk to hold them steady or because they were actively teasing the footman. Though contemporaries, the young men were obviously of a different rank than Drayton, thus leaving him unable to respond to their tomfoolery in kind. However, Drayton acted as if he didn't realize they were teasing him. His decanter followed their wavering glasses effortlessly, and one by one he refilled them all without spilling a drop, then bowed and walked away. The boys gave him a standing ovation as he departed, obviously impressed with his skill and his poise, and one of them called out an invitation to play cricket at the weekend.

"Such talent," Sarah said, eyeing Drayton's retreating form appreciatively. "And it doesn't hurt that he is easy on the eyes."

"Sarah!" Eliza swatted her friend with her fan. "You're incorrigible!"

"My dear, when you've been married as long as John and I have, you learn to take your jollies where you can."

"Not with my footman, you don't. He is a nice young man, practically a godsend, and I have no plans to part with him anytime. Although . . ."

Sarah whirled to her. "What's this? I smell a plan. Spill it."

"Oh, it's probably just the excitement of pregnancy, but I am feeling particularly maternal. I long to play matchmaker!"

"Oh, really! Let me guess! It's that sweet Emma Trask whom I have heard such talk about, isn't it? They say she has the air of a girl educated in a convent. Quiet as a mouse, subservient as a courtier to the tsars, and also quite lovely. She would make a good match with young Mr. Pennington."

"Emma?" Eliza said in a dismayed voice. "Oh no. I mean, yes, but not with Drayton."

"Let me see if I follow this. There is a single woman and a single man living in your house, both of the same age and station and worthy of a portrait by Titian, yet you are not planning on fixing them up together?"

"It's just too obvious, don't you think? Two penniless gentlefolk. Their opportunities are so very straitened. And Emma had an unfortunate childhood. She deserves a chance at a easier life."

"Aha! So you will fix Emma up with some rich middle-aged bachelor who desires a pretty, meek helpmeet to brighten the latter half of his life, and find some slightly older widow with a fortune she needs must lavish on a golden boy like Drayton!"

Eliza laughed. "It seems like Drayton isn't the only one reading the kind of novels Señor Cervantes made such fun of. Emma and Drayton are both too young and vivacious to be saddled with aging spouses. I have all but succeeded in maneuvering Emma and my brother together, and as for Drayton, I have heard tell that a certain heiress will be in town for the season, and I plan to make it so that she and Drayton see a lot of each other."

Sarah's eyes went wide. "My goodness, you are scheming. I don't know if this is extraordinarily liberal of you or if you are setting back the goal of American freedom by half a century."

"Sarah, please," Eliza protested. "I am not forcing them to marry against their will. I am only creating . . . opportunities, as it were, for nature to take its course."

Sarah laughed. "Well! I don't know who to ask about first. John? Or the identity of this 'heiress.' Spill!"

"My lips are sealed," Eliza said, mostly because she enjoyed watching Sarah squirm. "But look: There is Emma now, all but hanging on John's every word."

Sarah looked over and saw the girl, who

was indeed standing mutely before John and his cronies. Her face was as serene as a saint's in a painting. It was impossible to tell if she was bored or rapt by the conversation unfolding before her.

"Is she hanging on his every word?" Sarah said after watching the scene for a moment. "Or merely unable to get in a word edgewise? Though he has only been in the city a month, your brother's so-called skill as a raconteur has already made the rounds."

"Sarah Jay, my dear friend! Are you making insinuations about my brother?"

"What, no, of course not! I am merely saying that he has a reputation as a bit of a loudmouth." She laughed, and patted Eliza on the shoulder in a placating manner. "But what firstborn teenaged son of a rich man isn't a loudmouth? Their fathers teach them that the world belongs to them, and their mothers — or their mothers' maids — wipe their mouths and their bottoms until they're eight years old. They can't help being rather self-centered. They grow out of it eventually. The first time they lose their shirt in a business deal, usually, or when their wife turns her shoulder to their touch. Like colts, they must be taken firmly in hand, but any resourceful wife can handle the task with ease. I wonder if Emma has had quite that training though. She seems a bit too . . . docile for the job."

"Emma is an extremely steady young girl, which is just what John needs to settle him away from the distractions of the big city. I think they will make each other very happy."

Sarah frowned. "It is a lovely sentiment, but methinks you are being a bit naïve. And the other victim? I'm sorry, I mean the girl you have picked out for Drayton?"

Eliza merely mimed locking her lips with a key.

"No matter," Sarah said, "I'll get it out of Alex when he arrives. I know you cannot keep anything from him."

"I probably would have told him if I ever saw him these days. He is so busy though, that lately we only ever seem to see each other at parties and other social occasions."

"Perhaps. Or perhaps you're just trying

to throw me off the scent. At any rate, here is the man in question himself."

For at that moment, Alex had appeared in the doorway, looking a little tired but clearly happy to be home. Before he could enter, however, a panicked-looking Drayton hustled toward him through the crowded room, a silver tray sporting a cluster of empty glasses perched precariously on his fingertips above the heads (and wigs) of the guests. The footman darted in front of Alex, blocking his way, and spun toward the guests in the room. His tray whirled with him, but the glasses didn't even rattle, let alone fall.

"Mr. Alexander Hamilton!" Drayton shouted in a voice whose volume shocked the throng of revelers into silence. He stepped aside like a carnival barker about to reveal a trained bear or a bearded lady, revealing the stunned face of his employer.

"Well, uh, yes," Alex said to the staring audience, one eyebrow lifted in an amused arch. "That's me. Alexander Hamilton, at your service."

Without missing a beat, he snapped into a deft little jig, clapping his heels on the floorboards and ending with a spin and a heel click. He whipped off his hat as he bowed low to the applause of the crowd.

There was much laughter as he began to make his way through the room toward Eliza. However eager he was to join his wife, his progress to her was slow. As he moved through the crowd, everyone had to shake his hand or stop him to ask a question about trade tariffs. Still others made him pause in order to make a comment about the rumors of a constitutional convention to create a document that would replace the Articles of Confederation, or to inquire if there were any shares left in the Bank of New York, which Alex had helped found last year, throwing the scheme together before his law practice really took off.

Alex, a born politician, answered each question genially but tactfully, taking thirty seconds or two minutes to say what could have been said in just two words: *No comment.* It took a good ten minutes before he was at his wife's side.

When he finally arrived, he gave Sarah Jay a quick kiss on the cheek, then turned and embraced Eliza. His hug was different from the tentative touches of the male guests or the unfettered enthusiasm of the female. It was a hug that knew her body, for one thing, but it also wasn't about her, or, rather, wasn't about the baby (whose existence he had already celebrated many times). There was an urgency in his grasp — Alex clung to his wife as if she were the only thing holding him up.

"I miss you," he whispered in her ear.

"I miss you, too," she said. "You have been at the office far too late of late."

And Sarah, who could be as tactful as she was brash — she was a politician's wife, after all — immediately melted into the crowd, calling out for Drayton to "top off" her glass of honey wine.

"My love," Eliza said when the coast was clear, "is something the matter?"

Alex shook his head as if he were trying to clear it, then took a deep breath. "No, no, everything is fine, once I've unburdened myself — and loosened this damned cravat."

But Alex's words did nothing to quell

Eliza's worries. She reached for her husband's lace and adjusted the knot herself. "Has something happened?"

Alex accepted her ministrations meekly. "No, not really. Only I have told a little fib and I feel absolutely terrible about it."

Eliza stiffened slightly, then took a sip of her drink to calm herself. "I'm sure it can't be too serious."

"No, it's not. Only I don't know why I did it, and I feel just awful. You see, I took on a new client today."

Eliza frowned. "I thought you were in court today. The Gunn case."

"No, that was the fib. The Gunn case is still scheduled for Monday."

"I see," Eliza said, though she didn't at all.

"The client is a young married woman," Alex continued. "Her husband —" His voice caught in his throat. "I'm sorry, my darling, I don't know of a gentle way to say this."

"It's all right, Alex." Eliza squeezed his arm tenderly. "I am aware that not all men hold themselves to a gentleman's code."

Alex's lip curled in a grimace. "Well, this man is as far from a gentleman as Moll Flanders is from a lady. I'm afraid he — he strikes his wife."

"Oh!" Eliza's hands flew, not to her mouth but to her stomach, as if this simple act could protect the growing child there from the horrors of the world. "The poor woman!"

"Indeed." Alex took a moment to pat Eliza's hand, then, as if that weren't enough, leaned forward to give her a little kiss. "And, well, it soon emerged that she had neither a place to go to escape the brute, nor money with which to do so. So I took her to Caroline Childress's inn and ensconced her in a room there. She was so distraught, though, that I didn't feel it was safe to leave her for some time, lest in a panic she run out into the streets, or perhaps even back to him."

"I understand completely," Eliza said. "Only, why did you feel the need to hide it from me? Is she pretty?" She tried to make her voice light, but it sounded awkward to her ears.

Alex seemed about to say something, then stopped and grinned, tiredly but with the first real cheer since he had arrived home. "Why, Mrs. Hamilton! Are you jealous?"

"Jealous? How uncharitable of you, Mr. Hamilton! No, I only thought that, faced with the prospect of, shall we say, an extended period without romantic intimacy, you might find your eyes flitting to other, more beautiful vistas."

"Oh, you *are* jealous!" Alex crowed. "How perfectly delightful! No," he continued quickly, not quite able to wipe the smile from his face. "It has nothing to do with her looks. It's just that she is unable to pay me anything, and I know we've talked about me taking on more lucrative clients so that we can move to a bigger house and raise our children in a manner befitting the Schuyler name. And here I am paying for a room for her out of my own pocket."

"Out of your own pocket!" Eliza said quickly, then stopped herself. *Now who's being uncharitable?* she thought. "How very gentlemanly of you," she corrected quickly, though her tone didn't sound very convincing. "This Mrs. . . ."

"Reynolds."

"This Mrs. Reynolds is lucky that she found a man as chivalrous as you to see her through her time of need. Why, you make young Drayton here look like a proper boor."

She nodded at Drayton, who was pouring and bowing and clearing and bowing and serving and bowing like some cleverly manipulated marionette.

"Yes, I was going to ask you about him. That shouting thing . . . ," said Alex.

"It is rather jarring, but the guests are amused by it, and if I'm being honest it saves me the trouble of introductions. I can see why they do it at court."

Alex smiled. "Whatever my princess wants." He kissed her on the forehead. "I'm sorry about fibbing. It was a lapse."

"Hmph," Eliza said. "Princess? I don't see my mother around. That makes me the queen."

Alex laughed, and she could tell he felt forgiven.

There is nothing to forgive, Eliza said

silently, though she wondered if she were trying to convince herself. It was understandable that Alex should feel the need to drop everything and come to this woman's rescue, after all, but why lie about it? Clearly she had touched some kind of nerve in him. Eliza didn't think it was something she needed to be jealous of — she knew her husband adored her — but what, then, had so rattled him?

Who was this Mrs. Reynolds? And *was* she pretty? Eliza felt a little sick at the thought of her husband with another woman without telling her about it. But he did tell her about it, didn't he? He told her about it just now. There was nothing to worry about. She knew he loved her completely. But they had been married now for several years — she shook the thought from her head irritably. She trusted her husband.

Just then Drayton took up his post at the door. "Miss Elizabeth Van Rensselaer and Mrs. Cornelius Jantzen."

He stepped aside to reveal a pale blond girl of perhaps sixteen and a rather rotund matron of about sixty swaddled in widow's weeds.

"Elizabeth Van Rensselaer?" Alex turned to her. "Stephen's sister?"

"Her parents have sent her down for the season," Eliza nodded.

Alex groaned. "Please don't tell me she's staying with us."

"Ha!" Eliza said. "I gather Stephen has purchased a 'city place,' as he calls it, on Mulberry Street. It has six bedrooms and a ballroom large enough to contain our entire house. It is *we* who should be staying with *them.* But I will be seeing a fair bit of her. Peggy has asked that I chaperone her."

"Isn't that Mrs. Jantzen's job? And is that the same Mrs. Jantzen who accompanied you to Morristown all those years ago, when I so gallantly rescued you from a wrecked carriage?"

"You mean ruined my favorite frock and insinuated that I snuck into your hayloft at my parents' party?" Eliza teased, to Alex's consternation. "And yes, that is the same Mrs. Jantzen. Widowed now, the poor thing, so we must try to be accommodating. But still. She is a bit much for any young girl to have to deal with for six months."

"So it's Eliza Hamilton to the rescue again, is it?"

"What can I say?" Eliza said. "It's a calling."

"I sense there's more to this than a mere 'calling,' " Alex said, "but I'll get to the bottom of it later. Let's go greet our guests."

"Perhaps," Eliza said coyly as they made their way across the room. "By the way," she added. "You still haven't told me if she's pretty."

"If who's pretty?" Alex said, eyes wide in feigned innocence.

Eliza snapped her fan open and waved it coquettishly in front of her face and décolletage. "Just remember, it'll be a year before I am again your blushing bride, as they say. Indeed, I've heard sometimes the recovery takes as long as two."

"You will always be my blushing bride, no matter what," said Alex softly. "You have never been more beautiful." He lowered his face to hers and kissed her tenderly.

Eliza gave in to the deepening kiss, hiding them behind her fan, as Alex drew her even more tightly to him. So many couples lost their spark once children entered into the picture, yet to her he was still the dashing young soldier she first fell in love with, and she fervently hoped what he said was true. That she would always be his blushing bride.

"We'll see if you're still singing the same tune in a few weeks," she teased, pulling away to catch her breath.

In answer, Alex kept the fan firmly in place to kiss his wife again.

10

LIFE, LIBERTY, AND THE
PURSUIT OF ROMANCE

The Hamilton Town House, Rear Parlor
New York, New York
July 1785

When they had finally stopped kissing, Alex and Eliza attended to their guests. Alex entertained the menfolk with stories of his latest victory over Aaron Burr in court, and when he once again caught up with his wife, she was looping her arm through Betty Van Rensselaer's. Claiming that Betty must be exhausted from her travels, Eliza pulled her into the rear parlor, which was less crowded than the front — people always wanted to be near the door to spot new arrivals and claim any celebrity guest as their own.

"Drayton," Eliza called to the footman as they went. "Do please bring a decanter of Miss Van Rensselaer's brother's honey wine for her to drink."

"Drayton," Betty called in a mocking voice. "Do please *don't* bring a decanter of Miss Van Rensselaer's brother's honey wine for her to drink. Miss Van Rensselaer has drunk more of her brother's honey wine than is safe for any human being to consume. I fear if I have another drop I shall turn into a honeybee!"

"Oh, I see," Eliza said, and motioned for Drayton to wait. "What would you like to drink then?"

Betty turned to Alex with a wicked grin. "I have heard that the Marquis de Lafayette often sends you some of the cognacs and wines he produces on his estate in France. Perhaps you have a bottle on hand?"

Alex smiled at the girl's moxie. You certainly couldn't fault her taste. "Alas, those gifts, precious as they are, seem never to last very long in this household. I always mean to set a bottle aside —"

"— and we always wake up with it beside the bed," Eliza said with a laugh.

"I can offer you some of the wine General Schuyler makes on his Saratoga "estate," Alex suggested.

"Ugh," Betty said, then blushed slightly. "Begging your pardon, Eliza, but Peggy is always trying to get us to drink it at Rensselaerswyck. Barker, our butler, can't even get the servants to imbibe it, let alone the guests."

Alex covered his smile with his hand. He shared Betty's opinion of his father-in-law's wine-making abilities and knew Eliza did as well, but he never would have said it quite so bluntly.

"Footman," Betty said now, turning to Drayton, "what is Mr. Hamilton's finest liquor?"

"His name is Drayton," Eliza said in such a way that made Alex turn sharply to her. Alex knew that Eliza hated to see servants talked down to, but her tone was less critical than . . . personal, almost. It was as if his wife were introducing their footman to their sister-in-law. "Drayton Pennington."

"Speak up, Pembleton," Betty said with a wry grin. "I know my brother-in-law is holding out on me."

Drayton nodded deferentially, though

Alex couldn't tell if he was cowed by the girl's imperious manner or by the fact that a pretty girl was teasing him in front of a roomful of people. "From what I have seen, Mr. Hamilton esteems his Virginia bourbon above all other libations. It was sent to him by Mr. James Madison from his own estate, Montpelier."

Alex's mouth dropped. That bourbon was indeed delectable and was one of his prized possessions. There were only a few bottles left.

"Is that so? Well, then, that's what I'll have. Be sure to bring the whole bottle. I don't want to have to keep calling you. Not for drinks, anyway," she added, all but winking at the clearly embarrassed boy.

Alex couldn't tell if she was toying with Drayton or actually flirting with him. He had heard that Betty was headstrong and spoiled but good-natured. It would be just like a rich, pretty princess from the provinces to have a last fling with a handsome New York servant before going back to Albany to marry some first or second cousin fifteen years her elder and settling into a life of tea parties and children. At any rate, before Alex could think of a suitable protest — other than the fact that he wanted it all for himself — Drayton was gone.

"Well, what do you think?" Eliza said, turning back to Betty.

Again that familiar tone, as if some European baronet had just left the room and Eliza wanted to dish about the wax in his mustache or the extent of his vineyards. Alex was starting to wonder what his wife was playing at.

"Oh, the house is lovely," Betty said after a bit of a pause. "Stephen told me its diminutive size only added to the charm, and he was correct. I wouldn't mind another log on the fire though. These north-facing rooms do get rather chilly, even in July."

Eliza smiled, a bit painfully. "Thank you — our tiny little house does suit us, though perhaps we'll find larger accommodations when baby comes."

"What baby?" Betty said blankly. She looked around for a moment, then pulled her shawl around her shoulders.

"Didn't Peggy tell you? I am expecting."

Betty shrugged. "Maybe? I've never quite paid attention to pregnancy. It's so . . . unsightly, you know." With her hands, she described a rotund shape, frowning first, then laughing. "The figure never really bounces back either, does it? Even Peggy, who was once nearly as slim as I am, has thickened up since Cathy's birth. She has this cute little fold of skin below her chin now. I call it her wattle, which I think is quite funny, but she seems to think I am teasing her."

"She should wear it with pride," Eliza said, though it seemed to Alex that she sat up a little straighter, as if to smooth out the folds in her skin.

"Mmmm," Betty cooed in a noncommittal manner.

At that very moment a rattle sounded from the door. Drayton had returned with a bottle and sherry glasses balanced on his tray.

"Oh, Pemberly is back with the whiskey!" Betty said, clapping her hands. "Yay!"

Drayton hesitated but recovered

quickly. He set his tray down on a side-board and began pouring drinks.

Alex sighed under his breath. Even the bottle James had brewed his whiskey in was beautiful, exceptionally tall and slim, and blown from translucent heavy crystal. The liquid inside was golden brown — just like the color of Maria Reynolds's hair — why that occurred to him, he did not know, and he banished the thought quickly.

Drayton placed a glass on his tray and bent forward to offer it to Betty. She didn't look at it, and her hands remained in her lap. "Eliza, please don't forget to ask Dradington to stoke the fire."

Alex could see that Eliza's smile was forced. "Of course. I'll be sure to relay the information to *Drayton.*" She paused. "Don't you want a drink?"

"Oh, I'd love one!" Betty said, though she made no move to acknowledge Drayton's presence. The footman continued to bend forward like a clock whose hands have stopped at two thirty. Despite the tray delicately balanced on it, his outstretched arm was absolutely unmoving.

"It's, um, right there?" Eliza said.

Betty turned and abruptly looked at Drayton as if she had just noticed him for the first time. "What, this?"

Even Drayton was finding it hard to maintain his composure. "Er, yes?" he said, as if he doubted what he had poured in the glass before her.

"But I asked for whiskey, and this is a sherry glass," Betty said.

Drayton's mouth dropped open, and his cheeks went red. "Oh, I'm so sorry, Miss Van Rensselaer —"

"No need to apologize, Drayton," Eliza spoke over him. "The fault is all mine." She turned to Betty. "I told Drayton that where ladies are concerned, he should always serve brown liquors in sherry glasses. One wouldn't want them looking like boozing sailors, now would one?"

"Oh, ah, I see," Betty said, unsure if she had just been insulted or not. "In that case, thank you." She took the glass from Drayton's tray and held it in her lap without drinking.

Point to Eliza, Alex thought proudly, then accepted his own glass.

"Wait, why is he getting a sherry glass,

too?" Betty asked. "He's not a lady, as far as I can tell."

"Wait till you taste the whiskey," Alex said quickly. "It deserves a belled glass to encapsulate its oaky bouquet."

Betty sniffed at her glass, then wrinkled her nose. "Smells like whiskey to me," she said, then tossed her drink back in a single gulp. "Fill 'er up, Pennyworth," she said, holding out her glass to him.

Alex still couldn't tell if she was teasing Drayton playfully or if she was just being rude. He glanced at Eliza. Her face was equally puzzled, but there was also a sharpness to her eyes, as if she had some a vested interest in knowing which it was.

But he had more pressing concerns. He was quickly realizing that if he was going to get any enjoyment out of this bottle he was going to have to try to keep up with his sister-in-law. "Another for me as well, Drayton."

Drayton refilled their glasses, then turned to Eliza, who demurred, patting her stomach. "Very good, ma'am. Will there be anything else?"

"I think that's all for now. Perhaps Miss

Van Rensselaer will want a plate in a while, though, so do check back."

"Of course, Mrs. Hamilton," he said, bowing as he backed out of the room.

As soon as he was gone, Eliza turned to Betty. "Well," she said in the same excited tone as before. "What do you think?"

"Of the house?" Betty said. "I believe I said it was cozy? Am I imagining that?"

"Not the house," Eliza said with a smile. "Drayton."

"Who is that?" Betty asked, apparently serious.

"The footman?" Eliza said. "The one you were so clearly flirting with?"

"I was *flirting*?" Betty said incredulously. "With the *footman*?"

"You must admit he is quite handsome," Eliza said in a leading voice.

"Oh, is he?" Alex said now, feeling a flash of jealousy himself. "I hadn't noticed."

"Said the man hiding strange women in hotel rooms," Eliza said sharply, though she kept her gaze directed at Betty.

"There's nothing strange about Mrs. Reynolds," Alex said. "You very quickly get used to that third arm she has growing out of her side." He wagged a finger at Drayton, who was just visible in the front parlor, on the far side of the dining room. "What's this? What are you cooking up here?"

Eliza took a sip of her drink. "Why, whatever do you mean?" she said, in what Alex thought was supposed to be a Southern accent, though it sounded rather Irish to Alex's ears.

"Don't play innocent with me, wife. I am not the only person who likes to save people. Only in this case, I'm not sure it's saving you're doing, or sabotaging."

"What on earth *are* you two talking about?" Betty said, interrupting their banter. "And will someone *please* refill my glass?"

"I would be happy to, Birdy," a male voice said from the doorway. Alex looked over to see John entering the room, carrying his own empty glass. "I thought I smelled whiskey."

"Little Johnny Schuyler!" Betty exclaimed. "I had forgotten you were here."

"Am I so forgettable then?" John said, pouring a little whiskey in her glass and being rather more generous with his own. Alex noted sadly that the bottle was nearly half empty already. "You cut me to the quick, Birdy."

"What?" Betty said, pretending to look around for the source of the voice. "Oh! John! I had forgotten you were here!"

"Touché," John said, touching his glass to Betty's, then swilling half of his back in a gulp. "I tell you what. I won't call you Birdy if you won't call me Johnny."

"Well, what am I supposed to call you then? John is your name, after all."

"That's right, John is my name, not Johnny."

"Eggplant, aubergine," Betty said. "It's all the same to me. But whatever you want, *John,*" she finished in a heavy, teasing voice.

"What's wrong with Birdy? I find it charming," said Alex.

"John used to call her that when they were children," Eliza said, noting how cheerful John looked at the sight of their old friend. "He said she had legs like a

211

chicken's."

"My legs were *adorable,* thank you very much," Betty said. She extended one now, revealing a polished wooden heel and dainty foot clad in glove-soft leather and, daringly, a bit of silk-clad ankle. "Mama said I could have been a dancer, if it were not such a disgraceful profession."

"In the opinion of your mother and our mother," John said, "there are only three professions available to women: general's wife, gentleman's wife, or widow."

"Your mother got two of them," Betty tittered. "Does that make her a bigamist?"

"Betty!" Eliza gasped, sounding genuinely shocked to Alex's ears. "You go too far!"

"Oh, relax, sis, we're all family here," said John.

"But even so. A little respect for the women who raised us is only fitting," said Eliza.

"Mother? Raise me?" scoffed John. "I had to ask Nanny for permission to even see her, and it was Nanny's lap I sat on during the visits, not Mother's. Frankly, I'm relieved. Mother has such skinny legs. It would have been like sitting on a pair of fallen fenceposts. Nanny's lap was plump like a pair of pillows."

"Our mothers are from a different generation than ours," Eliza said. "Everything was formalized then. The rules came from the king down, and each step on the rung was clearly demarcated. Their roles restricted them, but it also gave them a sense of identity. Our generation is much more open to possibility. We can choose our own roles. We are not bound by expectations of family or class," she said. "For instance, in the United States, one is free to fall in love with a gentleman as well as with a footman."

Betty turned to John. "You said she had turned into quite the little sermonizer. I see you weren't exaggerating. I for one am happy with who I am," she continued. "My family built this country, both before and after independence, and I am only too content to continue their traditions. Stephen is Patroon, and I, as his sister, will have a special place on our lands. What woman would not want the masses to part for her when she walks by, like the Red Sea for Moses?"

"This woman, for one!" Eliza said, a bit irritated by the young woman's old-fashioned attitude. "How terrible to feel that one cannot interact with one's fellow human beings as equals. To wonder if everything they say to you is couched in fear of reprisal rather than honesty."

"But we are not all equal, no matter how Mr. Jefferson says we are created," John said now. "Too many people think that he meant we are born equal, when all he meant is that God *created* us the same all those hundreds of generations ago. But we are born into quite different circumstances. Male, female. Light-skinned, dark. And more tellingly: rich and poor, free man and slave. These circumstances shape us and make us all the more different from one another. To pretend otherwise is simply to deny the evidence before your eyes, and the inherent injustice of the current system."

"You certainly have a point. But by your own argument," Eliza responded, "you admit that people change over time. And if they can change in one direction, they can change in another. The high can come lower, the low can come higher, and we can all meet somewhere toward the middle. And slavery is the most unjust of all and must be ended at once."

"Hear, hear," said Alex.

John and Betty nodded as well. But Betty soon found her footing once more. "Still, it sounds so dreary. You describe the social version of porridge oats or strained peas. I for one like a little salt and sugar, some spicy pepper from the east!"

"Not to mention some delectable whiskey," John said, touching her glass to his and smiling at her warmly. They clinked and drank. Alex's heart sank a little more, but he was enjoying Eliza's sparring too much to say anything. Though he had had conversations like this with John Jay and James Madison and even Aaron Burr, it was a welcome spectacle to see his wife holding the torch for the American experiment in equality.

"So are you saying," Eliza said now, leaning forward to Betty. "Are you saying that there could never be anything between you and, say, Mr. Pennington?"

Alex's eyes went wide.

"I don't know who that *is,*" Betty said.

"Oh, for heaven's sake, Betty. Drayton. The *footman.* You have met him several times already tonight," said Eliza.

"Are we still on about the *footman?*" Betty clutched a hand to her chest.

"Yes, why not? In a new country, with new customs, do you think a landed lass like yourself should fail to find common cause with a lad as handsome and honorable as Drayton Pennington merely because he wears livery rather than a lieutenant-colonel's epaulets?"

"Good heavens, Eliza," John said. "It is almost as though you are challenging her."

Eliza shrugged. "Perhaps I am."

"Challenging me to what exactly?" Betty said. "I love a good challenge!"

"Eliza, darling," Alex said now. "A word?"

"Just a moment, dear," Eliza said, keeping her eyes trained on Betty's. "I challenge you to look at Drayton as what he is. As a boy, your age, with the same drives and ambitions we all have. To do something worthwhile with his time. To find love."

"Love!" Betty laughed. "Oh, Eliza, you set me a difficult task!"

"You are only here a few months," Eliza said nonchalantly. "If the experiment does not take, you can return to Rensselaerswyck none the worse for wear. The Red Sea will part, and you will be back in the promised land."

Betty just shook her head, but Alex could see her gaze was focused somewhere out of the room. He looked where she was looking, and saw the upright form of the footman. He was proffering a sandwich to Mrs. Jantzen as though it were an emerald ring on a pillow. He offered a winning smile, and Mrs. Jantzen responded by batting her eyelashes at him like a sixteen-year-old.

"I suppose he isn't bad-looking, is he?" Betty said musingly.

"That's the whiskey talking," John said darkly.

Betty shrugged. "Well, there's always more whiskey, right, Alex?"

Alex glanced longingly at the nearly empty bottle. "Indeed, Betty," he sighed. "There's always more whiskey."

11
SERVE AND MATCH

The Hamilton Town House, the Breakfast Table
New York, New York
July 1785

In the middle of the night, Alex startled awake. "I've got it!"

Eliza didn't open her eyes. "That's good, dear," she said, pulling his arm more tightly around her. "Now go back to sleep before I stab you."

The next morning at breakfast, with a dewy-eyed Emma and a somewhat blearier John seated between them, Eliza asked Alex what he had been raving about last night. He looked at her blankly. "I know I drank a bit and perhaps got a tad boisterous, but I should hardly think I was *raving*."

"You got up on an ottoman and recited Marc Antony's eulogy for Julius Caesar, but that's not what I'm talking about. In the wee hours of the morning, you woke up and yelled 'Eureka!' or some such. I worried that John was going to run in from across the hall to see what was going on."

John chuckled under his breath, though he didn't look up from his as yet empty plate, whose pattern he was studying as though it were a passage in Greek he was expected to translate.

Eliza ignored this as Alex considered his wife's question. At last he shook his head. "I have no memory of any eureka moment, alas." He smiled in mock self-pity. "No doubt I dreamed up some grand defense of a powerful central government that would bind the thirteen colonies together into a single nation instead of the squabbling confederacy we now are, and it has been lost to posterity forever."

Eliza rolled her eyes. "That's what I love about you, dear. Your modesty. But perhaps it was something closer to home? About work? Family?"

Another pause; another shake of the head. "I'm afraid nothing comes to mind. But then, my mind is a little the worse for wear after two bottles, ahem" — he glared at John — "of my reserve batch of whiskey."

John continued to stare into his plate.

"Perhaps about the Trinity case?" Eliza prodded. She didn't know why she felt it so imperative to help Alex remember, but his voice had been so joyous, so triumphant. She was sure it was something important, and she still recalled the elation she felt after her own dream revelation had returned to her.

Alex laughed ruefully. "Now that I *would* remember. But if ever there was a legal Gordian knot, it is the Trinity case. There is no untying it."

John's head snapped up, though his eyes still seemed unfocused. "I thought Alexander didn't untie it. He just cut it open."

"Perhaps I could explain the concept of a metaphor to you," Alex said drolly. "Or perhaps I could simply tell you how much each of last night's bottles of whiskey was worth."

Alex's words solicited a weak laugh from John. "If it makes you feel better, I can't even remember how much fun I had last night, *and* I have a raging headache."

"It would," Alex said, "if I were not in the same boat myself. Also, why are we talking so much instead of breakfasting? Drayton, may I have some coffee, please?"

Drayton, who had been standing by the sideboard like a member of the king's guard outside Buckingham Palace, stirred himself like a clockwork soldier whose spring had been unfastened. "Very good, sir," he said, stepping forward with the pot to fill his glass.

"Is this new?" Alex said, pointing to the pot but looking at his wife. It was an elegant silver decanter with slender, gourd-shaped body and a spout as long and graceful as a swan's neck.

Eliza batted her eyes at her husband. "It depends on what you mean by 'new.' I purchased it almost three weeks ago, but you are only noticing it today, so I suppose you could say it's new to you."

Alex grinned sheepishly, then took a

sip of his coffee. "So what you're saying is, I can't scold you for spendthrift habits since I have been too busy with work to notice the nice things you bring into our house?"

"And spiriting off pretty young women to private inns," said Eliza, who hadn't been able to get Maria Reynolds out of her mind.

"Excuse me?" John said, at last summoning the energy to look at his tablemates. "Did someone mention pretty young women and hotels?"

"I never said she was pretty," Alex said, pointedly ignoring his brother-in-law while clinging to his coffee cup like a life preserver.

"No, Eliza did," John said. "Do tell, sis."

Eliza didn't take her eyes from her husband's. "Get your mind out of the gutter, brother, lest you find another part of your anatomy there. Mr. Hamilton knows I am only teasing him."

"Mr. Hamilton is relieved to hear that," Alex said, though he still looked a little green around the gills. It could have just been the hangover, of course.

"Saucy!" John said to his sister. "You never spoke this way at the breakfast table at home."

"Neither did you," Eliza said, "but, to the best of my knowledge, only one of us has earned the right to such language, since only one of us is paying the rent on this house."

"Yes, and it's me," Alex said, trying to grin.

"Is that so?" Eliza said. "And whose parents furnished this house when we moved in and vouched for your ability to meet the terms of the lease?"

Alex looked a bit shocked at the acid of her comment, but Eliza did not seem chastened. She was increasingly discomfited that he had lied to her about his whereabouts the other evening, and even more irritated that it concerned a strange woman.

In a stage whisper that could've been heard down the block in City Hall, John leaned over to Emma and said, "Don't forget, she's an heiress."

Emma, who had been watching this

exchange as though it were a tennis match, tittered.

"Et tu, Emma?" Alex said. With a sigh, he reached for his copy of the *New York Journal* and unfolded it in front of his face. "If you need me, I'll be in the news."

Emma brought her napkin to her lips quickly, but another chuckle could be heard. "Drayton," she said quickly, "may I have some more coffee please?"

"Very good, Miss Trask."

"Oh, Drayton. You must call me Emma. It feels improper for you to address me as though I were somehow above you."

"Very good . . ." Drayton's voice faded. Fortunately for him, John jumped in before he could force himself to use Emma's Christian name.

Well, perhaps it wasn't so fortunate for him.

"Oh, come now, Emma," John said. "You are sitting at table. Drayton is standing to your left with a coffeepot in his hand. Under such circumstances it seems to me he cannot call you anything *but* Miss Trask. I am all for egalitarian-ism, but let us not throw out the baby with the bathwater."

"Really, John," Eliza said. "Given the riffraff with whom you've been socializing lately, I wonder that you would judge anyone for a little interclass fraternity. Not that I regard you as riffraff," she said to Drayton, her face going a bit red.

"Very good, Mrs. Hamilton," Drayton said. "Coffee?"

"Yes, thank you very much."

"Very good, madam."

"Drayton," John said now, catching Emma's gaze with a wicked glint in his eye. "May I have some coffee, too?"

"Very good, Mr. Schuyler."

The footman poured, then stepped back to the sideboard.

"Drayton," John said, winking at Emma. "May I have one of those scones?"

"Very good, Mr. Schuyler. Would you like blackcurrant or fig?"

"You choose."

"Very good, Mr. Schuyler." Drayton returned to the table with a small platter of scones and tonged one onto John's plate.

"Drayton," John said as the footman was walking back to the sideboard, "may I have some cream with my scone?" Another wink at Emma, who remained stony-faced, though her eyes were sparkling. Eliza couldn't tell if it was from amusement or anger.

"Of course, Mr. Schuyler. Very good, Mr. Schuyler."

Drayton set the scones down and picked up a salver, which held a cruet of cream. He spooned some onto John's plate, and as he was turning away John said, "Drayton," yet again. Eliza could only see the footman's face in profile, but she was pretty sure he winced.

"Could I have some jam with my scone and cream?"

"Very good, Mr. Schuyler." Drayton gave an inaudible sigh, setting the cream down. "Rowena has opened some grape, strawberry, and orange marmalade. Which may I offer you?"

"Hmmm," John said, as though he were considering whether to play his ace in a game of whist. "I think I will have . . . marmalade."

"Very good, Mr. Schuyler," Drayton said, returning to the table with yet another salver holding yet another cruet and spooning a mound of glistening orange pulp onto John's plate.

"On second thought," John said as Drayton was turning away, "I think I will have some grape jam as well."

"Very good, Mr. Schuyler."

It seemed to Eliza that Drayton's back grew just the tiniest bit straighter as he turned back to the sideboard. Another cruet appeared; the spoon sank into its red depths; a mound of viscous compote plopped onto John's plate next to the marmalade.

"Oh no." John sighed dramatically.

"John!" Eliza hissed. "Enough!"

"I'm so sorry, Drayton," John moaned. "But this color combination" — he waved his hand between the red and orange jellies — "simply will not do. Please, take my plate away and bring me another with just a few slices of melon."

"Very goo—"

"Well, it looks perfectly delicious to me!" Emma said, and, standing so suddenly her chair wobbled on its hind legs, she reached across the table, snatched John's plate before Drayton could clear it, and slapped her own empty one in its place.

"Oh ho!" John said. "The lioness wakes at last!"

"I am no lioness!" Emma said. "Merely someone who recognizes injustice when she sees it!"

"Injustice seems rather a strong term at nine in the morning," John said. "I was only having some fun."

"You have a strange definition of fun," Emma glared. "Perhaps it's one you learned in college. I am but a home-schooled girl myself. I rely on the more traditional meanings of words. Like decency and honor! Drayton!" she added harshly as the footman returned with a platter of sliced cantaloupe and honeydew. "Do *not* serve Mr. Schuyler. He has had his opportunity to eat and forwent it."

"Very good, Miss Trask," the footman replied, though he remained at John's side with the platter, his tongs at the ready.

"And call me Emma!"

"Very good, Miss —" Drayton's voice broke off in obvious consternation.

"Em-ma," John teased.

"John Bradstreet Schuyler, if I have to stand up again . . . !" Emma left the threat unvoiced. "Emma," she said to Drayton, sounding remarkably like John. "Call me Em-ma!"

If the footman had been an overwound clockwork toy a moment ago, he now seemed as if his spring had sprung. He stood there without moving, drooping slightly, his cheek twitching as Emma blazed at him, her cheeks fiery with passion.

John glanced at the two of them, raised his eyebrows, but kept his mouth shut for once.

Eliza glanced at Alex to catch his eye, but he had remained hidden behind his paper ever since she had made that comment about her parents financing their household. She supposed, as their hostess, she should try to make peace between her guests, but John had been incredibly rude, and he deserved it.

"Very good, Emma," Drayton whispered at last. "If that will be all, Mrs. Hamilton?" he added, turning to Eliza desperately.

"Thank you, Drayton," Eliza said sympathetically. "If we want anything else we will serve ourselves. You may flee."

"Very good, Mrs. Hamilton." Drayton bowed and somehow managed to make his exit from the room look like something other than scurrying.

She turned to her brother. "John Bradstreet Schuyler, I am embarrassed of you. What on earth were you thinking?"

John yawned, seemingly unaffected by his sister's remonstrance. "Well, I'll give him one thing," he said at last. "Drayton never once cracked. Good man. Kept his temper and can take a joke. And on that note," he continued, slurping up the last of his coffee cup and grabbing a couple of scones from the sideboard, "I must be off. I have a philosophy lecture I intend to sleep through."

■ ■ ■ ■

tween her guests... John had been incredibly rude... and he deserved it

Later on, when Alex had also gone off to work and it was just Eliza and Emma, the two ladies of the house took up a post in Emma's bedroom on the third floor. Before Emma had moved in, Eliza had been in the habit of spending her mornings there because it was the first room in the house to be flooded with sunshine, and even though it was early August it was a cool morning, and she was feeling a bit of a chill. She had furnished Emma's room with an overstuffed wing chair and a wooden rocking chair. Emma took her seat in the latter quickly. Eliza knew that the rocking chair, though quaint-looking with its wicker seat and ladder back, was not particularly comfortable, but she was feeling a little too pregnant to pretend to offer Emma the upholstered seat.

Her condition had also meant her work with the orphans had to cease for the time being, and Eliza missed it. Her doctor advised her to stay home and rest, but she continued to write letters on their behalf.

She and Emma had brought their embroidery hoops with them. Emma was working on a scene from Ovid's *Metamorphoses* for a decorative pillow — Perseus's liberation of Andromeda from the sea monster — while Eliza was doing her best to stitch her initials into a handkerchief. For some reason she could not fathom, the *E* looked more like a backward *3* than the first letter of her name.

"Mrs. Hamilton," Emma said once they were settled, "there is something that has been weighing on my mind."

Eliza looked up almost gratefully. "Oh, Emma, what is it? I hate to think of you in distress!"

Emma's voice was direly earnest, but even so, she didn't look up from her needle, either because she was too nervous to meet Eliza's eye or because she didn't want to risk a mis-stitch. It was a terrifically complicated pattern she was working on. Titian would have been jealous.

"It is my behavior at breakfast. I absolutely must apologize for it. I forgot my place, and I'm terribly sorry. I should not have yelled at your brother."

"Oh, Emma darling" — Eliza couldn't

stop herself from chuckling — "there is no need to apologize. John grew up in a houseful of girls, after all. He is well versed in the ways of tormenting our sex. And he did deserve a tongue-lashing."

"But it wasn't *me* he was tormenting. It was poor Drayton. He really had no call to speak to him that way," said Emma.

"Of course not," said Eliza with a sigh. "But they are both boys, after all, regardless of their difference in station. It's natural for them to spar a little, especially in the presence of a pretty girl. Besides, it wasn't Drayton who got so upset," she said. "It was you."

"But he could not allow himself to get upset. Let us not forget that he is your employee, though by birth, he is as much a gentleman as Mr. Schuyler or Mr. Hamilton."

Eliza laughed. "By birth, he is much more a gentleman than Mr. Hamilton, and it looks like the jury is still out on John." She smiled gently at her ward. "Oh, darling, you are so young. Poor Drayton was just a means to an end."

Emma risked a glance up. "What do

you mean, Mrs. Hamilton?"

"Despite his sometimes coarse tongue, John is quite attuned to others' feelings. He sensed that you were sympathetic to Drayton's position and needled the boy in order to get to you."

"To me! Why, whatever have I done to him?"

Another smile from Eliza. "Oh, you are *so* delightfully naïve. You have done nothing, of course, save for being a beautiful girl who is constantly in his line of sight!"

Emma's eyes dropped again, but Eliza noticed that her fingers had stopped their work. "I'm sure I don't understand you, Mrs. Hamilton."

"And I'm sure you do. As I've told you, I believe John is sweet on you, my dear. And in the manner of boys everywhere, he thinks the way to make you sweet on him is to tease and torment you and generally make you crazy."

"Me?" Emma laughed nervously. "But I am so far from a suitable candidate for . . . for Mr. Schuyler's feelings that I cannot believe he would . . . feel for me,"

235

she finished awkwardly.

Eliza reached forward and patted Emma on the knee. "If men and women only fell in love with suitable candidates, Mr. Shakespeare would have been out of a job. And this generation of Schuylers has a distinguished record of falling in love with not-quite-suitable candidates, as you say."

Emma frowned. "You mean Mr. Hamilton? But he is such a respected figure. Any father would be proud to see his daughter married to him."

"Remember that when I met him he was just a penniless, nameless aide-de-camp to General Washington. By his own admission, the main reasons he was hired for that position were that he spoke French and he wrote in a clear hand. He has a few more pennies now — enough to keep up with my spending habits, even, if he were not profligate himself — but such a prospect was not at all evident when I fell in love with him. And my elder sister, Angelica, eloped with a gun runner dogged by rumors of an abandoned family back in England."

"What?" Emma gasped. "How scandalous!" But the way she said it, it sounded more like "How romantic!" She continued: "But Mrs. Van Rensselaer certainly played by the rules."

Emma's assumption prompted a hearty laugh from Eliza. The idea of Peggy playing by the rules was just too rich. "In Peggy's case, *she* was the unsuitable candidate. The Van Rensselaers were not at all keen on the marriage. The romance persisted for more than five years before they finally allowed Stephen to propose, and had Stephen's father been alive, I'm not sure it would have happened at all."

"But the Schuylers are a most prestigious family! What on earth could have been the Van Rensselaers' objections?"

"What is it always? Money. If the Schuylers have an income of a thousand pounds a year, the Van Rensselaers have an income of a hundred thousand. If we own two hundred fifty acres, they own two hundred fifty thousand. Why, nearly all of upper New York State falls under the dominion of the patroonship. Some say that Rensselaerswyck is larger than Holland itself."

Emma's mouth fell open. "I knew that

Miss Betty Van Rensselaer was wealthy, but I had no idea she was *that* wealthy."

Eliza nodded. "The only family in the area that comes close to rivaling them is the Livingstons. Stephen's mother is a Livingston, and she wanted him to marry another of her clan, and so unite the two largest fortunes in the north. But Peggy has her ways. Poor Stephen never stood a chance, I'm afraid. It didn't hurt that Judge Livingston had made it clear that he was bestowing the bulk of his estate on his eldest son, Robert, and that his daughters stood to inherit nearly as little as Peggy."

Emma smiled wistfully. "But still. I am no Peggy Schuyler. Mr. John Schuyler cannot feel about me the same way Mr. Van Rensselaer felt about your sister."

"No? Who is it that John is always talking to when he is at home? Is it me, his sister, or Alex, who could help with his schoolwork or his future career? No, it is our lovely houseguest, Miss Emma Trask."

Emma smiled bashfully but didn't say anything. At last she picked up her needle and began to embroider again. She was working on Perseus's shield, which was emblazoned with an image of the Gorgon's head.

Eliza let her work for a moment, then gently prodded. "So tell me, Emma. Does my brother's attention displease you?"

Emma pulled a few more stitches, rendering the snakes of Medusa's hair with frightening vividness. "As I say, I am not as aware of it as you seem to be. But in general I do find his conversation witty. He likes to tease but does not seem to me to come from a cruel place. A tad impious perhaps, but I am such a shy person that I take a kind of vicarious joy in someone else's insouciance. Although I found his treatment of Drayton demeaning."

"*Insouciant* is a kind word for it," Eliza said, forgetting for a moment that she was supposed to be John's champion. "But I think you are right when you say that it does not come from a cruel place. Our family is so large that one has to squawk a little in order to be heard. I think that once he has spent some time in the world he will realize he doesn't need to try quite so hard. So," she added in a little tone, "his attention does not displease."

Emma took another long moment, punching her needle through her hoop and pulling the thread taut. But she did not answer Eliza.

"I do not ask you to return my brother's flirtations. Only . . . allow him to flirt with you," she beseeched.

Emma shrugged. "I do not see how I can stop him. Especially when I have apparently not even been noticing it."

"Rebuffing a man is an art unto itself, one that I hope you will never have to learn. Very well, it is settled. John will woo you, and you will be wooed. Yes? Perhaps I can get you to wear a brighter shawl, though? That gray is quite regal, but not exactly romantic. Something red, to bring out the blush in your cheeks?"

Emma's head snapped up, a look of horror on her face. "Mrs. Hamilton! I would feel — *brazen.*"

"Fine," Eliza said. "It was just a suggestion. And speaking of suggestions, I would like to propose an idea to you."

Emma took a moment to compose herself. "As long as it doesn't involve face paint and powder, I am eager to hear it."

It took Eliza a moment to realize that her normally prim companion was joking, and she laughed heartily when she understood. "No, no, nothing like that. I would like to establish an orphanage."

Emma looked up in confusion. "I'm afraid I don't understand."

"Children who lost their parents in the war have always been a special concern of mine, and I have endeavored to find homes for as many of them as I could."

"Indeed," Emma said. "I owe my own good fortune to your compassion."

"Thank you, my dear, though I was not soliciting compliments. I am motivated by more than a bit of self-reproach."

"Why, whatever for? You are one of the most generous women I know!"

"Once again, thank you. But this past month, as I have run around snatching up bolts of pristine linen and gilded bassinets and pale-flowered wallpaper to make a nursery for my child, I have been reminded of how arbitrary it is that I have so much when others have so little."

"That is just another sign of your sensitivity, Mrs. Hamilton."

Eliza wished Emma would stop complimenting her. She felt as though she was bragging, and that wasn't her intention at all.

"Sensitivity or guilt. It doesn't really matter. I would like to make a place for the orphans of this city I have come to think of as home. It is a grand city, full of energy and purpose, but for the same reason it can also be a callous city, grinding down those who are not well situated to survive its challenges."

"An orphanage," Emma said. "You mean, a permanent facility?"

"Yes," Eliza said eagerly. "With bright warm rooms like the one awaiting baby Philip, soft beds, warm clothes, hearty food, and a staff of matrons who will give them a measure of maternal warmth until proper homes can be found for them, and teachers to educate them so that they do not become waifs or urchins but can enter society as self-sufficient adults rather than fall between the cracks."

"Oh, it sounds like a wonderful place!

But how can I help? I am but an orphan myself, one who lives on the generosity of others."

"It is you who are generous with us," Eliza said. "With your warmth and diligence and assistance. I would like you to apply those same skills to running the orphanage."

"What? Me! But I know nothing of such things!"

"You know how to care, and if I'm being honest, you are twice as organized as I could ever hope to be. And of course we would pay you for your services. This would be proper employment, not charity."

"I-I'm flattered, and flabbergasted," Emma stuttered. "B-but where on earth will you get the money for all of this?"

Eliza laughed. "I have rich friends and a resourceful husband. I will find it somewhere."

Her eyes fell to her lap then.

"Oh, will you look at this!" she said, holding up her hoop. "I have written *ES* instead of *EH*! Although the *S* looks more like a five than a letter."

Emma regarded the handkerchief with pity. "You have many skills, Mrs. Hamilton. I am afraid embroidery is not one of them."

Eliza stared at her companion for a moment. "John was right. You *are* a lioness. I do look forward to the day you roar!"

12
MARIA'S STORY

*Ruston's Ale House and Inn, Mrs. Smith's
  Room*
New York, New York
August 1785

The first thing Alex did when he got to
the office was dash off a note to Maria
Reynolds, promising her that he would
come visit her in the afternoon or evening
and asking her to stay in Mrs. Childress's
inn during the day and not, under any
circumstances, to contact her husband.
He then sent word to a certain Señor La
Vera. Miguel was a direct descendant of
the conquistadors who had taken Mexico
from the Aztecs under Hernán Cortés.
He claimed that his ancestors had stolen
a "king's ransom" in gold from Mon-
tezuma's coffers in the early 1520s and
squandered it over the course of the next

250 years, so that by the time Miguel was born he was forced to labor in the fields alongside the peasants his family had once enslaved. At age fifteen he ran away, making his way to Cuba and thence to Florida. He joined an independence movement to drive the Spanish from Florida, a movement that was ahead of its time, and he barely managed to escape north to Georgia with his life.

He was just in time to join the Continental army, however, serving in the South Carolina 2nd Regiment. He was one of the few survivors of the Continental army's failed attempt to liberate Savannah in 1779, took part in the defense of Charleston in 1780, and wound up his service at Yorktown, where he had heard tales of Lt. Col. Alexander Hamilton's bravery, though the two never met — mostly because Miguel had lost his right foot and ankle to a cannonball and spent the ensuing months fighting for his life on a hospital cot. All this by the time he was nineteen years old. The hardy Mexican had survived, however, and eventually made his way to New York, where he looked up Alex and asked if he had any work. Despite his wooden leg and heavy Spanish accent, Miguel had proven himself to be a master of subterfuge and disguise, and had become Alex's primary investigator for cases of a less-than-savory nature.

He showed up at Alex's office just after noon in typical fashion. Alex had dipped into his files to look up something, and when he turned back around, Miguel was sitting in the chair in front of his desk. For a man with a wooden leg, he was surprisingly light on his feet.

"Colonel Hamilton, you called?" he said simply. He wasn't one for small talk. Miguel liked to refer to himself as an "Aztec warrior" and wore his long hair pulled into a unique topknot on top of his head.

Alex handed Miguel a sheet of paper. "I need you to find out everything you can about James Reynolds. His address is there."

"By everything, you mean everything illegal, I assume."

"Illegal, compromising, or otherwise unsavory. I want to make this man look as bad as I can."

Miguel blinked. "Ho, Colonel Hamilton, this guy must be some nasty fellow. I have never seen you take a case so personally before."

"In truth, I have never met the man. I do not know how he conducts his public life, but in his private life he is the most base kind of knave."

"You mean he mistreats the ladies?"

"He mistreats his wife." An image of Maria's bruised cheek flashed in Alex's mind. "I don't just want to destroy his reputation. I want to shame him. I want people to hiss and spit when he walks down the street, or cross over to the other side as if he were a leper. I want him to flee from this city with his tail in his hands."

"Don't you mean between his legs?"

"No, for I intend to cut it off, whip him in the face with it, and then throw it at his feet."

Miguel grinned. "I'm sure the situation is tragic, but I like seeing you like this. It's like the soldier we saw at Yorktown. A lone wolf charging a moose, fearless of the big antlers."

Alex tossed Miguel a coin purse. "For your trouble."

Miguel weighed the purse and pursed his lips. "Is she rich and beautiful, or just beautiful?"

"Go," Alex said, fighting back a grin of his own. "Bring me something good and there's another purse waiting for you."

"Oh, she's definitely poor," Miguel said with a laugh. "Men never waste money on a rich woman."

Alex spent the rest of the afternoon attending to work he had neglected for the past month while he tried to sort out the Trinity case. It was mostly rote paperwork, but there was a lot of it. Nippers, Turkey, and Bartleby had produced hundreds of pages of documents, each of which needed a review and a signature. By five o'clock, Alex's hand was cramping, and he barely recognized the letters of his own name. But he had billed for nearly a hundred pounds, which would — almost — cover the money Eliza had spent redecorating the house for John, Emma, and baby Philip.

There was one last stack of pages to go

through, and the light was still good. Alex normally would have persevered until it was done, but he knew Maria must have been anxious, alone in Caroline's inn without any knowledge of what was going on in the case that would decide her future. He packed a valise and headed for the door. The youngest clerk, Bartleby, sat at his desk staring idly into space.

"If you could make three copies of this for me for tomorrow," Alex said, depositing a document on the clerk's desk.

"I would prefer not to," Bartleby said, without meeting his eyes.

"Now *that's* funny," Alex said, and headed out the door.

Alex's office was heavily shaded by its neighbors, and he didn't realize what a hot day it had turned into. It was nearly six, but the sun was still high in the sky and beating down on Alex's hatted head. He had worn a smart but rather heavy wool coat in a deep burgundy (he hadn't planned to, but John had shown up to breakfast in a dazzling jacket in a color that could only be called shocking pink, and Alex wasn't about to outdone in his own house, and by a teenager to boot); this on top of a long-sleeved linen shirt, embroidered velvet waistcoat, and his undergarments. Within five minutes he was sweating; within ten he had taken his hat off and held it in his hand, and to hell with the disapproving looks of his fellow pedestrians. By the time he arrived at Ruston's Ale House a half hour later, he was drenched.

"Mr. Hamilton!" Sally exclaimed when he walked in. "You are a victim of your own sartorial elegance if ever I saw one."

Alex accepted the towel she handed him and mopped the sweat from his face.

"Thank you, Sally. You look lovely, too."

Sally had already swung behind the bar and knelt down to draw him a pint from one of the several barrels stored there.

"This will cool you off. We are trying a new thing here at the alehouse."

Alex was about to ask what the new thing was when he put his hand on the glass. It was ice cold. He thought perhaps the glass had been chilled, but when he sipped his ale he realized it was the liquid itself.

"It's . . . cold," he said wonderingly. He had never before had ale at anything other than room temperature.

Sally nodded. "The barrel is packed in ice. It is apparently quite popular in Boston, so we've decided to give it a try here."

Alex gulped down a good half of his glass. "It is certainly refreshing." Another long pull, the icy liquid rushing into his body and immediately cooling him. "This cold beer thing may well catch on."

"The ice is very dear, but our customers have responded well, despite the extra penny for the glass."

"It is certainly worth it," Alex said, standing up. "Please send a pair of these to Mrs. Smith's room in a few minutes."

"I do not know that Mrs. Smith is an ale drinker. A cider perhaps?"

Alex nodded. "Send a second pint of the ale as well. If she doesn't drink it, I will," Alex said, and headed for the stairs.

When he reached the second floor, he knocked on Maria's door softly.

"Mrs. Reynolds," he said in a quiet voice. "It's Alexander Hamilton."

There was no sound from within the room, but after a few moments he heard a key turning in the lock, and then the door opened. The first thing Alex saw was that Maria was wearing the same clothes as when they first met. Well, of course she was. She had run away from her husband without a coin purse, let alone a traveling case. Her dark blue dress had a simple cut, and this helped keep it fresh-looking, but it still looked as though it could use a pass with a hot iron.

In contrast, though, Maria's face looked remarkably fresh, as if she had passed her first good night's sleep in years. She had washed the powder from her skin, and though the bruise on her cheek was more visible, it was also obviated by the soft smile on her lips and the hopeful expression in her eyes.

"Clearly we have to get you to a mercer's," Alex said by way of greeting.

Maria's smile grew wider, and a bit more pert. "Well, that's certainly how every woman loves to be greeted."

Alex's face, already flushed from his hot walk, grew even warmer. "Oh, I beg your pardon! I quaffed an ale downstairs and it has gone straight to my head. I didn't mean to imply that you —"

Maria cut him off with a laugh. "No need to apologize, Mr. Hamilton. I understood what you meant, though I do not presume to rate a new dress, or even the fabric to sew one. You have already done so much for me." She stepped aside and waved a hand. "Do please come in."

Alex walked in and set his hat on the dresser. He could feel his sweaty shirt clinging to his back. "I don't mean to be presumptuous, but do you mind if I remove my jacket and waistcoat? Only it's rather hotter than I realized outside, and I overdressed for the weather. I am quite soaked through."

"Please, treat my room as you would your home. Shall I throw open a window?"

"That would be lovely," Alex said as he took off his jacket and hung it on a peg. "I am surprised you have them closed; it is such a warm day."

Maria did not answer immediately but only stared out the window. She was silent so long that Alex started to fear that he had somehow offended her.

At last she spoke.

"Do you know I have sat here in this chair all day, looking out this window? There is not much of a view — just the walls and windows of the buildings across Water Street, and the sunlight, and the clouds. Yet to me it is the sweetest vista imaginable, like the Alps in summertime, with their green sides and snowcaps, or the first glimpse of palm trees of the isles of the Indies appearing on the horizon, or the famous pyramids of Egypt seen across the majesty of the Nile. But this." She gestured to the window. "This looks like freedom to me. Freedom and the future. So great was my pleasure that I thought if I added even a single additional detail I would be overcome. I would wake from this dream and find myself back in the house of my oppressor. And yet —"

She put her hands on the sash and pushed the window up. A fresh breeze rushed into the room, and she inhaled as though it were the bouquet of roses or fresh-baked bread.

"And yet it is not a dream."

Alex had removed his jacket and waistcoat while Maria spoke, and now he walked to the second window and threw it open. He leaned out the window, and after a moment Maria leaned out hers, and they turned and faced each other outside the walls of Caroline's inn. The streets below were dotted with pedestrians enjoying the sunny day, and a few carriages carrying wealthier New Yorkers about their errands, or perhaps up north to their country homes to escape the heat, and wagons and carts ferrying their wares, and, directly below them, a couple of pigs, eating the garbage from the gutter.

"It is not a dream," Alex affirmed. "Today you open a window and stick your face out into the free world. Before you know it, you will be venturing out into this world, a free woman. The city shall be yours."

One of the pigs below the window squealed as if in agreement.

"Well, perhaps not the pigs," Alex said, grinning.

"I'll take the pigs," Maria said as they stepped back into the room and took up perches in the two chairs. "I'll take the bad with the good and everything in between. Only — only how do we do it? I have only ever heard of men being granted divorces, and then only in cases of the most flagrant infidelity. Women seem to be held to a higher standard of grievance."

"Matrimonial law is certainly not my area of expertise, but I know anecdotally that what you say is true. Alas, the law considers the fairer sex to be more dependent as well as more comely, and is less likely to believe that it is worth risking her vulnerability as a single woman than leaving her in the care of her husband."

"What nonsense!" Maria said. "During the war, nearly every woman I knew was living on her own — raising children, running farms and businesses, fending off redcoats and other threats, and generally enjoying the freedom of being out from under the thumbs of their menfolk, regardless of how dire the circumstances were."

"Indeed," Alex agreed. "Caroline Childress, in whose inn you are staying, ran this place on her own from 1776 onward, and I have represented any number of women, widows, orphans, or simply ladies who never chose to marry, who have thrived without need of a man's assistance. Yet with each new case I bring to trial, it is as if the court has forgotten about all the previous ones. It is not just legal opinion you are up against. It is society's. I have no doubt that one day, people will think differently, but I fear we are still some time away from that day. And of course there is virtually no chance that you will retain any property with which you entered the union, or that was added to it after your marriage."

"Well!" Maria said only half jokingly. "If your goal was to convince me of the hopelessness of my case, you have certainly succeeded!"

Alex smiled in apology. "I didn't mean to frighten you. I just want you to know what you are up against. Women have been granted divorces, but only in the case of, shall we say, rather extreme behavior on the part of their spouses."

He didn't phrase his words as a question, but Maria seemed to understand. She took a deep breath and sat up straight in her chair.

"You wish to know why I ran away from my husband."

Just then there was a knock on the door. Maria started, and turned toward it with a panicked expression.

"Mr. Hamilton? Mrs. Smith? It is Sally from downstairs."

Maria sighed as the door opened and Sally started in with a tray in her hand, then pulled up short.

"Oh!" she said in an embarrassed voice. "I did not mean to —"

Alex followed her eyes and saw that she was staring at his jacket and waistcoat, which he had laid open on the bed to dry.

Alex laughed. "Come now, Sally, you remarked on how wet I was when I first came in. I have simply removed my outer garments so that they, and I, can dry off."

"Of course, sir," Sally said as she crossed to a table and set the glasses down. "Only your shirt, sir. It is rather . . . transparent."

Alex looked down and saw that Sally was correct. "Oh, dear," he said, resisting the urge to cross his arms over his chest.

"Perhaps you would like my shawl?" asked Maria.

"Oh, ah, no," Alex said, glancing at the floral, fringed garment, which was decidedly feminine. "I wouldn't want to get it wet as well." *Nor would I want to look ridiculous,* he thought. "I'll simply, ah . . ." He pulled his shirt free from his skin as best he could. "It will dry soon in this breeze, and then decency will be restored."

"Of course, sir," Sally said with a bored air. Years of working in an inn frequented by sailors must have exposed her to far more risqué sights than a half-naked man. "Will there be anything else?"

"No, thank you, Sally. Have a good evening."

"You too, sir," Sally said, and took her leave.

Alex gave Maria her choice of ale or cider and she did indeed choose the cider. He took one of the pints of chilled ale for himself and returned to his chair. He checked that his shirt was still relatively modest, then turned back to Maria.

"To be clear," he began in a gentle voice, "I feel that it is the height of vulgarity that I should have to ask you about this, or that you should be compelled to tell me. I ask only because without the details of this narrative I have almost no chance to help you. Juries, rather like children, are seduced by a good story."

"I understand." Maria nodded. She took a sip of her cider followed by a deep breath, as if telling herself she was ready. Still, it was another moment before she began speaking.

"I was inspired to leave — if *inspired* is not too strange a word to use in this context — when I read the account of Mrs. Elihu Patterson, who was granted a divorce from her husband after he" — she summoned another breath — "after he behaved toward her in a decidedly ungentlemanly way in public. At her trial she testified that this was a pattern of behavior going back years. Her husband denied it, yet there were any number of friends, family, neighbors, and even passersby to support her claim."

Alex nodded. He, too, had followed the

story, which had featured prominently in the *New York Journal* and other local papers this past spring. He had found the accounts luridly distasteful, yet he had also been unable to tear himself away from them. He knew that people would follow the Reynolds case just as avidly. Everyone loved a tawdry scandal, but none more than New Yorkers.

As if reading his mind, Maria continued: "So I knew I would have to reveal my story publicly if I wished to be free. It took me some months to work up the nerve, not least because the idea of having my shame exposed as Mrs. Patterson's had been was mortifying to me. And I kept telling myself Mr. Reynolds would change, that the chance of success was too slim, that it wasn't worth the risk. Indeed, I knew that he had himself seen the Patterson story, and I fancied that it had scared him into a semblance of propriety, at least externally. And then . . ." She brought a hand to her bruised cheek, inspecting her fingertips as if the color had come off on them. "This kind of man doesn't change," she said simply.

Alex nodded but didn't speak. He knew she was working herself up and didn't want to jar her train of thought. A faint smile had come to her face, as if she were recalling a distant but fond memory.

"My parents were patriots," she said now. "My father joined the Sons of Liberty in Boston and was present at the Tea Party in 1773. When war was declared, he was first to the front. And, alas, among the first to die at Concord in '75. I was eleven at the time. My mother, unfortunately, was not one of those independent-minded women I mentioned earlier. She did her best, but there were six mouths to feed and almost no money with which to do so. When Mr. Reynolds began to show interest in me at the age of fifteen, she urged me to look favorably upon his suit. He was — is — much older than I, a widower and plainly coarse, but he had a solid income in trade, and there was no indication of his darker nature. I did not urge him on, but I didn't push him away either. He suggested assignations which —" She broke off, obviously embarrassed by the memory, but then summoned her resolve and continued. "That is, I was too innocent to know what, exactly, he wanted, but not so innocent that I didn't know to avoid them. I thought perhaps he would grow bored when his immediate urges weren't satisfied. I didn't realize then the obsessive nature of his character. He is one of those men who wants something that isn't his much more than something he already possesses.

"Still, I might indeed have been able to escape, had not my mother succumbed to illness during the winter of 1779 to 1780. My brothers and sisters and I had nothing to fall back on. We were parceled among our aunts and uncles like so many packages being distributed across beasts of burden to ease the individual load. I landed in the house of my aunt and uncle Willoughby, who made it clear that if I did not accept Mr. Reynolds's proposal, I would be turned out the minute the ice cracked on the Charles River that spring." She shrugged. "I had no choice. I was married in March 1780, just two months after my sixteenth birthday."

She paused for a moment, collecting herself. She stared out the window and took deep breaths of the fresh air. Alex thought she was unable to continue, and was about to tell her that he would be come back tomorrow when she started speaking again. As soon as the words began coming out of her mouth, he almost wished he had left.

"The horrors began on my wedding night. Mr. Reynolds had been married already, as I said, and, as well, it seemed clear that he had availed himself of — of certain unfortunate women after his wife left this world. The fact that I had not his experience in these matters seemed only to urge him on. My fear excited him. My pain brought him pleasure. He spoke of my innocence as a prize he was stealing from me. Afterward, he said I was just another fallen woman. I certainly felt like one."

It was Alex who taking deep breaths now, to steady himself.

"At first, the violations were confined to the nights," Maria continued. "But as time went by and I grew less afraid of him, he grew more jealous of me and constantly accused me of flirting with other men, or worse. If truth be told, Mr.

Reynolds had so soured me on the male sex that I wouldn't care if I never saw another one again, let alone courted one's affections. He punished me anyway, always with his words and sometimes with his hands as well, and as sometimes happens in these cases, I grew insensitive to his curses and his slaps, and taunted him with transgressions that I had not, in fact, committed. I soon learned that my husband's sadism was vested in my fear. He liked me to cower, not carp, and the more I showed him that his threats didn't hurt me, the less inclination he seemed to administer them. And so we persevered in this uneasy truce with but occasional eruptions, and I in my naïveté thought that somehow I could eke out an existence."

She paused again, turning her face to the window, which washed it in a golden glow. Alex saw with a start that the light had deepened considerably. The sun was going down. He was due home soon. Yet he was riveted to his chair.

"Alas," Maria said after nearly a minute of silence, "a villain's nature cannot remain sated forever. Mr. Reynolds's greatest pleasure was in my fear, but if I would not give him that, then he would take what he would get. After more than a year of relative tranquility, his outbursts suddenly redoubled and grew more pronounced. There were days, weeks, when I was not fit to be seen outside my own house or to entertain visitors within it. Here was Mr. Reynolds's new joy: making me a prisoner of my own politesse, my own shame. I realized soon enough that if I did not flee I would die in his house, and what's more, I would not even be missed, because I had not been seen outside it for so long by ought but shopkeepers. Even then it took months before I worked up the nerve to flee. And . . ."

Alex remained silent, waiting to see if she had reached the end of her story, or the end of her ability to tell it. Her face in the evening light was as serene as a Madonna's in some Italian painting, unlined, ageless, as if time had frozen for her five years ago, when she was sixteen and sold off to the highest bidder like a piece of chattel.

"And here we are," he said at length. "I must ask," he added after a moment.

"How did you choose me?"

Maria turned from the window to look at Alex for the first time in some minutes. Her eyes, he saw then, were not ageless, but filled with bitter experience, and even cunning. Suddenly Alex remembered that he was in shirtsleeves before a woman he barely knew. Again he had to fight the urge to cross his arms over his chest.

"I had seen your name, of course, and knew of your reputation for taking on lost causes. I did not connect it with my own situation, though, until I saw an engraving of you in court in the *Journal.*" She shrugged. "I thought you had a trustworthy face."

Alex couldn't help but smile as he thought of the image in question, which had appeared a few weeks ago. "That engraving looks nothing like me. In fact, it seems that the artist mistook opposing counsel's assistant for me. He's not a bad-looking man, I admit, but I do have rather more hair than him under my wig."

Maria cracked a little smile.

"I realized something was amiss as soon as I walked into your office."

Now Alex had to laugh. "I hope I haven't disappointed you."

Maria returned his laugh with a small but somehow self-assured chuckle. "No," she said in a soft voice. "I am not disappointed at all."

13

TEMPEST IN A TEAPOT

The Hamilton Town House
New York, New York
August 1785

When Alex finally got home for dinner
— to which he was an hour late for the
fourth straight night, or perhaps the fifth,
or fifteenth — Eliza found him unusually
silent.

"It's Mrs. Reynolds, isn't it?" she said
simply as she helped him off with his coat
in the front hall and handed it to Drayton. The footman had a stricken look on
his face, as though, by not getting to the
door first, he had committed some hei-
nous sin, like coughing up the Eucharist
or dropping a baby on its head.

"It is rather damp, sir," he said, inspecting the coat. "I shall take it downstairs
and hang it by the stove to make sure it

dries without mildewing."

"Thank you, Drayton," Alex said, as the footman scurried off with the garment, fluffing it with his white-gloved hand as he went.

Alex nodded his head and closed his eyes as he pulled Eliza into a tight hug and held her closely for several seconds.

"I have felt sympathy for my clients before," he said into her hair. "I have wanted to win their cases for their sake as well as my own. But no one has ever touched me quite like this woman. Her plight is truly heartbreaking."

After the party the other night, Alex had alluded to the strife that plagued Maria's marriage, though he had said he did not yet know all the details. Eliza sensed that he knew more now, though she wasn't sure if she should ask about them, or if she wanted to know. She stepped back and took his hands in hers and fixed him in the eye with a compassionate yet steely gaze.

"If you need to unburden yourself, I am here," she said in a voice that was at once diplomatic and full of sympathy.

Alex seemed to contemplate this, then

shuddered. "I would not . . . I *could* not inflict such violence upon you. There are things that your sex deserves to be sheltered from."

Eliza gave her husband a little kiss on the cheek. "Men always think they are sheltering us females, but it is usually *we* who are sheltering *you.* We are not as delicate as you think. If Mrs. Reynolds can survive the transgressions committed against her, I can surely survive hearing about them. But," she added quickly, as Alex seemed ready to protest, "I am not *asking* to be told anything. I am only letting you know that if you wish to share your burden rather than carry it alone, I am here to listen. Come, let us go in to dinner. I think a dose of family would do you well. I should tell you, though, we have a guest."

"A guest?" Alex said as they walked into the front parlor, brightly lit by a profusion of lamps.

"There you are," a female voice sang out as they entered the room. "I was just about to tell John to go look for the two of you!"

Betty Van Rensselaer sat in the wing-back chair Eliza usually claimed as her own, as it commanded the best view of the room. John had brought her home with him again. John and Betty had resumed their childhood friendship and had been out on the town together many a night. Eliza found the girl by turns charming and trying, immature and spoiled to be sure, but full of spark and not bad-hearted. John doted on her a little too much for Eliza's comfort, although Emma seemed not to notice, but Eliza thought she might be able to turn Betty's presence to her advantage.

Her brother was seated on the yellow sofa, closest to the open windows, while Emma had taken what was easily the hardest chair in the room, despite the fact that there were several more comfortable perches from which to choose. She had her embroidery hoop in her hand and was using a white thread to add incredibly realistic froth to ocean waves (she was still working on the liberation of Andromeda).

"And *I* was just about to tell Betty and Emma," John chimed in with a wink, "that we should head to table on our own while you two canoodle in the front hall."

From the corner of her eye, Eliza saw Alex color. Though they had been married for five years, and John was nearly a decade his junior, such was his respect for the Schuyler name that even the intimation of intimacy between himself and a Schuyler daughter could turn him back into a blushing fifteen-year-old. She expected him to say something, but clearly he was still caught up in whatever had transpired with the unfortunate Mrs. Reynolds.

"How funny!" she said, coming to her husband's rescue. "*I* was just about to tell Mr. Hamilton that we should head to table while *you* ride to Virginia to replace his bottles of whiskey."

"Touché!" said John with a grin.

The fivesome made their way into the dining room, where Drayton stood at the foot of the table as stiffly as a suit of armor in a musty old European castle. As soon as the diners appeared, however, he sprang forward to pull out Eliza's chair, which she sank into gratefully. In the last week it seemed that she had gained ten pounds, and she was starting to feel it in her feet. She noted that someone — presumably her all-attentive footman — had added a pillow to the seat as well. Grateful for his foresight, she looked up with more than the usual politeness. "Thank you, Drayton."

"Very good, Mrs. Hamilton," said Drayton, easing her chair in, then rushing to seat Betty. As he moved to Eliza's right, though, she saw him catch sight of Emma, and he pulled up short.

"Oh ho!" John chuckled beside Emma. "We have a situation! What is a poor hapless footman to do when there are two ladies to be seated and neither has clear standing over the other? On the one hand, we have Miss Trask, who would seem to have precedence as a beloved long-term guest of the hosts rather than an actual resident of the house. But if Miss Trask *is* in fact a resident of the house, then precedence would be granted to Miss Van Rensselaer, who is most definitely a guest here. Oh, it *is* a pickle! That's Shakespeare, by the way."

Eliza thought John was laying it on a bit thick, no doubt trying to impress the girls. Drayton wavered for another moment, but before she could say some-thing, Alex, who was standing behind his chair waiting for the ladies to be seated, started toward Emma's chair.

"What *should* have happened, John," Alex said in a voice that was half scold-ing, half mocking, "is that *you* should have seated Miss Trask, whose place is beside yours, leaving Drayton to assist Miss Van Rensselaer." He pulled out Emma's chair, and Emma took her seat.

"Oh, it's all such a bother," Betty said from the other side of the table. "A veritable tempest in a teapot. It's just a *chair,* after all. It's not a chest of drawers or a marble bust. I can pull it out myself." Which is just what she did. "You are a pretentious ass, by the way," she said, turning up her nose at John.

Drayton caught his breath.

"So close!" John said, plopping into his chair and looking at Drayton with feigned sympathy. "The chivalrous host had almost saved the evening, and then the boorish — or whatever the lady equiva-lent of boorish is —"

"Common, I think," Betty said drily. "Or maybe slatternly."

"The slatternly guest —"

"John Bradstreet Schuyler! Don't you dare!" Eliza shouted, but it was plain she was trying hard not to laugh.

"By which I mean, of course, the *misguided* guest loused everything up by *pulling out her own chair.* Will decorum ever recover?" John added in a stricken voice. "Is the evening lost to chaos over a footman's mistake?" He collapsed into laughter.

Eliza saw that Emma's eyes were flashing but that she kept silent, perhaps cowed by the presence of a guest, especially one as distinguished as Miss Van Rensselaer. *Although "distinguished" is putting a fine spin on it.*

Why did John take every opportunity to tease Drayton? It was as if he were jealous of him somehow. Was he? Jealous of the footman? Whatever for?

"Drayton, please tell Rowena to plate the roast," Eliza said finally. "It's nearly nine. I'm famished."

"Oh, darling," Alex said to his wife as Drayton hurried off. "You should have eaten something!"

"What makes you think I didn't eat something?" Eliza laughed. "My appetite has positively doubled in the past couple of weeks. As has my waistline."

"Oh, pshaw," Betty said. "You will be one of those despicable creatures who is delivered of her child and a week later is back in a corset, outshining everyone else at the ball. Whereas I, like my mother and aunts, will somehow manage to look fatter *after* I've had my baby! It is the *other* Van Rensselaer inheritance," she added. "The one we don't like to talk about."

"Why, Miss Van Rensselaer!" John said, turning his wicked attentions to her. "Are you thinking of having a child? Hadn't you ought to find a husband first?"

Betty rolled her eyes. "What do you think I am doing *here,* you silly goose?"

John coughed and sputtered, and Eliza bit back a chuckle. But it was Emma who cleared up the confusion.

"She means in New York City, Mr. Schuyler," she said in a quiet voice. "Not here in this house."

Betty looked aghast, then burst into

laughter. "Oh, you thought I meant *you*! Little Johnny Schuyler? My husband? Oh, that is the best joke you've told all night!"

John glared at Betty. "As if I would ever wish for a wife like you," he said.

Betty arched her eyebrow and looked him up and down. "I think that is exactly what you wish."

Drayton walked back into the room just as everyone at the table burst into laughter. John laughed so heartily he had to wipe his eyes. Everyone was laughing except Emma, Eliza couldn't help but note, and of course Drayton. Their shared sober countenances seemed almost conspiratorial.

After pouring some whiskey for Eliza and Betty, Drayton turned to Emma. "Some whiskey for you, Miss Trask?"

Emma started to shake her head but stopped herself. "As a matter of fact, I will," she said, "but only if you call me Emma as I have asked."

Drayton hesitated but soon nodded regally. "Very good, Emma," he said, in a voice that made it sound as though he were greeting a queen.

"Just a taste," Emma said, putting her hand up after Drayton had poured little more than a drop in her glass. "Thank you so much."

Drayton bowed once again, so that his ears turned a little pink. He poured Alex some whiskey next, before leaving to fetch the roast.

"How interesting," Betty said once he was gone. "Is there a little cross-class romance going on, Emma?"

"What? No, I — oh," Emma interjected then, cutting herself off. "You are too forward, Miss Van Rensselaer."

"Betty, please. Call me Betty. So, you have no interest in Drayton?" she asked pointedly.

"Of course she doesn't. Don't you know? Everyone's in love with *me*," John said drolly. "Even Emma, who disapproves of me but still finds herself vulnerable to my many charms."

"Oh, John, don't tease Emma," Eliza said now. "She has every right to disapprove of you. You have been acting like a total dissolute since you arrived in New

York City."

"Hmmm. I thought 'dissolute' was an adjective," John said. "I guess we are using it as a noun now."

Eliza turned to her husband. "This is why people who didn't go to college despise people who did."

"Oh, I don't think we need to single out this instance," Alex said merrily. "There are so many reasons to despise John."

"I don't despise Mr. Schuyler," said Emma. "I like him very much. He is a good friend."

"That I am," said John with a wink.

"Is he now?" asked Betty. "Is that all he is?"

"Of course not, I am also her beau," John said with a grin. "Jealous, are you?"

Betty huffed and ignored him. Emma shook her head and reached nervously for her glass and took a deep draft. She immediately bit back a cough as beads of perspiration appeared on her upper lip. "Oh! Whiskey!" she said in a shocked voice. "I forgot!" She opened her mouth and fanned her tongue. "I did not know it would burn!"

Alex, meanwhile, was staring at Eliza quizzically. His eyes flashed between Emma and John, clearly asking if there was something going on between them. Eliza just smiled her best wouldn't-you-like-to-know? smile and leaned back in her chair.

"He is joking; of course he is not my beau. He is Mr. John Schuyler, whose father is General Philip Schuyler, and I am but Emma Trask," Emma said meekly.

"Nonsense!" Betty said now, sounding a bit irritable all of a sudden. "Who cares who was whose father anymore? Aren't these the kinds of crusty old European ideas we're trying to shake off? Not inheritance or anything so radical — do not think I am giving up my fortune so easily. But why shouldn't I marry, oh, let's say, Drayton here? If we followed the old rules, Emma would marry Drayton, and John and I would be wed. But why should Emma get the hale and handsome lad, while I am left with the inbred stripling? And, yes," she added, looking at John with narrowed eyes, "I was definitely talking about you this time."

"I cannot protest," John said self-deprecatingly for once. "I am skinny as a rake. As for inbred, well, when you don't know whether to call someone at a party aunt or niece, you know that too many cousins have married one another."

"You are not cousins with Emma," said Eliza with a smile.

"Indeed he is not," said Betty, coloring from the whiskey or the conversation; it was hard to tell.

"And you are singing quite a different tune from our last party, Betty," said Eliza.

But before Betty could reply, Drayton arrived with the roast. Conversation lulled while he served it, the odors of Rowena's cooking so delectable that wit was made superfluous.

"Speaking of marriage," Betty said, inhaling the steam coming off the succulent slices of meat and glistening potatoes and carrots Drayton placed on her plate, "I would marry the person who made this meat regardless of class *or* sex."

"Whereas I would marry the meat,"

John said, wafting the steam toward his face. "God bless Cook," he said, "but she thinks water is a spice."

"Thank you, Drayton," Eliza said after everyone had been served. "You may leave the platter on the sideboard and we'll help ourselves if we want seconds. You should take dinner with Rowena now. It is getting rather late."

"Very good, Mrs. Hamilton," Drayton said, bowing and heading downstairs.

Eliza sat stiffly, expectantly, while Drayton made his exit. To the fellow guests, it probably looked as though she were merely waiting to eat, but she had something far different on her mind. "And why *shouldn't* you marry Drayton?" Eliza said to Betty as soon as the footman was gone.

"That's what I said before," Betty said as she tucked into her meal. "Oh! You're serious!" She put down her fork in confusion. "My goodness. Last month you were challenging me to a little romance. And now you have upped the ante to marriage," she said. She considered the idea. "Well . . . by all means why shouldn't I marry Drayton? It's a free

284

country, isn't it?"

John's face, which was already flushed, turned a shade of purple.

"And besides," said Betty, "Emma isn't interested in him."

Emma lowered her eyes to her plate and kept them there.

"Someone should be," said Eliza.

Alex addressed his wife in a warning voice. "Eliza? What are you on about?"

Eliza answered her husband with a mixture of innocence and exasperation. "Oh, Alex, don't make it sound as if I'm talking about some far-fetched scheme like building a fourth story on the house! Miss Van Rensselaer has already remarked that she finds Drayton attractive, and we are all aware of both his fine character and excellent mind. Why, Emma pointed out just the other day that he reads more than I do!"

"That's because you're lazy," John quipped.

"That's because she's busy helping the poor," Emma quipped back, finding her voice.

"I'll tell you why she wouldn't marry

285

Drayton," said John with a strange look on his face.

"Yes? What is it? Enlighten me," said Betty.

"You know perfectly why, Miss Van Rensselaer, heiress to almost all of New York State."

"Why, Johnny Schuyler, are you calling me a snob?!" Betty cried.

"If the velvet glove fits . . ." He shrugged.

Betty held up her hands. "What gloves? My hands are bare." She put her hands back in her lap. "I'll have you know, John Schuyler, that I am the farthest thing from a snob. If I *were* a snob, I would have stayed in Albany and accepted one of the many proposals I have received from a positive litany of first and second cousins — and uncles, for that matter — and one old gentleman who, though not technically my grandfather, is certainly old enough to be. I came down here to find a good husband."

"Well, you won't find him here," sneered John.

"Why not? She might," said Eliza. She

leaned back, feeling satisfied that she had planted the seed and now needed to step back and let nature do its work. "All I'm saying is do not think of Drayton as a man so different from you, Betty. This is a new country, not the Old World."

"But he is different," Alex said now, "and not just in class."

"Hmmm," Betty said, turning to Alex. "What are you implying, Mr. Hamilton?"

Alex smiled warmly. "Only that you are a confident, outgoing, and, dare I say, independent young lady, and Drayton is a . . . steadier sort of fellow. I do not see him rushing out onto the dance floor anytime soon."

"Especially not with a tray of canapés in his hand," John said bitterly.

"Drayton *is* steady," Emma said quietly.

"Can I get a drink around here? Where is our Drayton?" asked John.

"Perhaps he is getting ready for our wedding," said Betty airily.

John ignored her and nodded to his empty glass. "Well, he should hurry up about it then. Why is it I can never get what I want around here?" he said, frustrated.

"I beg to argue. You can get anything you want," Emma said, her voice suddenly hot. "Because you are John Bradstreet Schuyler, firstborn son, heir to the Schuyler fortune, and he can get anything he wants. Except, apparently, Miss Van Rensselaer."

John's jaw dropped even as Betty clapped her hands. "Oh, I like this Emma! Anyone who can leave John Schuyler speechless is welcome at *my* table anytime," she said.

"Who knows?" Eliza said. "Maybe one day she will host you at her own table."

At this remark, everyone but Emma turned to stare at her with confused expressions. Emma merely grabbed her fork and knife and sawed heavily into her roast. "If I do," she said, "I hope I'll be serving this roast. It's delicious!"

14
MARITAL ISSUES

The Hamilton Town House, the Hamilton
  Bedchamber
New York, New York
August 1785

That night, Alex sat up with some papers concerning the Reynolds case, while Eliza, who was perhaps thinking about her footman's reading more than she did, began cutting open the pages of her novel. A pair of lamps on the bedside tables were all that lit the room, casting the bed in a glow of light while its corners receded in shadow. Normally Alex loved this time of night, ensconced between the four pillars of the matrimonial bed with Eliza's beautiful face relaxed in sleep beside him. Tonight, though, the sound of her paper knife slitting the folio into individual pages seemed to saw through

289

his concentration, and the letters on the page he was trying to read danced in the flickering glow of the lamps.

Eliza sighed. Alex recognized it as the sigh of someone who wanted to talk. Perhaps more to the point, it was the sigh of someone who was oblivious to the fact that her companion had no desire for conversation. "*Moll Flanders,*" she said after a moment. "Have you read this one?"

"Apparently not," Alex replied in a distracted voice. "Else you would not have to cut the pages."

Eliza laughed as if he had made a great joke. "I didn't mean this particular copy, silly! I only meant the book. *Moll Flanders,* by Daniel Defoe."

"I am aware who wrote *Moll Flanders,*" Alex said.

At that, there was a little pause from the reclining form next to him, as if she had heard the shortness of his voice and wondered what it meant. Whatever her conclusions, though, they weren't enough to deter her. She brought the book into the light and opened the cover.

" '*The Fortunes and Misfortunes of the*

Famous Moll Flanders,' " she read off the title page, *"'Who was Born in Newgate, and during a Life of continu'd Variety for Threescore Years, besides her Childhood, was Twelve Year a Whore'* — oh! — *'five times a Wife (whereof once to her Brother), Twelve Year a Thief, Eight Year a Transported Felon in Virginia, at last grew Rich, liv'd Honest, and dies a Penitent.'* " She snapped the cover shut. "It sounds racy!" Her knife plunged back into the volume with renewed eagerness.

"It sounds like you don't need to read it. The title is rather . . . fulsome. Besides, it has been sitting unread for a while now."

Eliza's knife jerked in her hand, and from the corner of his eye Alex saw a page rip, not along its seam but along its face.

"Are you upset with me, Alex?"

This time it was Alex who sighed. A clear sigh of warning. "Why should I be upset with you?"

Eliza tossed her book aside and turned over, placing her hand on his stomach — or, rather, on the pages there — and rubbing softly, which had the effect of causing the pages to swirl around. "I don't know. That's why I'm asking."

"Eliza, please!" Alex said, snatching the papers and thrusting them onto the bedside table. "These are important documents!"

"I wasn't damaging them," Eliza protested. "I don't understand —"

"Only I don't know why you decided to cut your novel's pages just now," Alex interrupted. "It will take you twenty minutes to finish, by which time you will be ready for sleep and will have succeeded in doing nothing but preventing me from catching up on my work!"

"You *are* upset with me!" Eliza cried, pushing herself upright and turning to him. "Whatever have I done?"

Alex berated himself mentally. He had spoken out of turn, and now he would have to calm his wife down, or not only would he not get any work done tonight, he wouldn't get any sleep either. He set the rest of his papers aside and turned to her. "I am not upset with you, my dear. I am just upset. I suspect this Reynolds affair is affecting me more than I care to admit."

In truth, Mrs. Reynolds's story was too close to his own mother's plight, and it was bringing up memories of his childhood he had long suppressed and never shared with his wife, who had been born into privilege and love and stability. She wouldn't understand what it was like to be so impoverished. He felt Eliza's hand on his leg, and he moved his to cover it with his own.

"I have wondered as much myself," she said. "I have never seen you quite so bothered by a case before. Perhaps someone else would handle it better."

Alex snorted. "It is hard for me to imagine a lawyer in New York who would agree to take it on. Indeed, it is hard for me to imagine a lawyer who will condone my taking it on."

"Alex, no!" Eliza said. "Do you mean to say that this case will damage your professional reputation? People already say such vile things about you because of all the work you do for loyalists!"

"Do they now?" he said curtly.

"Oh, darling — I did not mean —"

"I think you did," he said shortly. "Why should I not work for the loyalists? They pay our rent and furnish our house and accommodate our lifestyle." Including, he thought, a footman who had delusions of grandeur and a permanent companion for his wife who was not quite a house-guest nor a lady's maid, yet commanded the privileges of the former and the salary of the latter.

"My parents furnished this house," she said quietly.

"As you keep reminding me," he countered, then immediately felt sorry for their disagreement.

"It is just that — I like to feel that I contributed, too," said Eliza. "Even if I do not bring in an income."

Alex turned to her. He had married her for her beauty and her great heart, had fallen in love with her quick mind and loyal nature, and it would never have occurred to him to think she did not "contribute." She was, after all, a Schuyler sister. She was more than enough. She was his partner, his equal, his soul, and he knew she loved him dearly. But would she still love him, he thought, if she knew everything about his miserable background? That his mother was never someone that her mother would ever consent to receive in her drawing room? Of course she would, and she did — but a little part of him never really believed he was worthy of her.

"Divorce is not a welcome subject in society," he finally said at last. "People feel that if one woman were to be granted divorce on the grounds of mistreatment by her husband, a hundred others will step forward to make the same claim. Indeed, it was the Patterson case that prompted Mrs. Reynolds to contact me."

Eliza cringed at the memory. "Oh, that was such a terrible story! I did not know which was worse: that her husband treated her so cruelly or that the details were bandied about so crudely in the newspapers."

"The press would not print the stories if people did not want to read them," Alex said reproachfully.

"Alex," Eliza said, and a different tone came into her voice. "Do you think perhaps you are having such a strong reaction to Mrs. Reynolds because she —

she reminds you of your mother's situation in some way?"

Alex felt his whole body go still. "Mrs. Reynolds? Like my mother? No, I hadn't thought of it."

Eliza's hand wriggled in his, and Alex realized he was squeezing it tightly. He did his best to loosen his grip.

"Only you told me that your mother left her first husband because he did not treat her kindly," Eliza said in a quiet voice, as though Alex might have forgotten. "And then your father left her when he found out that she was still legally married to the previous man."

"There is no need to refer to Mr. Lavien, as the man's name was, as my mother's 'first husband,' since she never legally married my father. He was, therefore, merely her husband." Alex's voice sounded chilling even to his own ears. This was exactly why he never wanted to talk about this with Eliza. Such tawdry details in his background, from his people.

"Don't be angry with me," Eliza said. "Your sensitivity to the plight of women is one of the things I most love about you. I know it is because you witnessed your mother's sufferings at the hands of caddish men that you are so attuned to our difficult station in life, lacking as we women do any real rights, save those bestowed upon us by our fathers or husbands."

Alex saw red, his ire raised by the image of his suffering mother, of whom he was always a bit sensitive. "I don't know why you feel the need —"

"Alex, please! Keep your voice down. John is sleeping directly across the hall and Emma right above us."

For some reason this only made Alex angrier. "I don't know why you feel the need to remind me of my mother's base character," he hissed in a voice that could have sawed through wood. "Do I talk about how your father ran your family into debt building his vainglorious estates in Albany and Saratoga, and was only saved from financial ruin because he was able to use his position to secure generous grants of land and cash from the government, even as hundreds of other men who served their country as bravely and ably as he did — if not more so —

were granted next to nothing, merely because their last name was not Schuyler?"

Eliza recoiled. Alex almost thought she was going to run from the room. "Alex! What's gotten into you?"

But Alex was on a roll and couldn't stop himself. The words poured out of him, and even though he knew they were not really directed at Eliza, still, she was the one next to him, and thus she would bear the brunt of his raw emotions.

"And now you have this harebrained idea that you will arrange a union between Emma and your brother on the one hand, and Miss Van Rensselaer and Drayton on the other. Your family's entitlement really knows no bounds, does it? Whether it's orphans, servants, *yeomen*" — he added extra bile to this word — "or gentry, you move people around as if they were pieces on a chessboard. Well, you won't move me around so easily!"

"I cannot follow you if you hop from one subject to —"

"No, of course you cannot follow me. While I am managing dozens of cases in order to keep you in the style to which your family accustomed you, you are sitting in this house dreaming up new ways to spend the money I make. You buy books and don't read them; you buy silver service we don't need merely because it looks good on the shelf; you have more dresses than I have stockings; and now you are acquiring potential brides and bridegrooms. Will I be paying for their weddings, too?"

Eliza had clearly moved past shock now and was angry herself. "I doubt it, unless you can put on a wedding that would rival one thrown by Philip Schuyler or Stephen Van Rensselaer, which seems unlikely, given how strapped you claim we are."

"I claim nothing. I merely state the facts. For every pound I earn, you spend a pound and sixpence."

"Don't try to put this all on me! Did I pick out a house on Wall Street, two doors down from Aaron Burr's? Did I rent a separate office at five pounds a month when there was a perfectly good room right here in this house?"

"A room that is now occupied by your

lady's maid. Or is she your best friend? I cannot tell the difference."

"I do not rent a room at Caroline Childress's inn for a damsel in distress!"

"She is a client!"

"I thought clients paid you, not the other way around!"

"What are you insinuating?"

"I was insinuating nothing — though your tone makes me wonder if I should be!"

"ELIZA! I WILL NOT HAVE YOU TALK TO ME IN THIS MANNER!"

Eliza's eyes went wide with shock.

For the first time Alex heard his own words and realized what he'd been saying. He was taken aback by his fury. He had never spoken to a man with such ferocity, let alone a woman — let alone his wife. The anger had bubbled up out of him from a deep well he didn't know he harbored, and now all he wanted to do was slam down the cover on it again.

He reached for Eliza's hands, but she pulled away. He knew better than to snatch at them. "Oh, my darling, I am so sorry! I don't know what's come over me. Please, darling, please forgive me."

Eliza turned away from Alex and stared into the shadows, yet Alex thought he sensed a softening, even though he knew he didn't deserve it. "I don't know why you think I am a spendthrift. That is unfair."

"It was, and I am sorry. I did not mean my words. I have been put off balance by this case," he said. "Will you forgive me?"

Still facing the wall, she nodded. "Of course. I will always forgive you. There is nothing to forgive."

"You spend all your time doing charity and good works, and the things you buy for our home are lovely, and I want them just as much as you do." He attempted a little laugh. "We are both a little too fond of frilly things for our own good."

"Perhaps. In any event, Miss Trask and I have decided to open an orphanage," Eliza continued without turning to him. "It is high time the city had one. It is shameful the number of urchins who sleep in squalor on our streets."

"Indeed it is. And I can think of no one

more qualified to establish one than you."

"You are going to help, too," Eliza said in a determined tone. It was not a question, let alone a request.

"Of course I am," Alex said, feeling a little trepidation. "What can I do?"

"You are going to persuade Trinity Church to give us a building in which to house it."

"Absolutely impossible." Alex nodded. "But I'll make them do it."

Eliza finally turned to him with a wan smile. "They say you are the man who can make the impossible happen."

Alex took his wife's hand, and this time she let it sit in his. "They only say that about me because they don't know you."

"Oh, they know me," Eliza said. "They just don't take me seriously because I am a woman." She squeezed her husband's hand. "We have never had a fight like this before."

"Not since the early days anyway," Alex said, "when you thought I was a terrible flirt."

"Oh, to be seventeen again!" Eliza

sighed and patted the softening center of her body, then leaving her hand sitting on her stomach. "I do not like to fight," she said, "especially now, when a new phase of our lives is beginning."

"I do not like to fight either," Alex said. "Under any circumstances."

"Perhaps I am being irrational, but I feel that something has changed since Mrs. Reynolds came into our lives. I do not like the effect she has on you. You were quite caught up with the Childress case last year, but it was more because you knew your professional reputation was on the line. This feels more personal. She is bringing up something in you. Perhaps it is memories of your mother, or maybe something else. But it is clearly upsetting you. Won't you talk to me about it?"

"I —" Alex broke off. He didn't want to admit Eliza was right, yet the things he had just said to her would have been unthinkable a few days before. His mother had died so long ago. She was just a distant memory, and Alex thought he had laid her — and the rest of his childhood — to rest long ago. But Eliza was right. Perhaps he had not reinvented himself when he came to North America quite as completely as he liked to think.

And he couldn't talk to her about it, couldn't lay out how terrible it was, how filthy, how dirty. He was lowborn enough; he did not want to burden his wife with his sordid past.

"I will be more careful," he said finally. He felt Eliza waiting for something more. "I cannot drop her case, Eliza," he said in a placating voice. "I gave her my word as a gentleman."

Eliza nodded at the darkness. "No, I suppose you can't. Only remember, however desolate she seems, she is not the first woman in your life."

"I could never forget that, my darling."

"No," Eliza said, lying back and relaxing into Alex's arms, but not rewarding him with her gaze or a kiss. "I don't think you could. But she can."

15
FUN-RAISING

The Great Houses of Manhattan
New York, New York
August 1785

In the morning, at breakfast, both Alex and Eliza made their countenances extra jolly, as if last night's fight were just a bad dream, and the only thing to do was smile it away. Yet Eliza could discern a certain stiffness in Alex's demeanor that wasn't there before. It was clear that, despite his chagrin, he was still ashamed of the things he'd said. *He should be ashamed,* she thought, and while she had forgiven him, she was still badly hurt by his words.

For her part, she found it all too easy to retreat into the chilly formality her mother had taught her to mask her feelings in a difficult social situation. She had started referring to Alex as "Mr. Hamilton" when she spoke to John or Emma, as she had when they were first married and she was too shy to use his Christian name to anyone other than him. Though her brother and houseguest both looked at her quizzically a couple of times, neither said anything, and soon enough John was off to school, leaving Eliza and Alex alone with Emma.

"I should be off soon," Alex said after John had left, "but first I wanted to ask you about the matter we discussed last night."

Eliza turned to him in alarm, but before she could beg him not to bring up the fight ever, ever again, he said:

"This orphanage you mentioned. I think it is a capital idea, yet I am not sure how to present it to Reverend Provoost." The words rolled out one on top of the other. Clearly he too had no desire to revisit last night's contretemps, and Eliza nodded a little too eagerly.

"I only asked because you mentioned that the church has so many buildings sitting empty. If they cannot collect rents on them lest they violate the terms of their charter, and if they cannot use them because they can't afford to keep them up, perhaps they could allow someone else to make use of it."

Alex shrugged. "Getting the church to part with valuable property will be difficult. They want me to make it possible for them to earn *more* money, not to give away potential future income."

"But isn't the church's mission to provide succor to people in need?" Emma chimed in here, but quietly, as if she were intruding on someone else's conversation.

"Yes," Alex agreed, turning to her. "But you are not asking the church to oversee the program, are you?"

Emma turned to Eliza, as if expecting her mistress to take over, but Eliza merely smiled at her. If the girl was to succeed in administering the orphanage — or in her suit for John's hand — she would have to learn to assert herself.

Just then Drayton appeared in the doorway, and Emma transferred her gaze to him. She smiled at him shyly, as if he might come to her rescue.

"Rowena asks if anyone would like

seconds, or can she stoke her fire and head to market? She says the fishmonger promised her fresh sole today, only she had better get there early because the catch has been skimpy lately," he informed them.

"Oh, I love sole!" Eliza said. "Yes, tell her to be off. Perhaps a little more coffee, though?"

"Of course, Mrs. Hamilton," Drayton said, retrieving the pot from the sideboard. He refilled her cup, then turned to her left.

"Emma?" he said in a hushed voice, still embarrassed to call her such, as she was sitting at a table on which he waited.

"Thank you, Drayton, but I am drinking tea, as I was the last time you asked."

She spoke in a quiet but firm voice, flashing her eyes at the footman, who colored visibly.

Silly girl! Eliza thought. *If she was half as cheeky with John, he would have already proposed!*

"I do beg your pardon, Miss Trask — Emma — of course, tea, just one moment —"

And you, you silly boy! If you continue to stutter around pretty girls like a schoolboy, you will never get Betty to see you as a man, let alone a potential mate! Well, she thought, *if the matchmaker's work were easy, there would be no need for matchmakers. Nature would just work things out on her own.*

"I'm fine, thank you, Drayton," Emma said merrily.

"Yes, very good," Drayton said, practically dropping the coffeepot on the sideboard and running out of the room.

"Hmph," Alex said. "I guess I shall refill my cup myself." As he stepped to the sideboard, he said to Emma: "I believe you were explaining to me the parish's role in your orphanage."

It seemed to Eliza that Emma fought the urge to look at her, but she managed to hold Alex's gaze.

"Yes," she almost whispered. Then, taking a deeper breath: "We Episcopalians have not the nuns and monks and Jesuit societies that the Catholics do, and, as well, I understand that the parish is in somewhat straitened circumstances, so it would be doubly impractical for them to

309

attempt to oversee such a large operation."

"How large are we talking?" Alex asked as he returned to the table with a steaming cup.

"By some accounts, the number of orphans in the city is over three hundred. There may be as many as five hundred if you count the villages in Kings and Queens Counties, as well as in New Jersey."

"My God! I hadn't realized the problem was so dire."

"It's just that they are so widely scattered," Emma continued. "Two here, three there, hiding out in haylofts and basements and squatting in the kitchens and basements of parish houses. Mrs. Hamilton and I have spoken to the rectors, priests, and rabbis of almost every church and temple in the city. The war left thousands of children without parents, and a good number of them converged on our larger cities, especially New York, apparently thinking that the opportunity for work or alms would be greater here."

"I suppose that makes sense," Alex

said. "And yet it seems that we were woefully unprepared for them."

"Part of it is the situation you yourself are dealing with," Eliza chimed in. "This problem of hamstrung finances dating back to the parishes' original charters from the Church of England. The Jews, Catholics, and other Protestant denominations have not these same restrictions, but their numbers are too small to make a big difference. Part of it, too, is the manpower lost in the war itself. Families are rebuilding their numbers as well as their finances, and few have the time or the opportunity to devote to others' needs, however much they might want to."

"By opportunity, I assume you mean money," Alex said.

"We thought we could fund the orphanage through yearly subscriptions," Emma said, "like Trinity's drive to raise to build a new church building."

Eliza felt the need to speak here, since this would be her primary responsibility. "I am hopeful that we can count on a few families to help us establish an initial endowment," she said, "from which

311

interest income will eventually accrue, while the day-to-day expenses can be underwritten by more modest annual donations."

"Endowments? Interest income? It sounds like you two have given this a fair amount of thought." Alex's voice sounded genuinely impressed, and even though he had directed his compliments at Emma, Eliza felt that things were returning to normal between them for the first time that morning. They were two young crusaders, working for the good of the city, their country, their countrymen.

Emma blushed. "Oh, it is all Mrs. Hamilton's doing. I am just here to file the papers, as it were."

"Emma, you are being too modest! The subscription idea was hers. I was just hoping that we could get Stephen to pay for everything," said Eliza.

Alex chuckled. "I've no doubt you will manage to extort a sizable payment from your brother-in-law, but Emma is right. Unless Stephen feels like parting with an unadvisedly large share of his ready income, it is unlikely that he will be able to do more than help you get the thing off the ground, leaving the issue of keeping it going year in, year out. But the ladies of New York society, much like their husbands, enjoy seeing their names on donor rolls. Though none of them may be able to give fifty or even twenty-five pounds, I am sure my wife knows enough women that she can easily raise the five hundred pounds or so that it would take to run such an enterprise."

"It will probably be closer to a thousand," Emma said.

Alex drew in a breath. "You are certainly aiming high."

Eliza laughed guiltily. "Credit to Emma, or blame, as you will. She pointed out that so many orphanages are breeding grounds for vice. The children are huddled together in wards and fed a subsistence diet, while they wait in vain for a family to come along and rescue them. She thought that we should not fasten our sights on the chimera of adoption but think of the institution more as a kind of boarding school, where we can educate our charges not just in Christian virtues, but in useful skills that will help them in trade or perhaps even in business, if they show an aptitude."

"I — I was inspired by your own story," Emma said to Alex. "It is well known how your own origins were not affluent, yet your intelligence was spotted early on, and you were afforded the education that enabled you to make something of yourself."

Eliza gazed hard at Alex as Emma said these words. She wondered whether her houseguest knew how close she was sailing to the troubled waters she and Alex had foundered in last night. Alex's eyes fell from Emma's to the table as the latter spoke, and his features softened. He was silent for a long moment after she finished. When he looked up, his eyes went first to Eliza's stomach, and then to her face, and she knew he was thinking more of the future than the past.

"A house full of budding Alexander Hamiltons? It sounds like an absolute nightmare." He chuckled, and then Eliza did, and then they were both laughing heartily while Emma stared at them as though they had lost their minds.

"And on that note," he said at length,

"I should be off. I will find the right way to present this to Reverend Provoost. It would help if I had some good news of my own to offer him, but I'm sure I can bluff my way through it."

He went around the table to Eliza and bent over to give her a lingering kiss, which, though it landed on her forehead, felt rather intimate.

"I love you more than I can say," he whispered in her ear.

Eliza felt her heart swell. She didn't reply but knew her shining eyes said all that needed to be said.

"Emma, your perspicacity in these matters is inspiring. I have no doubt the two of you will make a success of this enterprise. I only hope that my wife does not end up adopting all the children herself!" And with one final blown kiss to his wife, Alex made his exit.

The next several weeks were a whirlwind of activity as Eliza and Emma made the rounds of New York society in a hired carriage. The weather was fine all week, with just the faintest whiff of fall in the air, and they left the top down to enjoy the fresh air and sunshine, as well as the sights. The city was a hubbub of activity. It had fully doubled in size in the two years since Eliza and Alex had moved there, and though many of the new buildings and shops had a slapdash quality to them, there was still the undeniable smell of commerce and progress. The city, like the new country of which it was a part, was rife with uncertainty but also optimism. With the sun beaming down on a well-tied bonnet, the *clip-clop* of a trotting horse's hooves in her ears, and the hustle and bustle of pedestrians and laborers and businessmen all around, it was impossible for Eliza to believe that the city was marching anywhere else but the future — a bright, prosperous future that might just drag the rest of the country along with it.

The Jays were high on their list. John Jay had become Alex's most important mentor since they moved to the city, and Sarah had become a surrogate older sister for Eliza since Angelica moved to London with *her* John, transformed from a constant companion into someone who only existed on the pages of all-too-brief letters three or four times a year.

After the successful visit, the Jays invited the Hamiltons over for dinner the next evening, and now the two couples, with Emma and John in tow, were gathered together in the "triclinium," as Sarah jokingly referred to the small parlor that faced their garden, with three couches arranged around an elegant table, although it was really more like three dinners, with John Jay and Alex pairing off on one couch to discuss developments in the struggling Bank of New York, of which they were both trustees.

Soon enough, though, their conversation gave way to politics, although it was less a conversation than a lecture by John, who felt that Alex was neglecting his true calling. "You spend too much time in the courts," Eliza heard him say at one point. "There is a country to be built, and it will not be composed of property claims and petty grievances! We need not just laws but a document to govern them all and to tie us together once and for all. Out of all the men in this country, only you or Mr. Madison or

Mr. Jefferson could conceive of its contours, let alone write it. Mr. Jefferson is too much of an individualist to do so, and Mr. Madison is too rich to undertake such a vast endeavor without assistance. Your country needs you, Alex!"

Alex only nodded sheepishly and made occasional small sounds of protest — he was busy, he had not completely forgone his political work, he was still young, and there would be time for it once his law practice was stable. Eliza knew he was too proud to speak the truth more plainly — especially within the elegant confines of the Jays' sumptuous mansion — which was that he simply couldn't afford to work for his government for free when there was a growing household to support. It was easy to devote yourself to selfless activities when you had a thousand acres planted in Virginia tobacco or New York wheat to support you. A man who earned his own keep had to choose his priorities, and although Alex loved politics and his country, Eliza knew he loved his family even more and would always err in their favor. She only wished that he didn't believe (however much he might deny it) that being a self-made man somehow made him less than his aristocratic peers. He would save himself a world of grief if he did.

While the men engaged in their serious talk, Sarah and Eliza huddled on a second sofa to talk about plans for the orphanage. Their conversation ran much more smoothly than the men's: Sarah was immediately keen on the idea and wondered that it hadn't been done already. She said she knew of a dozen ladies in New Jersey whom she could tap for contributions and would make a special trip to her home state for that sole purpose.

That left Emma and John — who had invited himself, Eliza pointed out to a skeptical Alex — alone on the third couch. Eliza noted with glee that the young couple seemed to get along famously, with Emma frequently giving way to (modest, of course) laughter at something or other John had said, and John at one point even feeding her a little spoonful of berries and cream. Eliza was so pleased with this development that she barely thanked Sarah for her pledge of fifty pounds a year toward the orphanage and was halfway out the door when she rushed back in to give Sarah a big hug and kiss and thank her properly.

She had not previously considered the idea that these sojourns could be used to facilitate the connection between John and Emma, and cursed herself for not having brought him along on previous trips. After the smashing success of the Jays' dinner, however, which ended with a slightly tipsy Emma leaning warmly into John's arm and resting her head against his shoulder, she resolved to bring him along the next journey as well.

It was just a few days later that she received a note from John and Helena Rutherford informing her that they were in town from their New Jersey estate and would love to have them to dinner, and when Eliza wrote back she made a point of asking if John and "a houseguest, in whom the Schuyler heir has taken an interest" could join them. Helena wrote back that she would "delighted" to play hostess to a "budding romance." As it turned out, however, Helena had also invited Betty Van Rensselaer, along with William and Elizabeth (née Cornell) Bayard, and Robert Livingston, the recently appointed chancellor of New York, and his wife, Mary, who were in town from their country estate near Germantown, making it less of an intimate affair than a bit of a free-for-all.

Robert Livingston was a fine fellow, but he was rather full of himself as the heir to Livingston Manor, which meant that as long as there were no Van Rensselaers in the room he could assume he was the wealthiest, most powerful person present. He was an intelligent man, and civic minded, yet like most scions of family dynasties, he assumed that everyone wanted to hear every thought that went through his head, and even in another couple's house he had the unfortunate tendency to talk nonstop about whatever was on his mind, be it tariff laws or crop yields. On the night of the Rutherfords' dinner, he went on and on about the house he was erecting for himself and Mary to replace the one he had built when they first married. He had originally named it New Clermont, after the family seat, but recently started calling it Arryl House, which, he must have told each and every guest individually, was a play on his initials, R. L. " 'R. L.' *Arryl. Do you see how it works?*" he must have said a dozen times. Eliza found the name just the teensiest bit self-involved, since it was not only home to him, after all, but also to his wife and their children.

If he wasn't talking about building the house, he was talking about furnishing it; if he wasn't talking about furnishing it, he was talking about planting the gardens; if he wasn't talking about planting the gardens, he was talking about tending to the crops; and if he wasn't talking about tending to his crops, he was talking about tending to his father's, which then led him off on an entirely new dissertation about Clermont, which, being twice as large as Arryl House, and sitting on roughly one thousand times more land, required even more time to describe. Despite the fact that the dinner went on for nearly four hours, no one managed to get in a word edgewise.

No one, that is, except John and Betty, who were seated at the opposite end of the table from Chancellor Livingston and pointedly ignored him. The pair all but wrapped their arms around each other as they leaned close in conspiratorial whispers that often broke out into guffaws and gales of laughter that Robert either ignored because he had good breeding or didn't hear because he was so full of himself.

Alarmed by their camaraderie, Eliza tried to draw Alex's attention to the chatty couple throughout the meal, but he only smiled at her eye twitches and head jerks and turned back to Robert, whose every word he seemed to find as fascinating as Robert did. He always was a little too respectful of aristocracy, Eliza thought. Either that or he's the best actor in the world. They were still tentative with each other after their argument some weeks ago, and Eliza sometimes wished Maria Reynolds had never entered their lives.

She tried to get Emma's attention, but the poor girl was seated across from Robert and couldn't have intervened in John and Betty's confabulation if she wanted to. She sat in rapt silence, staring at Robert Livingston as though he were a preacher delivering the sermon that would guarantee her a spot in heaven.

At the end of the evening, though, the men retreated for a cigar, leaving the women at the table. It was Betty who brought up the orphanage, saying that Eliza was "cooking up a scheme," and they would all feel "left out" if their names weren't on the top of the donor rolls every year. In short order, Elizabeth Bayard and Helena pledged fifty pounds each, and Mary, after apologizing profusely for Robert's dominating the conversation, said that he would be mortified if they didn't give at least twice as much as everyone else, and promised one hundred.

"Oh!" Betty chimed in. She had been rather petulantly silent since the women and men had been quarantined from one another and she had no John Schuyler to tease. "In that case I shall have to get my brother Stephen to give two hundred. He couldn't possibly allow himself to be shown up by a Livingston."

Betty was grinning as she said it, but Mary snapped her fan open and began waving it in front of her face, which had gone pink and shiny. "My dear! That is an astronomical amount of money!"

Betty shrugged. "It's not our money, after all. The men keep it all for themselves. The least we can do is make sure they spend it on a good cause."

Mary continued to fan herself. "Well, yes," she said, nodding. "I suppose that's true. I imagine that I can persuade Robert to donate two hundred pounds."

"I'll get Stephen to give four hundred then," Betty said immediately.

"Betty!" Eliza exclaimed, feeling herself go as pink as Mary but resisting the urge to fan herself like an old woman suffering the change of life. "You will pauperize my sister and baby Cathy!"

"Ha!" Betty exclaimed. "Four hundred pounds is less than Stephen spends on clothing a year. Indeed, I suspect it is less than he spends on *lace* for a year — his collars and cuffs would make Marie-Antoinette jealous. He has grown into such a fop since he came of age. He will not even notice the money is gone." She peered slyly at Mary Livingston. "So what do you say, Mary? Think you can wheedle four hundred out of the chancellor?"

Mary's fan went back and forth so fast that Eliza thought her wig was going to be blown from her head.

"Well, I . . . that is, the chancellor does so like to be thought of as a generous man." She gulped audibly. "I think it can be done."

"That's settled then," Betty said. "I'll get Stephen to give eight hundred pounds, and you're set." She stood up. "My work here is done," she said, and waltzed out of the room.

Eliza was about to rush after her, but it looked like Mary Livingston was about to faint. She rushed over to the chancellor's wife and chafed her wrists.

"There, there, Mary," she said soothingly. "She was only joking. Your original contribution will be more than adequate. Stephen will never give that kind of money."

It took some minutes to calm Mary down, at which point Eliza rushed out into the hall. She was just in time to see Betty, with John rather cozily in tow, disappear out the front door. As she turned back to the dining room, she saw Emma staring after them, and she hurried back to her houseguest.

"Do not be alarmed," Eliza said quickly. "I'm sure Betty was just tired, and John is just seeing her home."

Emma blinked in confusion. "What? Oh, Mr. Schuyler told me earlier today that some of his schoolmates were having a party in their dormitory, and that Betty had asked him to sneak her in."

"Oh, that girl!" Eliza hissed.

"She is quite daring, isn't she?" Emma said, though Eliza wasn't sure if she was agreeing or disagreeing. "I sometimes wish I had some of her pluck."

"Bite your tongue, Emma dear," Eliza said (even though she had thought the same thing on more than one occasion).

Emma shrugged. "I suppose I should be more upset about it, but the truth is, it is not my nature. I *like* being calm. I'm sure there is someone out there who will appreciate that."

Eliza wondered that Emma was not more jealous that John's attentions were focused elsewhere, but she was still slightly woozy on her feet due to her condition and, for now, would have to just find a way to keep her brother away from Peggy's sister-in-law.

Plus, she had to leave Emma and return to the party, lest the evening's true purpose be lost. After several hours of soothing — and more than a few glasses of sweet wine — Eliza had raised quite a large amount, as the other ladies reiterated their pledges of fifty pounds each. On the romantic front, the night was a total wash, but on the charitable front, at least, she was continuing to make headway.

The next dinner was at Elizabeth Bayard's, who was so keen on the project that she threw together a soiree at which Eliza secured another two hundred pounds a year in funding. More events followed, at the Van Wycks', the Larsens', the Douglasses', and the Schermerhorns', each of which raked in more money. For the final push, however, Eliza decided to take an excursion up Manhattan Island, first to Inclenberg, the home of Robert and Mary Murray (the parents of Lindley, who had moved to England last year), then to the Beekmans' Mount Pleasant, and then on to Van Cortlandt House at the northern reaches of the Bronx and Morrisania where Gouverneur had written that he was eager to host them. Alex wasn't happy to be apart from his wife for a week or more, but she pointed out that he had left her alone a dozen times during their marriage when he traveled on business, and she was due at least one trip of her own.

"Besides," she said, patting her softening stomach, "I shall soon be showing, after which half of society won't receive me, so it's best to do this now while I am able." She had to make Alex understand this fast approaching deadline certainly added urgency to her fund-raising work.

Alex was not so easily convinced, but Eliza was implacable. And the truth was that between the Reynolds case, the Trinity project, and myriad minor lawsuits, he was busier than ever.

"Without me around as a distraction," she said, "you will have unfettered time to devote to your work."

"You are my favorite distraction, my dear," Alex insisted, kissing her hands.

"Perhaps," she said. "But I would rather be your focus than something you pay attention to between appointments. So, catch up with your work while I am gone, and when I return, prepare to lavish all your attention on me. I plan on being an exceptionally demanding expectant mother."

Alex grinned sheepishly. "Fair enough," he said. "I only hope that I shall be able to work for missing you. I look forward to being your obedient servant."

"Lovely," Eliza said. "You can start by getting me a slice of that pie Rowena made for dessert. Baby is hungry." She smiled, patting her stomach.

Eliza decided to bring Rowena with her and Emma, with the intention of leaving Rowena for the week at Mount Pleasant so she could spend some time with Simon, and she also brought Drayton to drive the carriage. Alex would be on his own for the week.

"Consider it your last bachelor hurrah," Eliza said as she kissed her husband good-bye. "Before you know it you'll be up to your neck in diapers!"

■ ■ ■ ■

PART THREE:
VOWS AND VICES

■ ■ ■ ■

16
New World Flock

Trinity Church
New York, New York
August 1785

In his mind, Alex imagined watching the carriage with his wife, houseguest, cook, and footman rattling down Wall Street until it disappeared in the throng of traffic, then returning to his empty house to wander the empty rooms, wondering how he was going to make it through the next six days alone.

In reality, he was already on his way to the office before the carriage had even turned north on Broadway. He didn't even have time to miss his wife, although he did. Their recent argument was still on his mind, along with the thought that his firstborn was on the way — the beginning of the Hamilton dynasty! A child of his own, a future torchbearer to his legacy! The pressure it put upon him was tremendous. He had so much to do, so much to prove, to himself, to his wife, to his city, to his country.

He had to get started. There was no time for sentiment.

First, he had his weekly meeting with his partner in the firm, Richard Harrison, then spent the rest of the morning and much of the afternoon at Federal Hall filing a series of relatively trivial motions. Around three o'clock, he headed to Trinity Church for the day's true work: a meeting with Reverend Provoost.

It was a meeting he'd been putting off for some time. It was not in Alex's nature to admit defeat, especially when it came to a matter of the law. In Alex's mind, the law was designed to facilitate solutions, not impede them — make people more free, not hem them in with unnecessary restrictions. But if there was a loophole or exception to the church's charter, he'd been unable to find it after months of scrutiny.

Reverend Provoost kept him waiting nearly half an hour before seeing him.

His waiting room turned out to be the chapel itself, which as an intimidation tactic Alex had to admit was pretty good. He sat in the straight-backed pew (not his, but one belonging to someone named David Sloane) and stared up at the sober wooden cross hanging at the front of the church. If he'd harbored any thoughts of trying to soft-sell the situation, let alone spin it, that cross banished all such ideas from his mind.

At last, a deacon came out and brought him into the office. As Alex entered, Reverend Provoost came out from behind his desk with a warm if tentative smile. He shook Alex's hand and directed him to a chair, while he sat on the room's leather sofa. "It's nice to see you, Mr. Hamilton. It's been so long that I was beginning to wonder if you'd forgotten about our little case."

Alex chuckled. "No such luck, Reverend. I think you know that my wife is expecting our first child. That has consumed much of our life these past months."

Alex groaned mentally as he heard these words leave his mouth. Blame the wife? What kind of second-rate attorney was he?

"It is a wondrous blessing, and I hope that it is the first of many," the reverend said with a serene, practiced face.

"Nevertheless," Alex continued, "I have had time to review your holdings as well as the pertinent statute law."

The reverend nodded eagerly. "And have you found us a way out of our predicament?"

Alex hung fire a moment. He felt like a general about to surrender his sword in defeat.

Finally, he decided that the easiest way to say it was just to say it.

"There are some things you can do," he began. "The easiest — and I use that term relatively — would be to transfer the bulk of the church's holdings to a separate corporate entity. Its trustees would be drawn from the parish officers, so it would be wholly controlled by Trinity. Its income would be separate from the church's, but could be funneled back to the church as needed."

Reverend Provoost frowned. "So we

would simultaneously own the land and not own it at the same time? That seems . . . complicated."

"It is a common arrangement among more profit-driven business enterprises."

"So the church's assets would be considered part of a — how did you put it? — 'profit-driven business enterprise'?" The reverend did not sound enthusiastic.

"Unfortunately, yes. You wouldn't be subject to any restrictions on your income, but you would have to give Caesar his due, I'm afraid."

The rector shifted uncomfortably. "You mean pay taxes."

Alex nodded. "Alas, there's no way around it. You would lose a not inconsiderable portion of your income, but the loss would be made up tenfold by the increased revenue — in a few years."

The priest nodded, but his eyes had drifted away. His head bobbed back and forth like a cat's grooming itself. At length he looked up. "You will forgive me, Mr. Hamilton, but your proposal has a whiff of Mammon about it."

Alex couldn't disagree. "I admit that it

is less than ideal."

"It makes the church look like a business," the reverend continued in a firm, slightly scolding voice. "And a dodgy one at that."

Alex tried not to wince. "You must remember that the church wouldn't be paying taxes; the external corporation would."

"An external corporation composed of the same people who run the church." Reverend Provoost did everything but roll his eyes. "It is semantics. And if you will forgive my saying so, it sounds as if the church would be trying to pull a fast one. That is not exactly the message of probity we wish to send to our parishioners."

Ouch, Alex thought, but the truth was, he knew the rector was correct in his assessment. It's why he had delayed so long in presenting the plan.

"You said this was one option," the reverend continued. "What are the others?"

"Just one other option. I confess that I am loath to even suggest it."

"It sounds extreme. Though after your first plan, I'm not sure how much more extreme one can go."

"It is," Alex said. He took a deep breath. "You could dissolve the church."

Reverend Provoost stiffened. His smile widened, but it was a reflexive action, as if a muscle had contracted in a spasm. "Dissolve?" he repeated. "Like . . ." He shook his head as he tried to think of something one dissolved. ". . . tapioca?" He shrugged helplessly. "I'm afraid I don't understand."

Alex nodded understandingly. "Trinity Church's charter, and indeed the charter of every Episcopal church in the New World, is ironclad. The Anglican church is, after all, an extension of the monarchy, and thus participated in the crown's attitude toward its colonies."

"I would like to disagree with you, but unfortunately I cannot. Many of us here at Trinity felt the Anglican church had lost a certain measure of ecclesiastical sovereignty over the years, which is why we supported the cause of independence."

"Your support lent incalculable credence to the soldiers' efforts," Alex echoed quickly, happy to find common cause with the reverend. "Nevertheless, Governor Clinton saw fit to carry over the church's original provisions rather than try to find some more tenable arrangement. This may have been an oversight on his part, or it might be that he didn't want any challenges to his power in his own region."

Reverend Provoost chuckled. "I will let that comment pass lest I incriminate myself."

"However," Alex continued, "there are as yet no laws governing the formation of new churches in our country, and thus no reason that they should have to be established on the same draconian terms crafted by the Church of England. You would have to change the church's name, of course, but that shouldn't be an impediment. You did it when you went from Anglicanism to Episcopalianism, just as the Anglicans did when they left the Catholic Church behind."

Reverend Provoost stared at Alex. "Do I understand you? You are not asking me to change the name of the parish. You are asking me to change the name of *the faith itself.* From Episcopalianism to, what, the Church of New York?"

"If you want. Or the Church of the United States of America. Or perhaps something more independent. Whatever it is, it would give you the freedom to renegotiate your charter from the ground up."

"A — new — *church?*" The reverend seemed dumbfounded. "A New World reformation, as it were? With who knows what new laws and customs to go along with the new name?"

"That is your area of expertise, not mine. I am only trying to make the church a stable financial entity so that it can fulfill its mission to succor the people of New York City."

"But that's just it, isn't it? We would, at least to outsiders, be making changes to orthodoxy for the sake of gold. It — it doesn't seem *seemly.*"

Alex did his best to remain calm. He knew the plan was outlandish, but having presented it, he felt he had to make the case. And why not be unseemly? It was a new country, after all. Americans had thrown off the British monarchy, which was seven hundred years old. The Church of England was three hundred fifty years old, and that had been tossed aside, too. Why not something as simple as a name?

"What is unseemly," Alex said now, "is that the colonial government of this land saw fit to use the church in its efforts to control its colonies. You would only be correcting that."

"By appearing to reject our faith and create a new one. Mr. Hamilton, the Reformation was several hundred years in the making and reflected the will of thousands of clergymen and untold millions of Christians. It was not cooked up, if you will pardon the expression, in a lawyer's office."

Alex took that one on the chin. "There was a reason why I led with the first option," he said, attempting a self-deprecating grin.

"Turning the church into a business. What, shall we start selling sausage rolls in street carts, too? Or tickets to heaven, how about that?" the reverend asked.

Alex swallowed his grin. "If I have offended you, Father, I do beg your pardon."

"It is not *my* pardon you need to seek, Mr. Hamilton."

Alex kept his face impassive, but inwardly he rolled his eyes a little. It was Reverend Provoost who had come to him, after all. Reverend Provoost was the one who wanted the church to make more money, not Alex. "It seems clear that my plans are not appealing to you."

"You are being droll," the reverend said.

Alex shook his head. "Merely trying to make my exit with what's left of my dignity."

"I do not mean to chastise you, Mr. Hamilton. You are young and well-meaning, and obviously your service to your country is not in question. But you must realize that the church's reputation is built entirely on appearances. If even a shadow of suspicion were to fall over our affairs, we would lose credibility with our flock. It is simply too great a risk."

Alex couldn't disagree. He really wanted to, but he couldn't. "I understand, Reverend."

"I am afraid you will have to try to come up with something else."

Alex's heart sank a little. On the one hand, he was grateful that he wasn't being fired. On the other, he had already devoted dozens of hours to this case with no progress — and no pay — and he had bills of his own. And he knew even better than Reverend Provoost that the church would not compensate him unless he succeeded.

"Of course, Reverend," he said, then continued: "This is perhaps not the best time to bring this up, but I wonder if I might speak to you about another matter."

The reverend shrugged amicably. "You're here, and you're always a pleasant interlocutor. What's on your mind?"

"My wife, Eliza. As you know, she has long been concerned about the plight of the city's orphans."

"A most warmhearted woman. She has housed many a young urchin in the rectory until finding a more suitable home for them."

"You are most generous to accommodate her. Well, now she has it in mind to create a 'more suitable home' as you say, for all the city's orphans. A more permanent one."

"You mean an orphanage?"

"Exactly, Reverend. She has begun a subscription service among the city's top families, and is even now embarked upon a trip north to see the Murrays, Beekmans, Van Cortlandts, and Morrises to secure their support as well. She already has a guarantee of more than six hundred pounds a year, and if I know her, she'll return with the last four hundred she desires for the facility."

The color drained from Reverend Provoost's already pale face. "A thousand pounds a year! That is a fifth of our income!"

"Indeed, Reverend. When Mrs. Hamilton sets her mind to something, she doesn't do it halfway."

"I should say not. Perhaps I should have hired *her* to work out this charter business instead of you."

Alex laughed good-naturedly and resisted pointing out that he hadn't been hired as much as lassoed. "Which brings me to my request, Reverend. Eliza still needs a domicile in which to house the new facility. I might have mentioned that the church has a few empty buildings it isn't using."

The reverend nodded. "I think I see where this is going. Well, what building did you have in mind?"

"It is a warehouse on Vesey Street. As I understand it, it hasn't been used since the city was liberated five years ago."

A laugh from Reverend Provoost. "I suspect you know better than I do at this point. What were the terms you were thinking of?"

"Terms, Reverend?"

"For the lease of the building."

Alex was a little taken aback. "Well, you see, Reverend, with the church's finances being what they are, you are not exactly in a position to, well, to make any more money."

"I know things are tight, Mr. Hamilton, but is it really so dire that we must give away our property?"

"According to my calculations, Reverend, if the property were developed in a manner commensurate with the buildings that surround it, it would generate income of about one or two hundred pounds a year. At this point, you could probably sell it for a thousand pounds, which is, as you know, a fifth of your income cap as defined in your charter. And you have dozens more properties like this one. Scores. Even using the most conservative valuations, the worth of your material assets alone, before any income is taken into consideration, exceeds the limit of your charter by two or three times —"

Alex broke off. A thought had just come to him. It was half formed as yet, but if he was correct . . . !

"Is something wrong, Mr. Hamilton?"

"Pardon?" Alex shook his head, then suddenly stood up. This idea would make his earlier scheme for a new church seem like a run-of-the-mill property claim. And yet not only would it be completely beyond reproach, it would save the church. "No, no, Reverend, nothing is wrong. Only I think I've just solved your problem."

"What? Do tell?"

"It's just a theory. I have to check a few things first. I don't want to get your hopes up. But if my hunch is true, I can completely free you from any restriction whatsoever."

"That is unbelievable," the reverend said. "Can you give me a hint as to what your plan is?"

"I'm sorry, Reverend, I'm not even sure I can put it into words just yet. Suffice it to say, that you will be only too happy to part with one of your buildings for Mrs. Hamilton's orphanage."

He shook the flabbergasted rector's hand quickly and dashed from the office.

17
OUT TO THE COUNTRY FOR SOME CASH

Inclenberg Manor and Mount Pleasant
New York, New York
August 1785

It was time to set off to collect more subscriptions to her cause. While Eliza had already raised a considerable amount, there were more wealthy families to solicit. And while this trip would take her away from Alex, she wondered if perhaps they needed the space. Absence made the heart grow fonder, or so she hoped.

Eliza wasn't sure when Drayton had had time to learn the city so well, but he piloted the carriage out of town with such ease, it would be easy to assume he'd been raised there. He veered off Broadway onto Park Row, past City Hall Park, and thence onto Bowery Lane and onward to the north as though he'd taken this route hundreds of times before.

"It's not a race, Drayton!" Rowena said, twisting round in her seat. "Mrs. Hamilton would rather arrive early this afternoon with her bones still connected to one another, than later this morning shaken all to pieces!"

In answer, Drayton flicked his whip over the geldings' withers, causing them to pick up their pace. Rowena lurched dramatically, as if a carpet had been pulled out from under her. "Drayton! Are you trying to throw me from the carriage?"

"If I wanted to do that, I would use my hands, Aunt," Drayton replied, turning around with a wink.

"For goodness' sake, keep your eyes on the road! We shall all be killed!"

Eliza winked back at the footman-cum-coachman. "I think we should leave the driving to Drayton, Rowena," she said soothingly. She hadn't been for a good bumpy carriage ride since she'd moved away from the Pastures, and had forgotten how much she enjoyed it. It made her feel like a little girl again. She was past the woozy stage of her pregnancy and beginning to feel like herself once more.

The only thing better would have been if she were astride a horse herself. In the country, it was perfectly permissible for gentlewoman to ride — sidesaddle, of course — but in the city it was considered gauche, and since the Hamiltons didn't keep horses of their own, she had given away her riding outfit. A rollicking ride in a tightly sprung carriage would have to do.

The air changed once the carriage passed Grand Street. The dust of the city's well-traveled roads, laced with an ever-present tinge of manure, was swept away by the sweeter air of the countryside. The buildings grew farther apart and were soon surrounded by split-rail fences holding in chickens and pigs, before giving way to small but proper farms and manicured estates (which were essentially farms surrounding bigger houses with more elaborate gardens). Cows and sheep grazed placidly on rolling fields; wives and daughters tended to their fruits and vegetables while husbands and sons split wood and stone to mend fences. The apple trees grew in neat rows, heavy with fruit that was almost ready to pick, while the wheat and barley fields lay neatly plowed after the midsummer harvest. The tobacco stood in bushy trails, its heady fragrance clinging to the ground, like an invisible, odorous layer of fog.

"I do not much care for pipe smoke," Emma said, "but I confess I find the smell of the growing plant to be quite pleasant."

"Truly," Eliza agreed. "It is like new leather and freshly turned earth and a hint of nutmeg."

"Mrs. Hamilton!" Rowena marveled. "Such powers of description! You could write the copy for apothecary bottles!"

It was a little over an hour to Inclenberg, or Murray Hill as people whose last name wasn't Murray tended to call it, because who really wanted to wrap their tongue around "Inclenberg"? The elegant five-bay house (Inclenberg Manor) had a large Greek gable spanning the central windows and a delicate widow's walk framing the roof. A woman in her mid-fifties appeared on the porch as the carriage drove up, not waving, but smiling warmly. Mary Murray, the mother of Lindley, an old friend of Helena and John Rutherford, was dressed in dark Quaker gray, but there was a mischievous gleam in her eye that suggested an inner mirth belying the outer sobriety. The plan was to take tea at Murray Hill before heading on to Mount Pleasant, where they would spend the night before heading farther north. A footman helped Eliza, Emma, and Rowena from the carriage, then directed Drayton to park it by the barn.

"Your man is welcome to join your maid in the kitchen if he'd like a bite to eat while we have tea," Mrs. Murray said. Rowena was already walking around to the rear of the house. "Perhaps he would like to join her for a smoke," she added with a little laugh.

"She is my cook actually," Eliza said, and, when Mrs. Murray frowned in confusion, added, "Her son is employed as a groom at Mount Pleasant. We are taking her for a visit."

"How very unconventional! I do not even enjoy sitting with my maid in the same carriage. She either refuses to say anything other than 'Yes, ma'am' or 'No, ma'am,' or else she goes on and on about domestic matters that are of no concern to me."

"I would think that the running of your household would be of great concern to you," Emma said, and only someone who knew her as well as Eliza did would have recognized the archness in her tone. Her blue eyes were flashing, which anyone else might have taken for vivacity, but Eliza knew was anger.

Mrs. Murray looked at Emma for the first time since they had been introduced. A single glance took in the ever so slightly faded nature of the dress, recognizing it as a hand-me-down from her mistress. She offered a thin-lipped half smile, and, though she didn't actually say anything, her pout said clearly, *poor relation.*

Eliza lagged a little as they went into the house to lean close to Emma. "Is there something wrong?"

"I just don't like seeing Drayton dismissed as a servant," Emma said in a quiet, if firm voice. "Or Rowena, for that matter."

"I wouldn't say Mrs. Murray dismissed him. She offered him a bite to eat, after all."

"A bite to eat," Emma repeated. "The leftovers of our own meal, which will be served on silver and china, while his is eaten off a dusty kitchen table."

"I only hope the table isn't dusty," Eliza tried to joke. "Rowena will have poor Mrs. Murray's cook in tears if she finds the kitchen untidy. Now, buck up. We are here to solicit money for the orphanage, not to make friends. In an hour we will be gone, and it may well be years before you meet her again. And I've heard she's a good raconteuse."

Emma offered her a weak smile but clearly wasn't mollified. By then they were being shown into an elegant parlor with a pair of tall windows that offered a view of a green field sloping down to the East River, less than half a mile away. Piles of sandwiches and scones and other delectables were indeed arrayed on ornate silver and china platters. A coffeepot was present, as well as, surprisingly, tea, which was only just starting to be an acceptable beverage since the Boston Tea

Party had transformed a once-loved quaff into an unsavory symbol of British oppression. There were also cider and perry, if the travelers wanted something cool.

"The cider is fresh, but the pear juice has been allowed to ferment," Mary said as she took a seat. "Mr. Murray and I are Quakers, but we do not insist that our visitors adhere to our sobriety. Coffee for me, Sheldon," she added, without looking at the footman.

"Very good, madam," the footman said. "Mrs. Hamilton? Miss Trask?"

Eliza had coffee, while Emma took a glass of cider. After their drinks had been poured, Sheldon approached them with one platter after another until they had laden their plates with a variety of savory and sweet items.

Then, even as Eliza was impatient to get to the reason of their visit, Mrs. Murray was telling them about her famous afternoon with General William Howe, the British commander who had taken Manhattan Island in September 1776, nearly capturing George Washington in the process.

"You might know that Lindley remained loyal to King George despite the fact that both Robert and I supported independence. It pains me, although I cannot fault him for it. It is a quintessentially American trait to stick to one's convictions even if they contravene those of your family. And on that day I was able to use my son's retrograde beliefs to my advantage, not least because Lindley always kept tea in the house, which we of course had long since given up. General Howe's horses needed refreshing, and he chose to commandeer supplies from Inclenberg, knowing that at least one loyalist lived in the house. While his horses were being fed I asked him in, saying that my son had a particularly fine Lapsang souchong on hand, which I had heard the general was fond of, as well as some decent Madeira. If Robert had been home I wonder if General Howe would have come in, but as it was just a lone woman of middle years, he didn't feel under any threat.

"Once he was seated, of course, I had him. The British are slaves to manners, and no gentleman would take his leave without the lady's permission. I simply made sure he never got an opportunity to ask for it. I must have told him the story of every tree we ever planted, every foal, calf, lamb, shoat, or chick ever born, every business deal Mr. Murray ever transacted, and of course Sheldon kept the wine flowing steadily and the cakes piled high. At one point I even proposed a toast when I thought he was about to depart — I, who have not touched a drop of alcohol in all my life! I fairly thought I would lose my head! In the end he was here nearly four hours, which time — General Washington later wrote me personally — made all the difference between the Continental army's capture and escape."

One would have thought this was the whole story, but it turned to be merely a précis. Eliza was more than ready to direct the conversation to the orphanage when Mrs. Murray, having given them "the bare-bones outline of the momentous afternoon," began going into the blow by blow of the encounter. Eliza could only smile stiffly, as she imagined General Howe had done.

An hour later, neither Eliza nor Emma

was in any doubt that the otherwise unremarkable woman sitting before them could have held a general captive. They had not managed to get a word in edgewise and were almost uncomfortably aware of the distinction between the milk given by Frisian, Ayrshire, Guernsey, and Jersey cows, which Mrs. Murray described the way a vintner talks about his finest wines ("Now, your Jersey, she may only give a few gallons each day, but it is of such creamy sweetness that it rivals butter in its natural state, with notes of walnut and sage rounding out the flavor").

They were saved by the timely arrival of Mr. Murray, a genial man with a bald head and a red mustache. Murray was well-known as one of the most successful merchants in the city, and kept Inclenberg largely as a country folly, but still took its stewardship seriously. He had just returned from his monthly survey of his extensive holdings and was tired and eager for his dinner.

"Have ye made your request yet?" he said, slipping into polite but brisk Quaker dialect. "You're here about the orphanage, are you not?"

Eliza nodded. "Of course I am. But it is also a great pleasure to finally see the inside of Inclenberg. It is such a lovely house. I have heard it praised many times, but the accolades don't do it justice."

"Flattery will get you everywhere, my dear," Mr. Murray said. "But so will social pressure. Your orphanage is a hotter ticket than the opera, which, being Quakers, Mrs. Murray and I do not subscribe to. But I told her that she should offer ye fifty pounds a year. I gather that is the going rate, and we would not wish to be seen as skimping."

"Oh, Robert, it is for the unfortunate children! Not for our reputations! Besides, there will be time for business talk later," Mrs. Murray said here. "We were just getting acquainted!"

Eliza did her best not to blanch. They had already been here nearly two hours and had still to travel on to Mount Pleasant. To her relief, Mr. Murray let out a raucous laugh.

"Yes, I know all about your 'getting acquainted' afternoons. General Howe, is it?" he said, turning to Eliza. Then, in a pitch-perfect imitation of his wife: " 'I must have told him the story of every foal, calf, lamb, shoat, or chick that was ever born.' What she didn't tell ye was that she tells every guest that story, and not just General Howe. The only thing different that day was the wine, which is like poison to her constitution, but she braved it nevertheless. She's a stout, brave lass, my Mary is, but ye'll never make it to Mount Pleasant if you don't flee now."

Mrs. Murray bore all this with a serene smile on her face and the good humor of one-half of a long-married couple to whom the other's moves are as familiar and impotent as a game of naughts and crosses.

As she took in the natural comfort between Mr. and Mrs. Murray, Eliza hoped she would be as placid one day when her husband teased her so. But their recent argument still festered like a wound. They should not have said those things to each other. She missed him and wished suddenly that she could turn back home right then, instead of waiting an entire week. Thinking of her beloved, she wondered what they would be like when they were as long-married as the Murrays.

"Send the bill to Mr. Murray's office on Vesey Street," Mrs. Murray said wryly. "I do hope you'll come back soon. I hardly had a chance to tell you about our prize ewe, who bore us not one, not two, but *three* sets of twins, all as jet black as a moonless night. And the milk! It has the earthiness of fresh-mown —"

"Run!" Mr. Murray said. "She's warming up, and there'll be no stopping her soon! Sheldon!" he added in a louder voice. "Come get these boots off my feet, my man. And bring me a slice of bread while ye're at it!"

Eliza and Emma shared a conspiratorial glance, and after thanking their hosts profusely, hurriedly took their leave out the front door to make their escape. There, they were joined shortly by Rowena, who came around from the back, and Drayton, who rode up from the barn in the carriage. His face lit up as soon as he saw the group, though Eliza thought there was a particular gleam in his eye when it landed on Emma. He all but leapt from his seat trying to assist the ladies into the carriage instead of allowing Sheldon to do it, as protocol dictated.

"Allow me, Mr. Sheldon," he said, practically elbowing the Murrays' footman out of the way to help Eliza into the carriage. "I have had an idle afternoon, and feel I need to earn my bread. Emma," he added then, extending a hand to her, which she took almost shyly.

Soon enough they were on their way. All in all, Eliza was pleased with how the visit had gone, though she found herself oddly tired. Perhaps the rollicking carriage was a bit more trying than she remembered? Or perhaps it was her pregnancy. She had to conserve some of her energy for the baby growing inside her. She allowed her eyes to fall closed during the ride to Mount Pleasant, which was hardly an hour away.

Like Murray Hill, the Beekmans' estate was located on the east side of the island, though rather closer to the river, and about a mile farther north. The light had begun to slant noticeably as the sun sank when the rambling mansion first came into view. It was larger than Inclenberg, though somewhat less formal in nature, being built into the side of a hill, with the stone foundation of the basement fully exposed on the west and south sides of the house, and the front door opened to an unadorned wooden staircase that led to a broad veranda. Still, it had a hominess to it that Murray Hill did not possess, reminding Eliza more of the Schuylers' summer home in Saratoga than the refined elegance of the Pastures. Despite its vast size, its facade was charming and warm, inviting rather than standoffish. The barns and paddocks and outbuildings all spoke of agricultural industry and gentlemanly indolence in equal measure.

"Oh, what a delightful-looking house!" Emma exclaimed.

"Is it not?" Rowena agreed. "Though it pains me to be so far separated from my beloved Simon, when I saw that he would be living here I could not be completely sad, for I knew that he would be happier in this place than in the crowded confines of the city."

"You sound as if you do not enjoy your

current living situation," Eliza said in alarm, rousing herself. She could not bear the thought of losing her cook. It wasn't just that her artistry with meat and vegetables and seasonings was unparalleled. She had been with Alex and Eliza since they first lived on their own, and felt like a part of the family.

"Oh, I am a city girl, never you fear, Mrs. Hamilton. I do not need to chase the deer out of my garden or shoo the foxes from my hens, and I am perfectly content to let someone else slaughter and dress my beef and ham. But my Simon cannot be penned in. He needs his space to roam, and here he has it in spades."

Just then, a horse galloped up the road toward the carriage, ridden by a slight figure who appeared to be hatless and jacketless to boot. Despite the blond locks, Eliza did not recognize him until he pulled up alongside the carriage shouting, "Mama! Mama!"

In the past year Simon seemed to have added four inches in height, and his skin had acquired the healthy glow of one who works in the sun much of the day.

"Simon!" Rowena called ecstatically.

"Oh, my only boy!"

At this heartwarming display, Eliza felt her hand search for her stomach and the new life taking shape there. It seemed impossible that in four or five months she too would be calling someone her "only boy," and that one day soon after he would be calling her "Mama." She felt a lump in her throat. She was so looking forward to meeting him.

"I don't care if Mrs. Murray is a Quaker and saved the republic," she said under her breath to Emma. "She is a terrible snob. It would take a heart of coal to deprive mother and son of such a joyous reunion."

Emma didn't say anything in response, but she clasped Eliza's hand in hers and squeezed it.

"Drayton Pennington, if you do not stop this carriage immediately I will leap from it and you'll be the cause of my death!" Rowena was saying now. Where a few hours ago she had complained that the ride was too rollicksome, now she was standing up and fiddling with the door of the carriage as if she would indeed fling it open and jump to the road.

In fact the carriage was moving at a fairly restrained trot, and it was but a moment before Drayton reined the horses in. Simon had already leapt from his mount, and now he yanked the carriage door open so suddenly that his mother almost fell into his arms. A moment later, mother and son were locked in an embrace while tears of joy rolled down Rowena's cheeks.

"Come, Mama," Simon said, without even acknowledging Eliza. "I have my apartment now that I share with the head groom, with a couch and table and bed and a proper stove! We shall spend the week there and it will be like when we lived in our own house when Papa was alive." Tugging at her arm with one hand, while holding his horse's reins with the other, he attempted to lead her down the hill.

"We'll not go anywhere, my young lad, until you greet Mrs. Hamilton properly," his mother remonstrated. "Without her kindness, we would not be having this happy reunion!"

Simon looked up to the carriage with a bright if distracted smile. "Oh, hello,

Mrs. Hamilton! It is so nice to see you again and thank you for bringing Mama to see me. Hello to you, too, strange lady, and to you, strange man! Mama, I have said hello," he said, turning back to Rowena, "may we go now?"

"Please, Rowena," Eliza said, laughing, "allow the young gentleman to lead you away, or I fear he will tear your arm off with his newfound strength."

The happy pair tottered off, their laughter and shouts floating to the carriage as, with a flick of Drayton's whip, it started back up the hill. As the main drive came into view, Eliza could see a pair of carriages on the gravel. One was an elegant gold-paneled brougham, the other a simple chaise like the one Eliza, Emma, and Drayton occupied. In fact, Eliza realized, it was all but identical, as if it had been rented from the same stable that the Hamiltons had acquired theirs. She didn't understand the significance of what she was seeing, however, until they had alit from their own carriage and were shown up the stairs to the verandah, where a pair of figures was emerging from the front door.

"Hello, sister!" a winking John smiled at her. "I thought you would never arrive! Mary Murray must have sucked you in like she sucked in General Howe."

"Oh!" Eliza said, surprised. Her eyes darted between her brother and —

"Oh, don't mention General You-Know-Who," Betty Van Rensselaer said. "You know he's a touchy subject around here." She smiled coyly then — not at Eliza, but at Drayton.

"Oh, hullo, Pennington," she said in accent that was so posh it sounded common, and getting his name correct for once. "Fancy meeting you here."

Eliza turned to see Drayton's face go red as an apple. To her surprise, she saw that Emma was blushing as well.

Her brother leaned over to greet her with a kiss, but Eliza pulled him to her in a rough embrace. "John?" she hissed into his ear. "What is going on? What are you and Betty doing here?"

"What do you mean?" John said innocently.

Now Eliza stepped back, and, heedless of James and Jane Beekman, who were emerging from the house to greet her, she pulled her brother aside. "What are you playing at, John Schuyler?"

"Nothing more than you are, Eliza Hamilton." He tried to smile, but a mischievous impulse twisted it into a smirk. "You wanted to play matchmaker, so we're letting you!"

18
ALL-NIGHT DINER

Ruston's Ale House and Inn
New York, New York
August 1785

Alex rushed from Saint Paul's back to his office, where he labored late into the night. He pored over the church's records of its holdings, totting up figures on page after page, double- and triple-checking his math until he was convinced he'd come up with the right number. He pulled his statute books from the shelf, cross-referencing British and New York law to see if there had been any major changes since independence had been declared. After nearly six hours of labor, he was convinced that the solution he'd come up with was not only legal but ethical, which is to say, Reverend Provoost wouldn't balk at it the way he had rejected Alex's previous proposals. More to the point, he was certain it could win in court. And if he did win, the benefits — to his reputation, to his practice, but perhaps most pertinently to his finances — were monumental. Neither the church nor his family need ever worry about money again.

Jubilant, he closed up shop and headed home, eager to share news of his victory with Eliza. It wasn't until he was halfway down Wall Street that he saw his darkened windows and remembered: His wife wasn't in. John had gone to stay with the Livingstons for a spell as he could not imagine life without servants.

He chuckled to himself but couldn't deny the pang of sadness he felt. He had, as Eliza herself had pointed out, left his wife home alone a dozen times and more since they'd been married. Not just when he went to war, but when he went to Congress in '82 and '83, and who knows how many more occasions on business, for a night, a week, a month, three. How dare she leave him by himself just once!

If he had a thought to try to stop her plans, thinking traveling was a bit rough on her condition, their argument the weeks before had held his tongue. Who was he to tell her what to do? Still, he was worried about her and hoped she was taking care of herself. There was certainly no one to take care of him at the moment.

"Oh, what helpless creatures we men are!" he muttered aloud as he let himself into the darkened, chilly house. With Drayton and Rowena gone as well, every single fire had burned out, and even the coals in the kitchen stove had gone cold. It took Alex an embarrassingly long time to light a fire in the dark — he had grown too used to having a servant take care of such quotidian tasks. All the while he worked the flint over the tinder, he was thinking how Eliza's face would light up when he told her his news. (*Light up,* he groaned inwardly, as spark after spark failed to catch flame.) He knew once he'd communicated the gist of it — and got her to understand how much money was involved — she was sure to be as ecstatic as he was. More so, even, because she would not only be happy for the family but for *him.* No one had ever celebrated his triumphs more than she had. Certainly not his family (what little he had); nor General Washington, who had always admired him, yet also seemed to look on him as Kronos had looked at Zeus: as a son whose natural abilities presaged far greater accomplishments than the father could ever hope for.

At last the tinder caught, then twigs, then logs, and soon heat began to radiate from the stove. Alex lit a lamp and inspected the larder, where half a dark loaf of bread and a crock of butter were all that greeted him. Rowena was an excellent baker, and Alex knew that her bread was as satisfyingly rich as a slice of beef, yet it was still . . . bread. Not exactly the most celebratory dinner in the world.

"Hang it all, I'm going out," he said aloud.

He sealed up the larder and stoked the stove — he wasn't going through *that* ordeal again! — looked in vain for his coat for nearly ten minutes before he realized he'd never taken it off, then locked up and headed back down Wall Street toward Water Street. In fifteen minutes, the curtained but still-lighted windows of

Ruston's Ale House came into view.

A man Alex didn't recognize was behind the bar when he entered. It had been nearly two weeks since his last visit, and though Alex thought Caroline might have hired a new barman, it was more likely that it simply wasn't seemly — or safe — for a woman to be working at this time of the night. There were four patrons scattered around the tables despite the late hour. All salts from the look of them, hoary gentlemen who were probably staying at the inn until they shipped out again, and seemed, to a man, to be deep into their cups. Alex thought he would ask to join one of them. He would trade his war stories for their tales of adventure on the high seas. Who knew? Perhaps one of them was from Nevis, or had stopped there, and would have tales of his home island.

Then he caught sight of her.

She sat in a shadowy booth in a corner of the restaurant. She was wearing a black dress like a widow and had probably dressed that way to repel the kinds of men who ate dinner at eleven at night. She herself was not eating, but reading a book, with a steaming cup beside her.

Alex considered ducking back out, not wanting to draw her attention, and not particularly desiring her company. Especially not while Eliza was away. But before he could, she had looked up and seen him. A smile crossed her face, but tentatively, as if she could sense his own hesitance, or simply because he had not been in touch with her in nearly two weeks.

Steeling himself, Alex walked across the room, his hand extended stiffly in front of him like a bayonet. "Good evening, Mrs. Reynolds. It is very nice to see you."

His voice rang hollowly in the quiet inn. He wondered whether she could tell he was lying.

Two weeks ago the investigator Miguel de La Vera had reappeared in Alex's office. He showed up in his usual way: Alex let himself into his locked office only to find Miguel sitting calmly in a chair just beyond the door. A grimace split his dark curly beard, which was the investigator's way of smiling. "So. As I suspected, this is not your usual case of a British loyalist who had his property seized from him by Governor Clinton."

Alex chuckled. "As you know, Señor La Vera, it is you who delivers information to me and not the other way around. For me to tell you anything about my clients would violate their confidentiality."

Miguel's grimace widened into a snarl of amusement. "Somehow I doubt James Reynolds is a client of yours. Perhaps it's his wife, who has been missing for almost a fortnight?"

Alex spread his hands in mock helplessness. "I can neither confirm nor deny your supposition, Señor. I only ask that you tell me everything you've been able to ascertain about Mr. Reynolds, including any material that pertains to his marriage."

Miguel snorted. "*Marriage* is a fancy term for his union. I find no records of a marriage certificate in Boston or New York in church or courthouse, nor could I find a clergyman or justice of the peace with any memory of Señor Reynolds. So whatever union he has is sanctified, if that is the right word, by a more provisional authority. If that, too, is the right word."

Miguel's Spanish accent was pronounced, but his English vocabulary was flawless. Alex often suspected that the accent was part of his disguise, like the articulated wooden appendage — instead of the standard issue peg leg — he wore inside a knee-high leather boot to disguise his missing foot. Alex wouldn't be surprised to find out the man's real name was Michael and he had been born in Charleston or Birmingham.

"Do you mean they are not legally married?" Alex asked, after weighing the information Miguel had just presented. "In that case, a formal divorce is un—" He broke off.

"You cannot dissolve what has never been established. Which is not to say that there is not a relationship between James Reynolds and Maria Lewis, as the state still knows her." Miguel smiled cunningly. "But you're not interested in Miss Lewis or Mrs. Reynolds, or however you would term her, right? You're only interested in the husband."

Alex kept his face impassive. "I'm

interested in whatever tells me more about the husband. If that involves information about his wife, or companion —"

"*Companion* is not quite the word I would use, Señor Hamilton."

"Señor La Vera, please. Despite the unusual state of her union, she is still a lady. Speak with respect."

"Begging your pardon, Señor Hamilton, but whatever else Miss Lewis is, she is no lady."

Such vulgarity made Alex physically recoil. "Señor La Vera!"

"Believe me, Señor Hamilton, it pains me to speak of a member of the fair sex in such a manner. But Miss Lewis's past, and her liaison with Mr. Reynolds, are the type of thing that you would prevent your own wife even to know about, let alone associate with."

"I am shocked to hear you speak this way, Señor. You and I both know more than most that a person is neither his ancestry nor his upbringing. Especially in this country. A person is what he makes himself — or herself, in Mrs. Reynolds's case."

"You mean Miss Lewis."

"I mean Mrs. Reynolds! She has been with him since she was sixteen years old!"

"Did she tell you that? If she did, she was lying. She has been with him no more than two years."

Alex couldn't help himself. He smashed his fist down on his desk. "How dare you!"

Miguel had fought in half a dozen wars and watched as a surgeon sawed off his own leg. He was not easily ruffled, and his affection for Alex was such that Alex's blow brought a smile to his face, albeit a rueful one.

"You know me, Señor Hamilton. You know I do not say such things lightly. But I've spoken to a dozen and more people who all testify that Miss Lewis is a woman of low morals, and that for the past two years Mr. Reynolds has been her . . . agent, if you will." He raised his hand to silence Alex before he could interrupt. "You charged me with investigating Mr. Reynolds, but it was very clear that Mrs. Reynolds was the real focus of your interest, so I asked around about her, too. I learned that she was orphaned young and ill-served by her family. I have no doubt that she was forced to become the kind of woman that she is, and that Mr. Reynolds preyed upon her vulnerability to keep her in that position. She is not the first girl he has mistreated in such a manner. But after a two-year liaison you have to ask yourself, why is she only leaving now?"

For perhaps the first time in his life, Alex was stunned speechless. Miguel gave Alex a moment before he continued: "People can change, Señor Hamilton. For the better, but also for the worse. By all accounts Miss Lewis was a fine lass. Perhaps one day she will be again. But do not assume that just because she is a woman she is incapable of making plans of her own. You do not know why she left her husband, or why she sought you out. You do not even know if she has really left him."

Alex laughed. "Now you're just talking nonsense."

"Have you ever known me to speak nonsense before?" Miguel didn't give Alex a chance to reply. "I managed to speak to the vile man. He tried to pretend that he knew where his wife was, but I don't believe him. But I also spoke to many people who tell me that he many times uses women to swindle honest men. Honest *married* men," he added pointedly. "Married men like you, Mr. Hamilton."

Even as his spine went cold, Alex felt his face flush at this insinuation or warning, he wasn't sure which. "Did you always know she was my client?"

Miguel considered Alex's words and offered a genuine smile. "It's what you pay me for, Señor Hamilton." He stood up to leave, pulling a thick envelope out of his pocket and tossing it on Alex's desk. "For what it's worth, Mr. Reynolds is pure filth. These documents will give you all you need to destroy him. For the good of all of New York, please do so."

The scene flashed through Alex's mind as he shook Maria's hand.

"I was just reading," she said, setting her book aside. "I get so bored in my room, especially with no visitors." If there was an accusation in her words, she kept it out of her tone. With a small gesture, she indicated the seat opposite hers. "Won't you join me?"

Alex looked at her sweet, open face. Could she really be the swindler Miguel said she was? Could she really be trying to swindle *him*? No, he decided. She was a woman alone in the world, a woman in a position not unlike the one his mother had found herself in — and his mother was innocent and deserved a better life. So did Maria Reynolds. She deserved his trust, and if he was honest, he was lonely.

Miguel had said she was false, but Alex couldn't believe that to be true. It would be like blaming his mother for her woes, and he could never, would never, be so disloyal as to think that of the woman who had raised and loved and yes — admittedly — failed him.

"Mr. Hamilton?" she prodded.

"I'd love to," he said at last.

19
MATCH POINT

The Mount Pleasant Ballroom
New York, New York
August 1785

While unbeknownst to her, Alex was in the company of a strange woman not his wife, Eliza was at the Beekman estate preparing for a ball.

She didn't know at what point the evening turned into a party. First Elias and Amy Van Huysman showed up, then Frederick and Constance Swanson, then a half dozen other guests whose names rang a bell, but whom Eliza had never met.

Even before the first guests arrived, though, Eliza knew something was afoot, because Betty Van Rensselaer had hooked her arm through Drayton's and was hustling him upstairs. Eliza had indeed hoped for Betty to see Drayton as a suitor, but this seemed rather . . . rushed.

"Betty? Where are you taking my footman?" she said, trailing after them.

"Footman?" Betty called without slowing. "What footman? I see only Drayton Pendleton, elegant, eligible bachelor from the wilds of . . . Kentucky, is it?"

"Ohio, madam," Drayton said uncertainly. "And it's Pennington, not Pendleton."

"Ohio! Even better! Half the people here will have never even heard of it, and no one will have been there! Ohio!"

"Begging your pardon, madam, but I don't —"

"And there'll be none of this 'madam' business tonight. Tonight we are all equals. Nay, you are our superior, for rumor has it that the Pendletons' Ohio holdings are as big as the New York estates of Livingston and Van Rensselaer combined!"

"Betty, what are you going on about?" Eliza said as she followed them down the second-floor hallway. She was only just showing, but she felt a half step slower than normal. "Drayton has been driving all day. I'm sure he's quite tired and would like to get a bite to eat and rest."

"Food he'll have a-plenty, and none of that servant's grub, either. As for rest, alas, there'll be no rest for anyone tonight. Tonight we dance!"

She threw open a door and pushed Drayton into what appeared to be a man's bedroom. "Out of that uniform, my good man!"

"Miss Van Rensselaer!" he protested.

"There's a wash basin and towel. Feel free to avail yourself of it. And don't stint on the lavender water. We can't have you smelling of horse." She pulled the door closed and then, to Eliza's surprise, locked it.

Eliza took her sister-in-law's arm. "Betty! What is going on here? Why have you taken Drayton prisoner?"

A hesitant knock came from the other side of the door. "Miss Van Rensselaer? I'm really quite confused."

Betty smiled wickedly as she dropped the key in her cleavage.

"What's there to be confused about?"

she said in a voice loud enough for Drayton to hear. "Tonight, as per your mistress's wish, we are doing a little experiment in class mobility. We are going to introduce you to a half dozen eligible bachelorettes and see if your innate charm is enough to woo them despite the — forgive me for being so blunt — the circumstances of your birth. Mr. James Beekman has been kind enough to lend you one of his suits for the evening to help with the charade. You are rather broader in the shoulder than he is, but the fashion is for men to wear their jackets open, so it should be suitable. Suitable!" she repeated. "Oh! I made a pun!"

"But this is absurd!" Eliza exclaimed. "Even if he does manage to fool everyone, what happens when they learn who he really is?" Eliza could not for the life of her understand how they had reached this pass. She had meant for Betty to take an interest in Drayton herself, not to introduce him to all of society as its most eligible bachelor!

"I thought he was a Pennington," Betty joked. "Look, Eliza, no one's going to propose to anyone tonight. And besides, I do not intend to let any of these hussies steal him from me. I am the real prize here, after all. Am I not?"

"I'm not sure *prize* is the word I'm thinking of right now," Eliza said drily.

"Mrs. Hamilton?" Drayton's voice came through the door. "What am I to do?"

"Come on," Betty cajoled. "If nothing else it will be a night of adventure for him and Emma. And maybe something will come of it."

"Emma?" Eliza repeated.

"Well, of course. Drayton is my project, and Emma is John's. You are set on your brother making Emma Trask your new sister-in-law and have been giving me more than a few nudges in Drayton's direction. Now's your chance to see if your matchmaking will catch flame. Matchmaking! Catch flame! Oh! I did it again!"

Eliza paused. Well, first she groaned at Betty's second bad pun, then she paused. She didn't think it was right to treat Drayton like a plaything, but if it meant that Emma and John could be drawn closer together, it might be worth it. And Betty may have been right: This could be an adventure that her footman would look back on later in life, if not fondly, then at least with amusement. And who knew? Betty was a flesh-and-blood girl, and Drayton possessed of undeniable physical charms. Maybe something *would* at last spark between them. Betty seemed hung up by Drayton's station and his uniform. Perhaps if he was dressed as a gentleman she would consider him as such and Eliza's plan could really take off?

But getting out of his uniform seemed to be exactly what Drayton was worried about. "Mrs. Hamilton?" he called again.

Eliza couldn't resist the intrigue of such an evening and decided it was worth a try. "If you don't mind, Drayton, please don the suit Miss Van Rensselaer has provided for you. I gather tonight is going to be a bit of a . . . masquerade."

"And let's not forget about you," Betty said. "Jane's mother just got back from Paris with the most sumptuous fabrics you've ever seen. Jane's got a dozen new dresses and she's promised us each one — your adorable Emma will have to put aside her Pilgrim gray for the evening, I'm afraid. I've picked out a dress for her that is of a golden hue so rich you could think it had been hammered out by smiths rather than sewn by seamstresses. And there's some precious metal for you too: the *most* stunning pink frock with real silver thread in the piping. It's like that dress you wore in that lovely portrait of you over your fireplace, but the *forte* version."

Eliza frowned. "Doesn't *forte* mean loud?"

Betty winked. "Just like the evening!" Then she turned and skipped off to her own room to change.

Three hours later, Betty's prediction had come true. Jane had impressed a trio of servants into musical duty, and though they weren't particularly adept at their instruments, they produced a lot of noise and managed to keep (mostly) on tempo. A succession of somewhat strained minuets, more comical than graceful, gave way to livelier jigs and reels, and the Beekmans' airy ballroom was soon toasty with the heat of bouncing bodies. The dancers were arranged longways, in two facing lines that spanned the length of the room, and partners were passed around liberally.

Before the first hour was up, everyone had danced with everyone else. Emma and John danced elegantly, if a little mechanically — no one would ever accuse her brother of grace on the boards — and at a certain point Eliza was pretty sure that Emma was leading him rather than the other way around. Drayton, however, had clearly had lessons out in Ohio, and he had a natural swagger as well, which had Betty beaming from ear to ear. Eliza was not surprised to discover that Drayton was a good dancer, despite growing up in a cabin in the Ohio wilderness, but it was somewhat more amazing to see Emma bob and bow and twirl, all with a radiant smile on her face. Pru Schlesinger was fond of a good party, and clearly she had not deprived her poor niece of the pleasure of accompanying her out and about.

When it was her turn to dance with

him, Eliza tried to ask Drayton if he was enjoying himself, but his gracefulness came at price: He concentrated so hard on the steps to their quatrain that he was barely able to acknowledge Betty's "amiability as a partner" as he twirled and turned Eliza around the floor. But when it was time for a second go-round, she begged off. She would never say it aloud, but Eliza was tired already. She didn't know whether it was the long day traveling or the dancing or the added weight of pregnancy, or some combination, but her feet ached as if she had been on them all day.

The boys protested, but she patted her stomach and was left alone, watching the revelry with a sigh. She remembered the first ball when she had met her husband, and how he had annoyed her, only because she was so attracted to him and did not want to admit it. Alex cut such a dashing figure and was a terrible flirt — she had been quite jealous of all the girls who clung to his side like burrs. *Like Aaron Burr,* she thought, a literal burr on his side as they often clashed in court and traded insults in the press. Eliza always thought they were more like enemies than friends, although Alex assured her it was all in good fun.

She turned back to the present and was pleased to see Betty sweep Drayton back out on the floor, and even more pleased to see John return to Emma. The footman and the houseguest had balked at the onset of the party, but Betty and John were not to be put off, and liberal doses of the Beekmans' homemade wine, which packed the punch of a good brandy, soon lowered their inhibitions, to Eliza's delight. Drayton whirled Betty around as though she were weightless. Emma gamboled about like a lamb in a meadow.

It was especially nice to see Emma shed her usual reserve. Her childhood had made her steady but perhaps too serious, and Eliza delighted in seeing her let loose for once and laugh like the girl she was. And why not? She was a beautiful, graceful, poised young woman. Though too withdrawn to ever be the center of a party, she was an amiable conversationalist and even better listener. Tonight, her golden gown was every bit as resplendent as Betty promised, with emerald and turquoise embroidery that only heightened its luster. There hadn't been time for wigs, much to everyone's relief (or at least Eliza's), but one of Jane's maids had managed to do some simple but lovely plaiting of Emma's hair, which coiled around her head in elegant loops and bows. A little powder highlighted the porcelain quality of her skin, *et voilà:* the "poor relation" Mary Murray had turned up her nose at was now as regal as a duchess.

Even the size of her dress didn't hinder her. For some reason Jane thought that she was going to keep the hooped bustle in fashion, though it had been steadily decreasing in size over the past few years. Emma's dress, like Eliza's and Betty's and Jane's, was an architectural miracle, half as wide at the hips as Emma was tall, and flaring out into a massive skirt that could have swallowed a card table. Indeed, with so many girls in such large gowns, the footmen had had to bring in extra sofas and armless chairs to accommodate them in the parlors, and even then they had to be widely spaced to allow for the ladies' spreading skirts. Yet

Emma, who rarely wore a corset let alone a bustle, handled it with pure elegance.

If the ladies were exuberant flowers — dahlias and hydrangeas and rhododendrons — the gentlemen were handsome branches on which they leaned. Even so, Drayton stood out from the pack. The suit Betty had selected for him was lovely. It was in a particularly striking robin's egg blue — pale but iridescent, bringing out the color of his eyes — although whenever Drayton was left alone he seemed to shrink a little into his own skin, as if he were trying to hide. Eliza was afraid this might give away his origins, but all it did was make him look like the rough-and-tumble son of a gentleman who had been impressed into ballroom finery by an older sister, which was almost true.

Eliza sipped some cool lemonade and rested her feet, proud of how well Drayton was doing at the party. He was such a naturally formal boy. Not cold or aloof, but respectful, even deferential, especially where women were concerned. Betty had dragged him off to a couple of chairs in a corner, and he sat with an attentive smile on his face while she went on and on about who knows what. Her hair, perhaps (she kept touching it), or her dress (she kept touching that as well — not to mention the curve around her cleavage). Drayton, poor boy, did all he could do to keep his eyes focused on hers. Being a boy of strong moral fiber, he succeeded.

If his eyes ever once dropped to Betty's chest, Eliza never saw it, although she did occasionally catch him glancing about the room. Or, no, not around it, per se: just at one particular spot. Amidst the bustling bodies, Eliza followed his gaze to the opposite corner, where John and Emma were sharing their own glasses of wine.

Here John was the seducer and Emma the stoic, though the smile on her face seemed genuinely amused at whatever (no doubt bawdy) anecdote John was relating.

It was sweet that Drayton was so concerned for Emma. Such the gentleman, always, but he needn't have worried. John seemed to be taking to his role as beau with enthusiasm. And why not? He and Emma lived in the same house, after all, saw each other every day, knew not just the social self but the more private, authentic individual. She knew he was more than the hard-partying college freshman, and he knew she had other sides to her besides the always-grateful ingénue who never wanted to offend lest she lose her place. She calmed him, he excited her: Together Eliza saw them as a more well-rounded, more interesting pair of individuals. A good match, and one she was right to have encouraged, Eliza thought with satisfaction.

The jury was still out on Drayton and Betty — who knew where tonight would lead them — but the more she saw Emma and John together, the more Eliza was convinced her instincts were correct.

"Matchmaker indeed," she said under her breath.

"Begging your pardon, Eliza?"

She looked up to see her friend James Beekman smiling at her. He held a decanter in his hand glistening with drops of moisture. It had obviously just been pulled from a bucket of ice.

"Oh, excuse me, James. I was just musing out loud."

"I shan't ask what thoughts could provoke such an interesting exclamation," he said tactfully. "I only came over to see if I could refresh your drink. My sister has, as usual, managed to fill the room with guests, and it is rather stuffy in here."

Eliza smiled gratefully and patted the seat beside her — well, as close as she could reach over her wide hoops. "Please, join me. I am afraid I am not as light on my feet as I was four or five months ago. Amuse me."

James sat down, refilling her glass fast with chilled perry — unfermented, as Eliza had requested — then topping off his own with the alcoholic version. "To be honest, I think it is you who have provided all the fun for the evening."

"And how is that?"

"Your two mystery guests," James replied, indicating Emma and Drayton. "They are charming everyone — when they can escape the orbit of Mr. Schuyler and Miss Van Rensselaer, at any rate."

It took Eliza a moment to recall that James wasn't in on Betty and Jane's little scheme, and she decided to play along rather than risk the story leaking out.

"Ah, yes. Mr. Penning— Pendleton, I mean, and Miss Trask. They are but recent acquaintances, although both have become quite dear to me."

"Betty has been telling the most outrageous stories about Mr. Pendleton. She says the family's Ohio holdings are as big as Belgium."

Eliza laughed. "You know how Betty likes to exaggerate. I don't think the whole territory of Ohio is as big as all that," though the truth was she was rather fuzzy about the size of the Ohio Territory, or Belgium for that matter. "But he is certainly a man of . . . singular wealth."

"Indeed. And so well-spoken. Jane said she could listen to him talk all evening."

"Has Jane taken a bit of a fancy, then?" Eliza asked as lightly as she could, though her heart was suddenly racing. Nothing would make Betty want someone more than a little competition. And Jane Beekman could hardly be considered a bad catch herself.

"Who knows?" James laughed. "My

sister falls in love almost as often as I do, and her infatuations pass almost as fast."

"Have you fallen in love with someone then?" Eliza asked, even as James's eyes flicked in Emma's direction.

When James looked back at Eliza, he saw that he had been found out. He grinned sheepishly. "Oh, I think I am rather out of my depth tonight. And to tell you the truth I enjoy being a bachelor and would not sully Miss Trask by playing Lothario."

Eliza had heard that James liked to toy with ladies' affections, if not their honor, and appreciated this discretion on his part. "She is indeed remarkably pure. Her life has not been blessed by great fortune or the most stable of family situations, and yet all the strife she has endured seems only to have made her stronger and more benevolent."

James turned to admire the lithe form of Eliza's houseguest once again. "Be careful, Eliza, lest you awaken a passion in me I cannot control."

"Oh, James!" Eliza said, patting his knee lightly. "You are such a lad! But in all seriousness," she added, "if you trifle with Miss Trask I shall have to hurt you."

The two shared a laugh, though James's was a little strained. Eliza's tone was light, but it was clear her warning was quite the opposite.

"As I said, I think I am out of my league anyway. As is, dare I say, your brother."

Eliza looked over at the love-struck pair. John was leaning in, attempting to make eye contact with Emma, who was looking coyly away.

"Yes, they do make —" Eliza broke off. "Wait, what? John is out of his league?"

"How long have Miss Trask and Mr. Pendleton been wooing each other?" James asked in an innocent voice. "They seem quite well suited — both so steady and well-mannered. They could teach us all a thing a two."

"Who?" Eliza asked. "You mean Emma and . . . *Drayton?*" Yet even as the words left her mouth, she had the nagging sensation that she had been missing something that had been right in front of her eyes all this time. Had she been so caught up in her own plans — for a family, for the orphanage, for Emma and John and Drayton and Betty — that she could have missed an entirely different romance taking shape in her own house?

No, she told herself. *It's not possible.* Yet even in her mind, she heard the whinge of protest.

James sat back slightly. "You didn't realize?"

Eliza tried to laugh off her obvious surprise as her mind spun. "I fear you are mistaken, James. Emma and my brother are quite in love, and Drayton would never presume —" She broke off at James's confused look. "That is, it seems clear that Drayton has his sights set on uniting the Pendleton fortune with the Van Rensselaer name." But even as she spoke she was following Emma's averted gaze, and realized that she wasn't avoiding John's eyes as much as she was seeking out Drayton's.

James chuckled. "My mother told me never to contradict a lady. Nevertheless, I have to disagree here. I have rather a little experience in these matters, and if Miss Trask and Mr. Pennington or Pendleton or whatever his name is aren't in

404

love, I'll eat my hat."

"An easy promise," Eliza said. "You're not wearing a hat."

"I have twenty," James said. "I'll let you pick. Some of them are *quite* large, and the fur trim is particularly chewy."

Eliza looked between Emma and Drayton. Though each seemed to be paying attention to their respective partner, they each glanced the other's way every few moments, and once, when they managed to look at the same time, they exchanged shy smiles. And now that she thought of it, their eyes seemed always to be straying to each other — at parties, at table. Even when they were in the carriage earlier, when Drayton would turn around to rib Rowena, it was Emma's eye he would catch. Emma he would wink at. Could James really be right?

"But — but this cannot be. It is not an advantageous match for either of them." The minute Eliza said it, she regretted it. Was she as terrible a snob as Betty Van Rensselaer? She was taken aback by the notion. After all, why couldn't Emma and Drayton be together?

James shrugged. "One is poor, the other

is rich and owns all of Ohio, and both are comely. It would seem to be the most advantageous of all unions."

Eliza stood up abruptly. "I beg your pardon, but I am suddenly feeling rather tired." She patted her stomach. "Could I trouble you to send Emma up to my room to help me from my dress?"

"My sister has set aside a maid —"

"In my condition," Eliza cut him off, patting her stomach rather more pronouncedly, "I prefer the assistance of a familiar pair of hands. Thank you for understanding," she added, then turned and exited the room.

20
JEWEL IN THE DARKNESS

Ruston's Ale House and Inn
New York, New York
August 1785

The barman came over to ask if Alex would like a pint of ale and a bowl of stew, both of which he accepted like a drowning sailor grabbing for a life rope.

"I, er, have to go fetch it," the barman said when Alex reached a hand out for a dish the barman wasn't carrying. Alex put his hand down sheepishly. "Very good, my good man!" he said with forced brightness. He winced inwardly at his own words. Had he stumbled into an Elizabethan drama without realizing it?

"It is so pleasant to see you, Mr. Hamilton!" Maria said after the barman had departed. "I was beginning to think you had forgotten about me!" Maria's voice was too loud, too bright as well, too desperate in the nearly deserted inn, and Alex realized he wasn't the only nervous one.

"I do apologize for the long absence, Mrs. Reynolds. Work has been exceptionally demanding lately." In comparison to his client, Alex's voice had gone too quiet, too flat, too dishonest.

"I'm sure," Maria said. "I understand that you have to prioritize your paying clients." Alex thought he heard a note of disappointment in her voice, not so much in him as in life. It was as if she had been dismissed in the same manner many times before.

"It's not that . . ." Alex's voice trailed off as the barmen returned with Alex's order. He and Maria stared at each other in silence as the heavy crock and stein were set down on the wooden table.

"Anything else, sir?"

"If Mrs. Smith would like anything . . . ?" Maria shook her head. "That will be all then. I have a tab," he added. "Alexander —"

"Hamilton, yes sir." The barman nodded. "You're well-known in Ruston's, and in this city, dare I say?"

Alex flustered and automatically put his hand out. "Pleased to meet you, Mr., ah —"

"Thomas, sir," the barman said, shaking his hand. Alex wasn't sure if it was the man's first or last name, and didn't ask.

"Is that it?" Maria said after the barman had gone. Alex turned to her in confusion. "You're afraid to be seen with me? You think someone might recognize you? Or, even worse, might recognize me?"

Alex's hand clutched at his glass. "Why would you say that, Mrs. Reynolds?"

Maria rolled her eyes at this weak attempt at a dodge. "It has been two weeks since I heard from you, Mr. Hamilton. I —" She gulped, and her cheeks flushed with color. "I have been abandoned before. I know what it looks like."

Alex sat up with a start. It stung to be accused of such callow behavior, even if he knew that was exactly what he had done. A vague thought troubled the back of his mind. This behavior reminded him of someone, but he couldn't think of who. And then in a moment of clarity, it hit him: his father, who had left his mother to her fate all those years ago.

"I have not abandoned you!" he almost shouted. "Why, I'm here now!"

Maria's smile was a frightening thing, full of a worldly knowledge Alex did not like to associate with such a young woman. He had seen a smile like that before, though he could barely remember it. But he could picture it on his mother's face when his father disappeared, and when the next man came into her life, and the next, and the one after that. She had worn it on her deathbed, too, a knowing smile that told Providence to do its worst, because she had already seen it all.

"Can you look me in the eye," Maria said with that cunning smile on her face, "and tell me that it was *me* you came to see tonight?"

Alex was able to look her in the eye, but he wasn't able to speak those words. It was all he could do to blink the visage of his mother away.

"Eat your stew," Maria said after a moment, sounding just like his mother. There was no triumph in her voice, only defeat. "It's getting cold."

Alex tucked in. He had been ravenous when he arrived, but now the savory beef concoction tasted like mud. Still, it was better than speaking.

But Maria wasn't about to let him off that easily. "What did he tell you?"

At first, Alex thought she somehow knew about Miguel, but then he realized she meant her husband. Her sort-of husband. Her — what was Miguel's word? — *agent.* "I assure you I have not spoken with Mr. Reynolds."

"No doubt," Maria agreed. "A gentleman of your class has middlemen he employs for such unsavory communications. You would not like to sully yourself by coming too close to my world."

"I think you judge me harshly, Mrs. Reynolds."

"Do I? Or do I judge you just harshly enough?"

Once again, Alex could not muster a reply.

"You see I have learned a thing or two about men in my life. Even men of your station, so above my own."

"Mrs. Reynolds, please. I beg of you. Do not speak of yourself so."

Maria sighed. "Why did you come here tonight, Mr. Hamilton?"

Alex hung for a moment, then shrugged. "My wife is away, and she took our cook with her. I worked late and needed some dinner."

"So you came here, as opposed to the Fraunces Tavern, which is just around the corner?"

"I have never been fond of the Fraunces. And, as you know, I have a long-standing relationship with Mrs. Childress."

"New York is a big city. I'm sure there are other taverns still open at this hour. Yet you chose to come to the one where you have a client. A client whose letters and person you have ignored for quite a while."

Of course, he had to ignore her. Miguel had warned him away from her. Moreover, she had been the cause of an

412

argument between him and his wife, when he and Eliza had never argued like that before. And the moment Eliza was gone here he was, by her side. Why couldn't he keep away? Why didn't he have another clerk in his office take care of this business? Why didn't he just send Nippers?

Alex chewed mechanically on the stew in his mouth, swallowed without tasting it. "A moment ago you suggested that I did not come here to see you. Now it seems you are saying I did."

"A man can desire a thing and yet not realize he desires it. There are parts of ourselves that only God knows, and that remain a mystery to even the most self-aware of souls."

Something funny happened in Alex as Maria said these words. On the one hand, he admired her perspicacity. To have acquired such wisdom at so young an age, and without the advantage of an education, spoke to a first-rate mind. Yet on the other hand, he was aware of how she had likely acquired it. The unnatural experiences she had had, and that had forced knowledge on her like Satan had forced the apple upon Eve. Alex had always taken the Eden story as a kind of parable, not literally true. Knowledge had always been his god. Yet now he felt that there were some things better unknown. The thought that a woman as obviously sensitive as Maria knew these things repelled him. Yet it held an undeniable attraction as well.

She knew the world as it was, like he did, the cruelty and the coarseness, she knew abandonment and deceit and hunger and survival, just as he did. They were alike in a way that Eliza would never understand.

"It is true that I have been out of touch these past two weeks," he admitted now. "It is also true that I hired a man to investigate your — your husband," he said deliberately. "It cannot come as a surprise to you that the investigation unearthed unsavory things not just about him but about you."

Maria regarded him with a level, eerily calm demeanor. "You may speak frankly, Mr. Hamilton."

"I think I am speaking as frankly as I am able," Alex said. "Your husband says that he sent you to entrap me, for the purposes of blackmail."

Maria sat back in horror — but not, it seemed, at the accusation. "Does he know where I am then?"

Alex restrained himself from taking her hand to comfort her. "It does not seem so."

Maria seemed doubtful. "Then how does he know I am with you?"

"He did not mention me by name. He only told my man that he had sent you out to 'do a job.' My man thought he was fishing, and I do, too."

"Fishing?"

"He was trying to find out where you were. Naturally my man told him nothing."

Maria considered this for a moment. "So, you do not believe him?"

"I do not," Alex said. "Yet I cannot deny that you actively concealed the truth from me either. Such behavior doesn't inspire trust."

"No," Maria said bitterly. "I would imagine it does not. Yet what would you have done if you knew the truth about me?"

Alex shrugged helplessly. "I am not sure that I *do* know the truth about you. I know a few facts. But a life is more than its plot points as it were, no matter how shocking."

Maria sighed wearily. "Are they shocking?" she said in a voice whose nonchalance made her words that much more bitter. "To me, they seemed . . . commonplace. Inevitable even."

"Our maker gave each of us the right to choose, Mrs. Reynolds."

Maria laughed. "Did the slave choose his fate then? No, Mr. Hamilton, our maker gave people the right to suffer, but only some of us actually get to choose the causes of our suffering. And we women have rather less opportunity than men to steer our fate."

"I want to understand you, Mrs. Reynolds. I really do. Yet how does a woman like you, who so obviously knows better, end up with a man like Mr. Reynolds?"

Another laugh, even more jaded than the previous one, but it tugged at his heart. Maria looked so delicate, so help-less, in the dim light of the tavern. She was a blossom that needed sun, not dark-ness. A jewel without tarnish, no matter what she had borne. It pained him to see her so low.

Alas, he was no longer thinking of his dearest Eliza, only of his mother, who had also been similarly discarded, and who deserved so much more.

"How could I not? I had no home, Mr. Hamilton. I had no kin, no income, no means of getting employment. I tried to find a place at inns like this, yet they always cast me out because my clothes were too dirty or my accent too coarse; and when I did find employment, there was always some man there to demand more from me than a stein of ale or bowl of stew, or a wife to chase me out before her husband could overstep his bounds. If it wasn't the owner, it was a patron. If it wasn't a patron, it was a deliveryman. If it wasn't a deliveryman, it was just a man on the street. There is only so long one can hold out when one has no place to sleep but the boardwalk and nothing to eat but the scraps she finds there."

Alex's mind flashed back, not to Nevis but to St. Croix, where his mother had taken them after his father left. The dark, sooty, sweltering rooms, the threadbare clothes, the endless bowls of watery rice unrelieved by pork or mutton or even poultry. "I never had a chance," his mother had said to him just a few weeks before the fever carried her away. "But you will, because you are a man." He had been eleven at the time and had not understood the full import of his mother's words, and now he realized he never fully grasped their significance. Not until this woman sat across from him and showed exactly how unjust men could be to women, even as they professed to adore and protect them.

He didn't stop himself this time. He put his hand out and took Maria's. "Please, Mrs. Reynolds, I beg of you. Accept my apology. I allowed myself to be blinded by innuendo and forgot the honorable woman who entrusted me with her care. I won't let you down again."

Maria looked wearily down at his hand, then pulled hers away. "I know you

418

believe what you say. But I also know how the world works. Nevertheless," she continued before Alex could protest, "I have no choice but to trust you." She stood up. "You should head home, Mr. Hamilton. It's late." She nodded at the bartender, who was staring at them openly. "People will talk."

21
CASTLES IN THE AIR

En Route to Van Cortlandt Manor
The Bronx, New York
August–September 1785

Eliza was terribly wounded by what she felt was Emma's deception. All along she had believed the girl to be enamored of her brother when all along she had feelings for Drayton. Hence Eliza had pretended to be ill when she went to bed last night so she could keep Emma from returning to the party, but also force her to sleep in a spare bed rather than share with her, as they might normally have done. A pair of footmen carried a narrow bedframe into the room and spread a mean-looking feather mattress across it. Eliza peevishly directed them to move it closer to the fire so "her Miss Trask" wouldn't freeze to death.

As it happened, it rained during the night and it was Eliza who turned out to be cold beneath her single blanket, but she curled herself into a ball and stoically (or rather, stubbornly) refused to ask Emma to join her for a little extra body heat, even though she could hear her friend tossing and turning on her narrow, thin bed, and knew they would both be more comfortable if they slept together as they had done during the entire trip.

In the morning, after a fitful night's sleep, Eliza was genuinely feeling under the weather — although it might have just been the weather. Thick fog gave way seamlessly to heavy clouds hanging low in the sky, so that the air was a solid sheet of suspended water, and the mercury had dropped almost thirty degrees. It seemed clear a heavy rain was coming, yet Eliza still insisted that they make the trip up to Van Cortlandt House that morning.

"We have work to do," she told Jane, who counseled waiting until the weather had cleared. "It is only six miles, and the carriage has a hood. We shall be fine."

"Your footman is certainly a robust

lad," Jane said, shrugging her shoulders. "I suppose he'll be fine, too."

It stung Eliza when a sweet but, if one was honest, somewhat pampered girl like Jane Beekman cared more about her servant's well-being than she did, but she was still so miffed by James's revelations (rather obvious, in hindsight, but still shocking) that she continued to insist on the journey. She was irritated that she had not seen Drayton and Emma's budding romance, and felt keenly betrayed by it. With her brilliant plans, she had been trying to improve their stations, and how did they pay her back? By falling for each other?

Infuriated by the thought, she retreated to the library, where she pretended to read a volume of Fielding, in order to avoid Emma, who was charged with packing up their things, and Drayton, who loaded them onto the carriage.

By ten o'clock they were ready to depart. A subdued Emma climbed glumly into the rear-facing seat, while a confused Drayton, swathed in an oilskin rain hat generously provided by one of the Beekmans' footmen, waited in the driver's seat. One of the horses looked back at him with an expression of "Really? In this weather?" then pointedly lifted its tail.

Jane came around to give Eliza a little farewell kiss. "You are a bit warm, Eliza. Are you sure you're fit to travel? Why don't you at least wait until John and Betty have awakened so you can give them a proper good-bye."

" 'John and Betty,' " Eliza parroted. "You make it sound like they are a couple."

Eliza expected Jane to look shocked — she wanted to shock people as much as she had been shocked last night — but all her friend did was wink.

"Well, actually —" she began. "I do believe your brother is quite taken with her. And she with him."

"Johnny and Birdy?" Eliza said, aghast. She thought of the insults they traded — "inbred stripling" Betty called him, while he thought her a horrid snob — or did he? And did she? Now that the blinders were off, Eliza could see quite clearly. Did she and Alex not trade barbs during their courtship? Did she not think him arrogant and cocky and do her best to pretend she did not swoon at the sight of him?

Oh dear Lord, she had gotten it all wrong. And if she could not see what was clearly in front of her, what else in her life had she missed?

She missed Alex terribly, though she'd been gone only one day. Why had she insisted on this trip — especially in her condition? She had been stubborn and single-minded and bossy, and she was hurt by his words and wanted to punish him a little. Let him miss her, as she had missed him.

Jane recoiled at Eliza's tone. "Eliza? Are you quite well?"

"I am *fine,*" Eliza said, though she was mortified at her behavior, and all she really wanted to do was climb back into bed. "Duty calls!" she added as gaily as she could, and without waiting for a footman's assistance hauled herself into the carriage. Once the door was closed, she banged on the wall behind Drayton's seat like an overzealous valet, and a moment later they were on their way.

Eliza had insisted that Emma don one

of her finer dresses for the journey —
"Can't show up at the Van Cortlandts
looking like a pair of country lasses, can
we?" — and she herself had worn a
bustled skirt, requiring her to sit bolt
upright on the carriage seat to avoid
crushing her ribs, which were already
tightly squeezed by the bodice of her
dress, which had been tailored last year,
when her stomach was substantially
smaller than it was now. There were
several minutes of rearranging as the
women shifted around yards and yards
of canopied silk in an attempt to get
comfortable, and more than once one of
the women stepped on the other's toes.
At last they came to rest, their dresses
intermingling like a flood of spilled
strawberry jam (Eliza) colliding with a
tipped-over pot of honey (Emma).

"Are you quite comfortable, Mrs. Hamilton?"

"Emma, please," Eliza said in a castigat-
ing tone. "We are friends. Call me Eliza."
It sounded like an order rather than an
entreaty.

"Of course, Eliza," Emma said in the
voice of a child who has been punished

for a transgression she is unaware of.

They rode on in silence for a few moments. Then Eliza, remembering herself, said: "And are you comfortable, Emma?"

"I'm quite comfortable," Emma answered. Then, after a pause: "Thank you for asking."

Eliza wasn't sure if she heard the slightest bit of sauce in Emma's voice. No doubt she was imagining it. Her friend was far too meek for cheek.

Too meek for cheek! she thought, and grinned crookedly. *Ha!*

Emma looked at her in confusion. Just then there was a crack of thunder. Emma started and peered out the window nervously. "It looks like it's really going to come down soon."

"Nonsense," Eliza said. "You have spent too long in the city and have forgotten how to read the sky. It's just a heavy fog. It will burn off within the hour."

Emma squinted at Eliza's transparent lie. Finally, she just shrugged and said, "I do hope you're right. It is five hours to Van Cortlandt House. That is an awfully long time to be out in the rain."

"We are not out in the rain," Eliza said peevishly, tapping the flimsy roof of the carriage. "And it is hardly five hours to Van Cortlandt House. Four at the most."

Emma looked at Eliza in consternation. "I was not referring to us. I was thinking of Drayton."

Eliza literally felt her eyes roll. "Of course you were."

"Mrs. Ham— Eliza?" Emma said anxiously. "Have I done something to offend you?"

"What?" Eliza said in faux innocence. "Of course not. You are by far the sweetest, most docile, and obedient girl I have ever met in my entire life."

Emma bore this acidic outburst as stoically as she could, but a warm flush had crept up her cheeks, and her eyes looked as watery as the sky.

"Only I would hate for you to think I was not extraordinarily grateful for everything you and Mr. Hamilton have done for me."

"Call. Him. *Alex,*" Eliza said almost vehemently. "We are your friends — your benefactors maybe — not your employers."

Emma shrank into her seat.

"I'm sorry, Eliza. I really do appreciate everything you have done for me."

"Yes, you already said that; you needn't harp on about it. You would think Alex and I invited you into our home just so we would have someone around to praise us for our good deeds all the time."

Emma opened her mouth, then closed it. Her lower lip trembled slightly, but Eliza refused to relent. "Only why," she said suddenly, "why do you refuse my brother's affections and instead dote on someone who can offer you none of the advantages John can?"

Emma tried to pretend she didn't know what Eliza was talking about, but her eyes flashed heavenward, to where Drayton sat just above her.

"Mr. Schuyler —"

"John."

"Your brother doesn't care for me. He flirts with me because he flirts with all the girls."

428

"Yes, he *flirts* with all the girls. He *woos* you."

Emma surprised her then. She laughed. "I should hate to tell you about your own brother, Eliza, but your brother would no more marry a poor girl than — than Miss Van Rensselaer would marry a poor boy!"

"Emma! I do not like to hear you speak of my brother and my friend in such a manner!"

"Friends don't tell friends how to speak, Eliza," Emma said tartly. "Or am I in fact your lady's maid, Mrs. Hamilton?"

"Drayton is not a good match for you! Why isn't that as obvious to you as it is to everyone else? The two of you will be penniless and — and servants!"

"There is no shame in being a servant, Mrs. Hamilton. It is honest work, and we cannot all be so fortunate as to have inherited money. And at least if I were a maid or governess or schoolmarm I should know my place and not always feel like I am overstepping my bounds when I call people by their Christian names, or sit at table with them and feel like I am eavesdropping on someone else's conversation. You like to pretend that America is a classless society, and while that may be true in Mr. Hamilton's speeches and essays, in real life the world is still very much divided by how much money one has, and for how long. There are still rich and poor, and the former still have very strong ideas about the latter's place."

"Emma Trask! Are you calling me a snob? I am the opposite of a snob!" Eliza cried, truly hurt.

"Indeed you are not a snob, Mrs. Hamilton. But a snob like Betty Van Rensselaer is easier to deal with. And at least she is honest about her place in the world and has a sense of humor about it as well."

Eliza was shocked into silence. Emma's chest was heaving, as if she were just as surprised by her words as Eliza was, but she didn't stop speaking.

"Money is money, Mrs. Hamilton, regardless of education. It might surprise you to learn that not every poor person makes mud pies for amusement or relishes opossum stew or thinks baths are an idiosyncrasy of the rich. We may work longer hours than you, and at less scintillating tasks, but we still find time to edify ourselves as well. As near as I can tell Drayton has read more books than you have, but he is still a footman."

"You just love to insult my reading habits, don't you?"

Emma scoffed. "There is no habit to insult."

Eliza gasped. "You forget your place, Emma."

"No, Mrs. Hamilton, I remember my place every day. It is you who forget *my* place. I live on the largesse of a couple I barely know, and though I go to sleep grateful each night to be installed in a comfortable bed above stairs, I wake up each morning wondering if today my mistress will suddenly remember who I am and banish me to a cot off the kitchen. Like she did last night."

Eliza didn't bother pointing out that Emma hadn't slept in the kitchen last night, but she couldn't stop herself from saying, "That was not a cot. It was the same size bed I slept on once upon a time."

"Until you were how old? Eight? Ten?"

"Twelve!"

Emma mumbled something under her breath. A flush spread across her face, but so did a self-satisfied grin.

"What was that?" Eliza demanded.

"Nothing, Mrs. Hamilton. I only said that you are a bit of an undersized thing, so it probably fit you."

"Why, I am bigger than you!"

"You are now," Emma said, her eyes flitting to Eliza's stomach.

Eliza stiffened. "I appreciate that our tempers are hot, but mind how you speak to me. There are limits to even my tolerance."

"You see? I am your friend when it suits you and your servant when it doesn't. It is a choice only a rich person can make."

"Well, if you married John you would be rich, and you could be as capricious as me."

"If I married John, I would be miserable as it is quite clear he is in love with someone else."

"What?"

"It is only you who are blind to it, as well as John and Betty themselves. They don't seem to realize they are quite taken with each other and resort to taunting each other instead," said Emma. "Besides, even if I married John, I would spend all my time thinking about Drayton, because I love him!"

Eliza gasped, even though she had heard it last night already. "You do?"

Emma's eyes had been flashing with anger, but now they fell to her lap. In a moment she was her usual self again, save for the flush that clung to her pale cheeks. "I do," she said in a quiet but determined voice.

"And does he love you?" Eliza asked in a defeated voice.

"He does," Emma answered, beaming.

Eliza processed this in silence for a moment. At length she reached out and took Emma's hand. "I only wanted to help you, Emma."

Emma squeezed Eliza's hand for a minute before pulling hers free, clearly not ready to forgive and forget just yet. "I know you did, Mrs. Hamilton. But

433

Cupid is remarkably independent. Almost as independent as you," she added in a questioning voice, as if unsure if she could make a joke so soon.

Eliza barely heard her. She was seeing an entire summer's schemes go up in smoke. How could she have been so blind? Not about Emma and Drayton, but about herself?

Was she a terrible snob? The worst kind, as she was ignorant of the fact? Yes, yes, she was. She had to do better, she thought, as she punched the side of the carriage. She had been upset to think about Emma and Drayton as it appeared they were throwing their futures away, when rich marriages could be made if they only let Eliza pick them. She had only wanted the best for Emma and Drayton, as she would for her own child. She laughed inwardly. How she had turned into her mother! This was Catherine Schuyler speaking, wasn't it? Still, it was hard to see her castles crumble.

The next eight hours were pure torture. Though Eliza and Emma didn't fight anymore, they sat in mutual silence that was more painful than their sparring words. Eliza couldn't tell if Emma was no longer angry at her, or simply too tired to continue dueling. For her part, she was torn between continued indignation that Emma had spurned her help — not to mention her brother! — and mortification at her behavior. She was hard-pressed to recall a time in her life when she had ever spoken as harshly to someone as she'd just spoken to Emma, and though she didn't want to admit it, she knew that one of the reasons she'd acted so vehemently was because she could. She was the rich one. She was the mistress. Emma was dependent on Eliza, for shelter, for food, for an eventual job as a governess or lady's maid, and was essentially helpless to respond in kind. The fact that she had lost her temper was testament to just how far over the line Eliza had stepped.

Yet Eliza couldn't bring herself to apologize just yet. It was hard to let go of such a well-planned scheme. She'd had her heart set on it. Emma could make John happy, and John could make Emma comfortable, and in time they could come to love each other. Maybe not the kind of love that she and Alex shared, but how many marriages were blessed with that kind of passion? And how many of those passions persisted over time? Every year growing up there would be a story of some love-struck swain or smitten maiden who ran off in the dark of the night, only to wake up a month or a year later beside someone who could not give them what they wanted. That would be Emma and Drayton. If they did marry, it would be a stroke of fortune if they even managed to live in the same house. More than likely Drayton would serve in one place and Emma in another, and their marriage would be like a sailor's, with brief unions snatched between interminable periods of waiting. And it wasn't just their own poverty they were guaranteeing. As servants, they would never be able to educate their children so that they could raise themselves up. It would be generation after generation of straitened circumstances. Why couldn't they *see* that?

But love is blind, and Eliza knew that truth better than anyone. Hadn't her own mother told her Alex was unsuitable? And hadn't Eliza ignored her and pursued him anyway? And hadn't it all worked out? Every couple was entitled to a fight now and then, and it would be alarmist to make more of it than it really was. On some level Eliza knew she was describing the situation as she wanted it rather than as she knew it to be, but when all was said and done she had faith in Alex and their love. That was enough, wasn't it?

While all these thoughts were darting around Eliza's head it started to rain in earnest. The wind picked up as well, and the flimsy lid of the carriage rattled on its hinges and let in mist-laced drafts that sprayed both ladies. To make matters worse, a steady drip soon started from a frayed seam more or less directly over Eliza's seat, and such was the width of the bustle she had insisted on wearing that she could not slide out of its way.

For the first time in half an hour, Emma spoke.

"Oh, Mrs. Hamilton, you should switch with me. You'll catch your death of cold, and in your condition it's not worth the risk."

The anger was fully gone from her voice, and in its place was the kindness and concern of which Eliza had grown so fond in the past few months. But Eliza's guilt at her own bad behavior was still too raw to allow her to accept Emma's generous offer.

"I am quite all right, thank you, Emma," Eliza said briskly. "It is just a few drops of water."

"But it is soaking through your dress!"

"Nonsense. It is just a damp spot," Eliza lied, piling as many layers of soon-to-be-ruined silk atop her thighs in an effort to shield herself from the freezing water. "It shall blow over in a moment, and then we'll lower the top and the sun will dry my dress in no time at all."

The mound of fabric kept her dry for a few more minutes, but such was the steadiness of the drip that soon it had soaked all the way through to Eliza's petticoat and pantaloons, chilling her legs as though she had stepped into an icy mountain stream, but still she refused to change places with Emma.

"It is almost done raining," she said every time Emma protested. "I can see clear skies on the horizon."

The storm did indeed blow over, but not till nearly two hours later. By then the damage was done. Eliza was soaked through and shivering, and, what's worse, the roads had been rendered a sodden mess. What should have been a five-hour journey took nearly eight.

Eliza was in a daze by the time the carriage slowed in front of the Van Cortlandts' stern gray stone manor house, which was little more than a dark shadow against the glowering sky. It took both Drayton and one of the Van Cortlandts' footmen to get her out of the carriage. Her last clear thought was saying, "I can stand on my own," before she fainted into Drayton's arms.

When next she opened her eyes, cold but bright bars of sunlight were angling into a strange bedroom. A roaring fire burned in a grate, and a thick, fluffy quilt swaddled Eliza up to her neck. She felt delightfully warm.

"Mrs. Hamilton? Are you awake?"

She turned and saw a blond girl in a prim gray dress staring at her with a concerned expression. Her otherwise smooth skin was creased with worry lines around her mouth, and there were dark circles under her eyes, as if she had not slept all night. Eliza had no idea who she might be.

"Do I know you?" she asked. She attempted to sit up but found she didn't have the strength for it.

The girl bit her lip, then took a moment to calm herself. "It's Emma, Mrs. Hamilton. Emma Trask."

For one more brief terrifying moment, Eliza stared at the girl dumbly, and then suddenly it all came back to her: the errand to the Van Cortlandts, the carriage ride, the fight. Her hands rushed to her stomach, to feel the mound of growing life there. It felt strangely . . . bigger. And then, even more strangely, it *moved.* With a tremendous start, equal parts terror and love, Eliza realized her baby was *kicking.*

"How — how long have I been asleep?"

Emma smiled at her gently and took her hand. "It has been three weeks you've tossed and turned with a fever, Mrs. Hamilton. We were afraid we were going to lose you."

"But . . . but it was just a chill," Eliza said, thinking Emma must be teasing her. And yet, the weakness in her body attested to the truth of Emma's words. Her limbs felt like putty, as if they had not moved in — well, in three weeks.

"Alex," she said at last. "Is he here?"

"Mrs. Van Cortlandt only wrote to tell him that you were ill. He is so overwhelmed with work that it seemed needless to send for him, as there is nothing he could do."

This seemed peculiar to Eliza to say the least — she was pregnant, after all, and tossing in delirium in a fever! And she wanted her husband by her side, badly. But before she could inquire further there was a knock at the door, and Drayton entered bearing a tray containing a teapot and some biscuits.

"Oh, Drayton!" Emma exclaimed, jumping up from her chair and rushing to the door. "She is awake! She is awake!" she said, grabbing Drayton's arm so excitedly that she almost upset his tray.

441

"Easy, my love, easy," Drayton said, giving Emma a little kiss on the forehead. "You will spill Mrs. Hamilton's tea, and then she may sleep for another three weeks."

He set the tray down, then turned to the bed. "Good morning, Mrs. Hamilton. It is good to have you back with us."

He seemed suddenly to realize that Emma's arm was still looped through his, and he grinned sheepishly and put his hand over hers.

Eliza laughed weakly at the folly of her plans. "You make a beautiful couple," she said. Her former plans were a distant memory, and melted like shaved ice in the summertime. She told herself that she and Alex would help settle the young couple so that they could rise above their station, and they would see that America was not England, and not stratified in the same manner. Their happiness made her melancholy, however, as she realized how dearly she missed her own husband.

22

TEMPTATION AND TRAGEDY

Ruston's Ale House and Inn
New York, New York
September 1785

He had gone there to comfort another. Not to seek comfort for himself.

He had gone there to celebrate his greatest accomplishment since Yorktown. Instead he had been handed his greatest defeat.

He defeated himself.

It was a bitter pill to swallow, especially as the day started in triumph. Three weeks after Eliza's departure, Alex had arranged a private meeting with a magistrate and Reverend Provoost to review the church's charter as a preamble to an official hearing at a later date. He walked into Judge Tankert's chambers in City Hall brimming with confidence. After a brief greeting, he spread his papers out and began his speech.

"In 1697," Alex began, "the Church of England, under the auspices of King William and the Lords of the Treasury, Trinity Church was established as the principal parish of the colony of New York. Its charter granted it some fifty acres of land at the lower end of Manhattan, to which were added some two hundred more under Queen Anne in 1705. Subsequent deeds by the Church of England, with the full knowledge and cooperation of the crown, increased the church's holdings to nearly four hundred acres over the course of the next seventy years.

"But while the church's properties grew vastly over that period, its original 1697 charter remained intact and unchanged. This charter, as both of you know well, declared that the parish could not 'use, lease, grant, demise, alien, bargain, sell, and dispose of' property 'exceeding the yearly value of five thousand pounds.' In effect, Trinity was chartered as a medieval fiefdom. Should its earnings exceed five thousand pounds, they would be siphoned off by the parent church back in England."

Alex saw Reverend Provoost flash Judge Tankert a look at the word *fiefdom* — strong language to describe the ecclesiastical body to which, up until a few years ago, both men had served faithfully. But to both his and the reverend's relief — and delight — Judge Tankert was nodding his head in agreement.

Alex continued in a bolder voice:

"Yet all the while this stipulation was in effect, the parent church was busy loading Trinity down with properties it knew the church could neither develop nor utilize for the betterment of its own parishioners. Trinity was constantly forced to entreat for dispensations so that it could attempt to fulfill its mission for the spiritual, physical, and mental health of its congregation. In this sense, the church treated its colonial offshoot no differently than the crown treated the colonial government or the colonists themselves. Trinity's every action was hobbled by the mother church, lest the colonists grow too independent. This, gentlemen, is a policy forged in oppression, pure and simple, and it has no place in a liberated and free United States."

Alex paused for a breath. Up till now, he had merely been summarizing the facts of the case, and adding a political gloss that he knew would go over well with the rector and the judge, both of whom had been staunch patriots during the war. But the time had come to dazzle them with his legal mind.

"Now, I know what you're thinking," he continued in almost an offhand manner. "You're thinking that even if this is true, it is of no consequence: Trinity and the government of New York State agreed to renew the church's charter under the original terms after independence. And this, too, is true. Yet the renewed arrangement was entered into on the presumption that Trinity's original charter had been maintained according to English law for the duration of its existence. And there, my friends, we find that that is simply not the case. You see from these documents" — Alex handed each of the men a sheaf of papers that Nippers and

Turkey had copied out — "that the value of the land that the crown bestowed upon Trinity exceeds twenty thousand pounds in value. You heard me correctly, gentlemen. *Twenty thousand pounds.* And that is the undeveloped land, mind you, completely separate from any farming or manufacturing or domicile that may exist upon it. And so, I ask you, how can a document that stipulates that Trinity be limited to assets not exceeding five thousand pounds be considered valid when the issuer of that document itself violated the terms of the agreement? I'll save you the trouble of answering: It can't. The Trinity charter has been rendered null and void by the Church of England itself, and as such, cannot be extended to another governmental overseer, British, American, or otherwise. I submit to you, gentlemen, that Trinity is a free church, unbound by any laws save those that govern the citizens of the state of New York and the United States of America."

Reverend Provoost and Judge Tankert stared at him in amazement for nearly a full minute. Eventually the judge bestirred himself, asked a few questions, made a cursory examination of the documents in his hands. As a representative of the state of New York, he was no doubt aware that Governor Clinton would be less than pleased by this development, but Alex's reasoning was ironclad and he knew it. The Church of England had been hoist by its own petard. Trinity was free.

After Judge Tankert dismissed them, Alex had a quick meeting with Reverend Provoost. A formal hearing would still have to be held, and a new charter would need to be worked out with the state government in Albany. Alex knew that Governor Clinton had hoped to use the church's charter against Trinity in order to coerce it into surrendering a large portion of its lands to the state, from which it could reap tens of thousands in business deals and taxes. Clinton wouldn't be keen to give up the potential revenue from seizing the church's land without something in return. Alex had a big job ahead of him. But in the meantime, the church was free to develop its properties as it saw fit, which gave it enormous financial leeway and freedom. And part of that freedom was the ability to pay Alex a fee that would ensure his and his family's prosperity for years to come. If the job wasn't so pressing, Alex would rent a horse and set off after Eliza to deliver the remarkable news. A letter would have to do.

Reverend Provoost clasped Alex's hand firmly, then surprised him by pulling him in for an embrace.

"The church appreciates your ingenuity and your hard work, Mr. Hamilton. We look forward to a long and prosperous relationship."

"As do I, Reverend. Perhaps we might start with the matter of my wife's orphanage?" He was imagining the delight on Eliza's face when she read his letter informing her not just of their newfound riches, but the success of her scheme to help the abandoned children of New York. He could think of no better way to apologize for his outburst.

The reverend laughed. "If this scheme of yours plays out as you and Judge Tankert seem to think it will, I'll see to it that Trinity not only donates the Vesey Street warehouse to Mrs. Hamilton, but refurbishes it to her specifications as well. It is not an overstatement to say that you have saved us, Mr. Hamilton. Trinity Church is forever in your debt."

Alex left the rector's office walking on air. Wait until that odious Mr. Burr heard about this latest victory! He would be drowning in envy!

It was barely noon, yet Alex couldn't bring himself to go back to his office. Instead he headed home, but once he got there the emptiness of the place was more than he could take. Again he thought of taking off after Eliza. He was lost without her. But it simply wasn't possible. There were motions to be filed on the morrow, in this and in other cases. He was going to have to stay on his toes to make sure Governor Clinton's men didn't try to cut their own deal with the church that might deprive Alex of thousands of pounds.

But he simply *had* to tell someone his news. He was desperately lonely, and his wife had been gone for much too long. And so, ten minutes after he'd walked through his front door, he was heading back out into the late summer sunshine.

Ruston's was doing a bustling lunch-time business. Sally was working the ale room with two other barmaids. Alex asked her to send up a cider and one of those chilled ales — better make it two — then made his way upstairs. Later he would remember that he had been on his way to see Caroline Childress when he caught a glimpse of Maria's open door from the stairwell. When he told the story to Eliza, he would say that he went to her because he feared something was wrong, but the simpler truth was, that for whatever reason, it was Maria he wanted to celebrate with, not Caroline. It broke his heart how broken she looked the other night. Perhaps it was because he needed someone to apologize to, and Eliza was far away. Perhaps it was because Maria reminded him of his mother. Or perhaps it was just because he wanted to put a smile on her face.

He hurried down the hall. To his relief, he found Maria sitting in the window, staring out at the cloudy sky, which threatened rain.

"Mr. Hamilton!" she said brightly. "I

451

saw you approaching on Water Street. I had hoped you were coming to see me."

"I, ah, of course I was," Alex said, a curious statement that he realized was both not true and true at the same time. "May I come in?"

"Of course," Maria said, indicating the room's other chair.

Alex stepped inside, then hesitated by the door. He wasn't even sure why he was hesitating, until he realized he wasn't sure if he should close it or not.

You're being silly! he told himself. *She is not some maiden with her mother listening in from another room, and you are not her love-struck beau! She is a guest in a private inn! Close the door and stop acting like a fool!*

He pushed the door shut, resisting the urge to look up and down the hall. He had no idea why he felt like a fugitive, but he did.

He took a seat in the wooden rocking chair. He felt suddenly warm, and took off his hat and fanned his face with it.

"To tell you the truth," Maria said after a moment, "I wasn't sure, after our conversation the other day, if you would be back or not. I half expected Mrs. Childress to evict me the next day."

Alex's flush increased, and he fanned himself more ardently.

"Oh, Mrs. Reynolds, you must know that I would never do that! There is no doubt I was taken aback by the knowledge of your . . . of your deception, but after a night's reflection it seemed clear to me that any falsehood you told was for the sake of self-protection, and not to harm or misuse me. Indeed, as I look back on it now, I believe I overreacted. It seems unfair of me to have expected you to trust me, when so many people — so many men — have treated you so poorly before. And so, from the bottom of my heart, I entreat you to accept my apology. My behavior was not chivalrous and simply unworthy of you."

Alex wasn't sure where the flood of words had come from. Indeed, he wasn't even sure if he believed them. She *had* deceived him, after all. And for what? She couldn't have expected him to pay for her to stay at an inn so she wouldn't have to go back to her husband — it was hardly part of an attorney's modus operandi — and she must have known that if she wasn't legally married to Mr. Reynolds, then she had no need of a lawyer to help her with the divorce. Which raised the question: What exactly did she want from him?

He realized he was still fanning himself like a dowager trapped in a stuffy drawing room. He quickly set his hat down on the windowsill. Maria stared at it as though it were a bird that had flown in, and she was wondering whether to feed it or shoo it away.

"When you came in you were smiling," she said at last. "You are not smiling anymore. I am sorry to have put you in such a dispirited mood."

"Oh, it is not you," Alex said too quickly. He could not stand to see the frown on Maria's face and hear the self-reproach in her voice. What had she done wrong, save for being the victim of men of low principles? "It was just that when I came in I was thinking about something else. A legal triumph, if you will. I won't bore you with the details."

"Please," Maria said, half a smile creeping onto her face. "Bore me. I have sat in this room for a month now with no interlocutors save the barmaids, who started out friendly enough, but seem to have come to distrust me as time has gone on. I don't know if they have learned something about my past, or if it is just the usual fear that attaches to a single young woman, who is always, eventually, perceived as a threat by all the other women around her. It is not our sex's most admirable feature, though I suppose men are as capable of jealousy as women are."

"Indeed," Alex agreed. "We most certainly are." He had no idea what he meant by his statement, yet he suddenly felt jealous of Maria as well.

There was a silence, and then Maria prompted: "You were going to tell me about your legal triumph."

"Oh yes!" Alex smacked himself on the face. "How silly of me!" He regained his composure. "Confidentiality compels me to keep the name of the relevant party to myself, but I think I can fill you in on the gist of the narrative. Suffice to say that there is a certain venerable organization in our city whose financial hands, as it were, have been tied behind its back by a discriminatory charter that hearkens back to colonial times."

Maria smiled blankly. "I'm sure I have no idea what you're talking about. Indeed, the only word I'm relatively sure I understood in that sentence was *city.*"

Alex laughed. "Yes, I suppose it does sound rather cryptic. Well then. Let us say the organization was a church, and its charter — its license to do business, if you will — was structured in a way designed to prevent it from making money, rather than helping it to do so."

"But why does a church even need to make money?"

"Well, to serve its parishioners, of course. To build houses of worship and rectories, for a start, but also schools and hospitals and, and orphanages." His voice fell on the last word.

Maria looked at him searchingly. At length she said, "Is it true that you are an orphan like me?"

Alex was stunned by her question. He knew that his past as a man who had come from less-than-privileged begin-nings was fairly common knowledge in the states, but he did not think that the particulars of his childhood were widely known outside of his immediate circle of family and friends.

"In a way," he said finally. "My mother was called home when I was a boy of eleven. My father is living still, but he betook himself from the family when I was only an infant."

"Betook himself hither?" There was no suspicion in Maria's voice, as if she merely assumed that he had set off for some distant port to earn his fortune like so many other men.

Alex shrugged. "The last I heard he was on the island of Antigua, though that was some fifteen years ago."

"His business kept him away?" Maria's voice was still guileless, though a note of curiosity had crept in.

Alex shook his head. "I'm sorry to say that he abandoned my mother before I had turned two."

Maria gasped. "Oh, that is so awful! Why on earth would he do such a thing?"

Alex felt his head growing hot again and resisted the urge to reach for his hat or loosen his cravat.

"There were . . . irregularities . . . in my mother's . . . status."

Maria stared at him blankly for a moment. Then she surprised Alex. She threw back her head and started laughing.

"Oh, men!" she said. "*Irregularities! Status!* You think that by putting the real name to things that you will cause them to take shape, seemingly forgetting that they already exist."

Alex was unnerved by Maria's sudden turn to mirth. "Mrs. Reynolds, please. This is my mother we are speaking of."

"Actually, it was your father we were speaking of. A man callous enough to abandon his wife and child because of, how did you put it, irregularities? In her status?" Maria said with another mocking, bitter laugh.

"There were two of us, actually," Alex said after a pause. "My older brother, James, and myself."

"So he is twice the scoundrel is what

you're saying? Well, come on. Think of me less as a delicate female than as Moll Flanders come to life, full of wisdom about things of which you yourself pretend to be innocent. So tell me, what were the sins of which your mother was adjudged guilty by your father?"

Alex sighed, and then, almost against his will, he heard himself say: "She was still married to another man when she took up with my father."

It shocked him to hear the words come out of his mouth. He had never said them quite so plainly in his life, not even to Eliza, who had taken the better part of a decade to piece together the barest outline of the story.

"And this first gentleman. Did she leave him, or was he just another abandoner?"

"My mother left. The man was —"

"Violent? A womanizer? A drunkard? All three?" The bluntness with which Maria said these words brought a blush to Alex's cheeks, but he found them strangely liberating as well. It was so refreshing to hear things called what they were, rather than skulk behind circumspection and propriety. Yet he couldn't bring himself to speak quite so freely.

"My mother did not talk of him often, but I gather that he was not innocent of any of the malfeasances you describe."

" 'Any of the malfeasances you describe.' I say, Mr. Hamilton, that is a very fine way of putting it. Only I should wonder that your tongue isn't in knots from having to categorize such simple behavior thus."

"There is no call for using vulgar words to describe vulgar actions, Mrs. Reynolds."

"The truth is never vulgar, Mr. Hamilton, no matter how unpleasant it may be. What is vulgar is concealing it behind flowery rhetoric, as if that could minimize the very real horrors that were inflicted and endured. Do you think a bucket brigade can put out a conflagration if they are forbidden from saying the word *fire,* or a surgeon can treat a disease if he cannot bear to look at the infected parts of the body, or a general can make effective use of a cannon if he doesn't know how it rips an enemy combatant's head from his shoulders? Vice, like any other obstacle in life, can only be conquered by understanding it, and it can only be understood by describing it honestly, accurately, and fully. So enough of these *irregularities* and *malfeasances. What happened to your mother, Mr. Hamilton?"*

Alex shrank before the force of Maria's words. How dare she! It was as if she were asking him to rip off a scab at the dinner table. It was unseemly. And yet, and yet . . . and yet the truth was no scab. The wound was still fresh and would only begin to heal, as she said, if it were examined openly.

Still, it took all his effort to answer her question.

"Her first husband beat her," he spat out bitterly, "and she fled from him to the arms of my father, who abandoned her when he found out that the previous marriage had not been dissolved according to the letter of the law. And so, her reputation ruined, she was forced to drift from man to man on whatever terms they would have her, until at last she contracted fever and died. And when the notice of her death was published, her first husband appeared and confiscated what few possessions she had left to me and my brother, leaving us on the street to live or die as chance would have it!"

A long silence hung in the room after this outburst. At length, Maria said gently, "There now. Don't you feel better?"

He did. She listened well, and he felt free to unburden himself in a way because she knew the rough edges of the world in the same way he did. They were alike, the two of them. They were survivors.

They talked for the rest of the day. The deluge, once the dam had been breached, could not be held back. Alex told her the full story of his early years in St. Croix and Nevis. All the things he had never told Eliza, for fear that she would reject him for being too common. The meals taken with servants and stable boys, the expulsion from the Anglican school for being the bastard son of an adulteress, the pain of being ripped apart from James at the age of twelve, never to live with him as brother and brother again. Dressing in clothes that were little better than rags. Reading the same books four, five, six times because there were no others to be had. The constant need to prove he was ten times smarter, harder working, and more determined than every other boy. And even though he knew the circumstances of his birth had nothing to do with him, still, he could never shake the shame of it.

It was not quite accurate to say that they talked, however. It was Alex who talked. Maria listened, her face attuned to his, her eyes filled not just with sympathy but with understanding in a manner he had never received from his wife.

Maybe it was because Eliza, for all her independence and empathy, was still a woman of her class, a little too inclined to think of the poor as projects rather than real people, as evidenced by her meddling in the love lives of Emma Trask and Drayton Pennington, or maybe it was because he had never shared this part of his past with her, or maybe it was just because Maria was there, in front of him, and Eliza was hours and hours away. And though they had parted warmly, there had been a distance between them that hadn't been there before. They tried to ignore it, but the sting of their argument still felt fresh.

His monologue was fueled by frequent visits from Sally or one of the other barmaids; those ice-cold ales went down one after the other a little too smoothly. As the afternoon wore on, he sent for some mutton and vegetables, and later he added a slice of pie. The sun was long gone by the time he felt spent. He must have talked for ten hours or more.

"I apologize," he said finally. "I really don't know what came over me."

Maria shrugged as if she, too, hadn't noticed the passage of time.

"I hope I am not keeping you from anything."

"No, no," Alex said quickly. "The day's labors were completed early, and my wife and servants are away, so the house is empty."

"Empty houses are funny things," Maria said. "When a house is crowded, all one longs for is solitude. And yet when everyone has gone all you want is for them to come back. But I have learned from my month here that if you sit with it long enough the emptiness can come to seem quite full."

"I am afraid I am not much cut out for solitude," Alex said. "I am much too needy."

"Well then. I am glad I was able to be here when you needed someone."

"You are truly a remarkable woman, Mrs. Reynolds. I must apologize again for ever thinking less."

"All I did was listen."

"A vastly underrated skill. Some people — people like me — listen for information. But others listen for what's being said behind the words. It is a much rarer trait. You do it exceptionally well."

"How do you know? I mostly sat here in silence."

"*Because* you sat in silence. Like a priest in his confessional, you knew that if you gave any appearance of prurience or even curiosity, I would have stopped talking. And you knew, too, that I was only saying these things aloud to make them real, not to engage in the usual back and forth of genuine conversation. I did not want to investigate my past, only to

465

air it out like a musty rug, so that the odors would dissipate in the breeze."

Maria greeted this with still more silence, and Alex laughed.

"I fear I am just talking now to delay my departure. Truly, an empty house does not hasten one home."

"Of course," Maria said. "But don't let me keep you."

"It is I who am keeping myself," Alex said, standing up. "However, now I must be off. Somehow it is only Tuesday, and the bulk of the work week lies ahead."

Maria stood, too, to walk him to the door.

"Good evening, Mr. Hamilton. I shall always treasure this day as one of the pleasantest in my memory."

"As shall I," Alex said. And then, surprising himself, he leaned in for a hug.

Maria was surprised as well. But instead of turning her cheek to one side, she turned her face up to him.

Alex would remember thinking that he should have pulled away. Rather than heed this warning, he felt his arms go to her waist. Then her arms were on his shoulders. They pulled each other close.

"Maria, I can't do this," Alex whispered hoarsely. "I love my wife."

He did love her.

He loved her so much.

But Eliza was away, and Maria was here, in his arms, and the easiest way to get rid of temptation, it turned out, was to give in to it.

23

THE HARDEST PART OF GETTING SICK IS GETTING BETTER

Van Cortlandt Manor
The Bronx, New York
September 1785

Eliza spent three weeks being ill and another two recovering her strength. The doctor told her that he would have released her from bedrest sooner had she not been pregnant. However, it was of prime importance that she be fully fit before attempting the fifteen-mile journey back to Wall Street. Fall had come on early and damp, with chilly showers drizzling almost every day, and sodden, rutted roads making the journey substantially longer than it normally would be. Mrs. Van Cortlandt said she could not in good conscience allow Eliza to leave before she was "full hale and hearty." If worse came to worst, she said, Eliza would stay until after her time, and she and baby could return to the city in the spring.

"Tis better that ye return alive than that ye return anon," she said in her old-fashioned manner. "Ye must think of the future and not just your longing for the comforts of home and husband."

Still, Eliza longed very much for both.

Last week, when Eliza's fever had taken its dire turn, the Van Cortlandts, after consulting with Emma, had made the decision to keep the severity of Eliza's condition from Alex. It was the doctor's judgment during the first week that each night she survived was a miracle. It was unlikely that a messenger could even deliver news of his wife's illness to Alex before she succumbed to it, let alone make it from the Bronx to the southern tip of Manhattan.

"Let the man bask in ignorance," Mrs. Van Cortlandt had said to Emma. "The awful truth will be upon him soon enough. And if there be no sad news, then we have saved him the anguish of unnecessary grief."

469

But Eliza was strong, and though she did not even seem to realize she was ill, she still fought her fever valiantly. After a week the doctor pronounced Eliza out of danger, and now the decision was made to keep Alex in the dark for the sake of not needlessly worrying him (though Emma suspected that the Van Cortlandts also wished to keep the secret of their conspiracy a little longer, because Alex would undoubtedly be furious when he learned that his wife had nearly died and no one had told him). With the Van Cortlandts' permission, Emma penned Alex another letter saying only that Eliza's fever had been more severe than initially diagnosed, but that she had pulled through and was now on the mend, though still too weak to write. This was not exactly true — while her fever had indeed broken, Eliza remained in a delirium for two weeks more — but Emma was much too respectful of the Van Cortlandt name to contravene their wishes. She concluded by telling him that his presence would likely only distract Eliza, who would feel the need to attend to him rather than the other way around, and that he should not abandon his work to serve as nursemaid to his wife. Emma was in attendance, and Drayton, as well as the vast household of the manor, which counted more servants than Van Cortlandts within its walls.

In truth, Emma thought that Alex would ignore her admonition, and she expected him to show up any day. But when a full week had passed with neither word nor sign of him, she began to fear that her letter had not been delivered, and she wrote another. The description of Eliza's condition was the same, as well as the entreaty that he not burden himself with the journey north, but she did add a pointed comment about his silence, inquiring if he had received the previous letter (the Van Cortlandts had paid dearly for a farmhand to deliver it to his doorstep) and, if so, if everything were all right with him.

And though they hadn't heard *from* Alex, they were certainly hearing *about* him. News of his Trinity triumph had spread all over the island, putting the Hamilton name once again on the lips of every Manhattanite, urban and rural. The

Van Cortlandts, who were as thrifty and enterprising a Dutch family as ever sailed out of the Port of Amsterdam, took the pragmatic view that Alex was simply overwhelmed by the responsibilities of negotiating a new church charter as well as handling what must undoubtedly be dozens of requests by new clients, who would surely be banging down the doors of the most brilliant lawyer in New York.

Emma did, however, overhear Augustus Van Cortlandt, a fine-boned gentleman of sixty who never emerged from his chamber without his ascot knotted tight beneath his chin and his wig firmly in place, mutter under his breath: "Does the man have blood in his veins, or fish oil?"

To Emma's surprise, another week passed in silence. She had had a brief, concerned note from John, who seemed ready to abandon his studies to rush to his sister's side, but he didn't mention the whereabouts of his brother-in-law. Emma wrote back to say that his presence would likely do more harm than good, and he should pass along the same message to Alex. But though John wrote to say that he was ready to come at a moment's notice, he once again failed to mention Alex in his letter.

Another week passed, and another. Eliza awakened and began her painfully slow convalescence. Emma found herself lying to Eliza, telling her that she had heard from Alex on several occasions while Eliza was in her delirium, and that now, knowing his wife was out of danger, he was attending to matters of business that he had neglected out of worry before. She hated to lie to her friend and mistress, but Eliza was so weak that she did not dare say that no one had heard from Alex in over a month, lest the shock trigger a relapse. It was possible that Alex had been called away unexpectedly. Although he was not directly involved in the political sphere, he remained close to many of the senators in Philadelphia, and they continually turned to him for advice. For all she knew they had summoned him to Pennsylvania to attend to some urgent matter — a financial question, at which Alex was particularly adept, or maybe even a military one. Everyone knew England was far from content to lose its North American colonies and was scheming to get them back, and other European powers saw the fledging nation as ripe for the picking.

But in her heart she couldn't help but feel that something was wrong. Alex would have found a way to get a note to Eliza if he were well, even if it was just to say that he would be out of contact for some weeks. What a dark hour it would be if both Hamiltons were struck low at the same time, but fifteen miles apart! She was on the verge of leaving Eliza in the Van Cortlandts' care and making the journey herself, when at last communication appeared, in the form of John Schuyler and Betty Van Rensselaer.

They arrived in a golden brougham that Emma recognized immediately as the Beekmans'. The carriage, which was one of the finest in New York City, was known about town as the "Chariot of Apollo," and Emma's heart immediately lifted when she saw it. Such a magnificent conveyance could not possibly deliver anything other than good news. Which made the sense of horror she felt that much greater when John emerged from the opened door with a face that was at once distraught and, so it seemed to Emma, infuriated.

"I need to see my sister," he said by way of greeting.

Emma quickly explained that Eliza's condition remained fragile and he could not possibly approach her in such a dark humor. At this, the emotion in John's face deepened — the sadness as well as the fury.

"Has something befallen Mr. Hamilton?" Emma asked in a trembling voice.

"That base scoundrel!" John hissed. "If Burr doesn't kill him, I will!"

A terrified Emma was prevented from asking John what on earth he meant by the untimely arrival of Augustus Van Cortlandt, who had stepped down from the porch to greet his guests. John summoned all his Schuyler steel, acknowledging Mr. Van Cortlandt formally but briefly, then asking to be escorted to a private chamber. The visibly concerned old gentleman brought them to his own study on the first floor.

"My dear boy," he said. "What on earth

is the matter?" By now his wife had joined them, and both stared at him expectantly.

But John only shook his head. "No doubt all of New York will know the tragic tale soon, but for now, at least, I shall protect my sister's reputation," he said, pointedly shutting the door in Mr. and Mrs. Van Cortlandt's faces.

It was all Emma could do not to grab John's hands in entreaty. "Mr. Schuyler, please," Emma said. "You are frightening me."

"Be frightened now," Betty answered in a tone of disgust, "because soon all you will feel is rage."

Emma whirled on Betty. "With respect, Miss Van Rensselaer, you are not helping. Would someone *please* tell me what is going on?"

Just then there was a knock at the door.

"Emma?" Drayton's voice called, and Emma rushed to the door to let him in.

"If you please, Emma," John said, "this is not exactly news for servants' ears."

"Drayton is my fiancé," Emma said. "Anything you can say to me, you can say also to him." She said it proudly, although their engagement had been marred by concern for her mistress. She didn't find the heart to celebrate while Eliza was still so sick.

"As you will," John said. "I have not the energy to argue. And congratulations, by the way."

Drayton was allowed into the room, and the door shut up again. When everyone was seated, John began. "I cannot think of a way to say this delicately, so I shall just say it. My brother-in-law has contravened the bonds of his marriage."

Emma felt her head spin. She groped blindly for Drayton's hand. "I — I'm afraid I don't understand, Mr. Schuyler."

"This Reynolds woman whose case he took on back in June. Apparently she is a regular Moll Flanders and seems to have used her wiles to seduce my sister's husband."

"Oh, John, don't," Betty said in a peeved voice. "I told him," she continued to Emma and Drayton, "it matters not who the woman is and what she did. The responsibility lies full with Alex. Even if she did attempt to seduce him, it is he who consented to stray. She didn't force him."

"But this is quite unbelievable," Drayton said. "Mr. and Mrs. Hamilton love each dearly. He could never —"

"He could, and he did," John said, waving Drayton silent. "This Mrs. Reynolds — yes, she is married, too, or at any rate partnered with a man — is housed in Ruston's Inn on Water Street. It is a busy establishment in the heart of the city, and word has gotten out that Alex visited Mrs. Reynolds there and did not leave until near dawn the following morning."

"But . . . b-but . . . ," Emma stuttered helplessly. "I cannot believe it. How do we know anything untoward happened? Perhaps he was just comforting her."

"Is that what they're calling it these days?" Betty snickered.

"Betty, please," John said. "This is no time for levity." He turned to Emma sadly. "I, too, wanted to believe that it was merely a misunderstanding. But when I went to ask Alex about it, he refused to see me. He has been sleeping at his office. If these are not the actions of a guilty man, I don't know what are."

"Oh, but this is horrible, horrible!" Emma moaned. "Mrs. Hamilton is still so weak. The shock of this news could kill her!"

"Obviously we will not tell her until she is fully well," John said. "By then the news may be even more grim, though that could turn out to be a kind of blessing."

"What do you mean?" Emma asked.

"Do you know Aaron Burr? He is a lawyer and sometime opponent of Alex's, as well as our neighbor on Wall Street." Emma and Drayton nodded, and John continued: "Apparently the enmity between Mr. Burr and my brother-in-law has increased since Alex defeated him in court last year, to the point that Mr. Burr decided to chide Alex for his infidelity in open court. Alex was so incensed that he called him out."

"You mean . . . a duel?" Drayton asked incredulously.

John started in Drayton's direction, clearly unused to being asked questions by a servant, and unsure whether to answer. At length he turned back to Emma.

479

"They are to meet this evening at midnight at Mount Pleasant. A rather ironic choice of venue, given the activity in which they engage, but James Beekman has accepted the role of second to my brother-in-law, if only so that the ritual is performed properly."

Emma's head spun. This was all so unbelievable, and yet so easy to believe. Hadn't her own life been blissful one moment, then torn asunder the next? God had made humans frail creatures, and if men were the stronger in body, it was Emma's experience that they were weaker in spirit. Only rarely was it the venality of corruption that undid them. It was momentary infatuation and gilded temptation — one good push at just the right time, and they were knocked from the straight and narrow forever. Hadn't she seen it happen with her father?

She shook her head in an attempt to clear it. "Would you excuse me for a moment? I must retire to my chamber."

"Of course," Drayton said before John could answer (which caused the latter to glare at him in consternation). "Let me help you, my darling."

"Don't worry, it is nothing undue. I will be but a moment."

She let herself out of the room and ignored the stares of the Van Cortlandts as she made her way upstairs. As she rounded the landing, however, her pace began to quicken, and by the time she reached the second floor she fairly flew down the hall. She raced to Eliza's room, slipped inside, and locked the door behind her.

Eliza looked up from the pages of her book. She had asked the Van Cortlandts to bring her a copy of *Moll Flanders,* but she had once again failed to make it more than twenty pages into the novel, which rested open atop her white-sheeted, plump stomach, like a little hut at the top of a snowy hill. Eliza's hands rested to either side of the book, and there was a rapturous smile on her face.

"Come quickly," she said, waving Emma over. "Philip is awake and moving about! It is as though he is running a foot race!"

Emma could think of no way to refuse. She walked over to the bed, where Eliza grabbed her hand and placed it on her stomach. There, indeed, were the shifts and thumps of a writhing form beneath the cotton, beneath the skin. She did her best to smile.

"Oh, my darling, you look so distraught. Do not fear. He doesn't hurt me."

Emma didn't answer, just stepped back and pulled a chair over to the bedside and sat down. Eliza stared at her with a puzzled expression.

"Is that the Beekmans' carriage I heard outside?" she said when Emma did not speak. "Are James and Jane here?"

Emma stirred herself from her reverie.

"You can tell it is the Beekmans' carriage by the sound of the wheels?" she said in a reproachful voice. "You have been up again, haven't you, Mrs. Hamilton?"

"Ugh, I am so *bored*!" Eliza wailed. "I know I am not yet at my full strength, but I do not understand why I must languish in bed like someone with plague. I long to be home!"

Emma's face went white as a sheet.

"Emma! My dear, what is the matter? You look as though you have seen a ghost!" Suddenly Eliza's heart jumped with a thrill of terror. "Have you heard from Alex? Is something wrong?"

There was a knock at the door then, and the doorknob rattled.

"Miss Trask? Are you in here?"

"Is that John?" Eliza said, a confused half smile appearing on her face. "Emma, what on earth is going on? Why have you locked the door? And why do you look so frightened?"

Emma gulped visibly. "I have something to tell you, Mrs. Hamilton. I hate to do it and I am terrified of the effect it may have on you, but Mr. Hamilton's life hangs in the balance."

"What!"

Another, louder knock at the door. "Miss Trask, I command you to let me into this room this instant!"

"Go away, Mr. Schuyler," Emma called in a quiet but determined tone. "You are disturbing your sister. If you do not leave immediately, I shall ask Drayton to remove you. I know he is there beside you."

There was a pause, followed by the low murmur of voices, and then John's voice came again: "I am stepping away, but I beg of you: Do not do what I think you are doing."

Emma didn't reply, and after a moment footsteps could be heard walking down the hall. Eliza stared at Emma in helpless terror. She had flung her book aside, and her hands clung to her womb as if to protect the child within.

"Emma, please. Tell me what is going on."

Emma pulled her chair close to the bed and took Eliza's hand in hers. Slowly, haltingly, she began to speak. She had not John's bluntness, and it took her some minutes before she was able to communicate the gist of the situation. With each subsequent revelation Eliza's face grew paler and more remote, as if she were shrinking inside her own skin. Finally Emma reached the news of Aaron Burr's confrontation and the duel to be fought that evening.

Eliza was silent for several minutes after

Emma finished speaking. Her hand in Emma's was as tiny and limp as a fledgling fallen from the nest.

"Mrs. Hamilton? Are you — are you ill again?"

Eliza's silence persisted another moment, and then suddenly she roused herself as if awakening from a nightmare.

"I have to go!" she said, sitting up suddenly and flinging the quilt from her legs. "Emma, help me dress!"

"Mrs. Hamilton, no. The doctor says you are still too weak to travel!"

"Listen to me, Emma!" Eliza said, grabbing Emma's arm with taloned fingers that betrayed no hint of weakness. "I am going to Mount Pleasant to prevent this duel one way or another. If you or anyone attempts to prevent me, I swear I will bash my way out of here with a fire iron and throw myself atop the first horse, mule, or ass I see. Now help me change, or begone!"

She started to strip her nightdress off, and after a confused moment, Emma began to help her. She fetched undergarments and a simple woolen dress and helped Eliza slip into them. The dress had laces so that it could be let out to accomodate Eliza's pregnancy, and Emma left all but one undone, as Eliza was more than six months along now, and her belly had grown quite large. One time she tried to remonstrate with Eliza, but Eliza turned on her with such wild eyes that she fell silent. If something were going to stop Eliza, it would not be a single girl. And the truth was, she was not sure she wanted to stop her. She was furious at Alex for his betrayal, yet surely there was another answer besides death? And if anyone could stop this duel, Eliza could.

When Eliza was dressed and shod, Emma opened the door. The hall was empty. Drayton must have taken John downstairs.

"Take us out the back," Eliza said. "We shall commandeer a carriage and driver in the barn."

They tiptoed down the hall to the servants' stairs and made their way into the kitchen. But when Eliza pushed open the door and slipped into the room, she found Drayton standing there, clearly waiting for her.

Before Eliza could tell him to get out of the way, Drayton spoke.

"We'll take the Beekmans' chariot," he said. "Quickly now. Mr. Schuyler is shut up with the Van Cortlandts, and we can be away before they realize. They have not a carriage harnessed, and the horses are all in the pasture. By the time they can ready one, we will be too far away for them to stop us."

"Thank you," was all Eliza said, and the threesome hurried outside.

Eliza's mind was a whirl of images, yet somehow through the fog and fear, she felt the damp air on her face and in her weakened lungs, where it simultaneously burned and chilled her. It had been five weeks since she had been outside, five weeks since she had smelled naught but fire-warmed, smoky air, and the shock was as intoxicating as a glass of spirits. Her head swam.

"Mrs. Hamilton, please," Emma entreated. "You are still too weak."

Eliza merely shook her head and pressed on to the golden ball mounted on its four tall, spindly wheels.

"I am fine," she rasped.

A moment later and the ladies were seated inside and Drayton had clambered into the box. There was a whipcrack, and the carriage lurched into motion.

Eliza sank back into the plush leather cushions and let her eyes close. The short walk had taken every bit of her strength. As if from far away, she felt Emma adjusting the car rugs around her. They felt luxuriously soft and warm, and she opened her eyes.

"Leave it to the Beekmans to furnish their car with sable," she said in a weak voice. "Well, for once, I cannot chide them their extravagance." She laughed wetly. "Is anyone following?"

Emma lifted a shade and peered out. "We are already out of sight of the house," she said after a moment. "But no one is on the road at least. We are safely away."

"If I know John, he will commandeer a horse and come after us. A saddled rider will be much faster than a carriage." She paused for breath. "Well, never mind. He can shout at us, but he cannot stop us. Unless he brings a gun," she added after a moment.

"Mrs. Hamilton!"

"Calm yourself, Emma. No one is getting shot today. *No one,*" she repeated in a firmer voice.

They passed the five-hour journey in virtual silence. To Eliza's surprise, John didn't appear. Perhaps he realized that he couldn't stop his sister, or maybe he didn't want to. Eliza was the only one who could compel Alex to call off his duel, after all, and however grave the charges against him, he must have understood that she wanted her child to enter this world with both parents still in it.

Of the charges themselves, she didn't allow herself to contemplate them. That was another matter, for later. She did not want to think about it. She couldn't think about it without crying and she did not have time to cry.

She had no idea what would happen after. If she thought she might forgive him, or if she would remain married to him but live forever apart from him like so many couples, or if she would force him to give her a divorce. She only knew that she could not allow him to die before she had had a chance to wring his neck. His son could not grow up without a father. She had seen what it had done to Alex, after all. She would not inflict that on her own child — she would not allow Alex to pass on his own misery.

The Chariot of Apollo was by far the finest carriage she had ever been in, with every modern advantage to smooth the ride. But nothing could soften the passage over roads rutted by more than a month of constant rain. Every jolt hurt Eliza's bones, and she half wished her bouncing head would fall off her neck like it felt it wanted to, because it was throbbing so badly she could hardly see. But she bore the pains in silence and instead sat with her hands on her womb, soothing the growing life beneath her dress.

"There, there," she whispered over and over again. "Shh."

The sun set just as the moon started to rise. Eliza could see Emma peering nervously out of the carriage's windows at the lengthening shadows, and the jolts seemed to increase with the darkness. Under normal circumstances Eliza would have suggested they stop somewhere for the evening, but these were far from normal circumstances. She was in a race to save her marriage. No, not that. She was in a race to save her husband's life.

"The moon is nearly full," she said to Emma in the calmest voice she could muster. "It will provide enough light for Drayton to see."

Emma nodded but didn't say anything. The carriage juddered on its way. The squeals of the axles and the squeaks of the leather cushions seemed to grow louder as the nighttime silence deepened, a soft counterpoint to the rhythmic *clop-clop* of the horses' hooves. It had an almost martial cadence, Eliza thought, like the players at the head of a military column. She remembered Alex telling her about his march from Morristown to Yorktown near the end of the war, how at the end of days of marching, the steady beat of the fife and drum corps was the only thing that kept soldiers' feet moving. *I'm a soldier,* she thought. *I'm march-*

ing to war.

She must have fallen asleep, because she was suddenly aware of a strange sensation and realized they had stopped. A creaking sounded above them as Drayton clambered down from the box and the door was pulled open.

"We are here, Mrs. Hamilton."

Eliza took a moment to summon her energy. Her body felt as bruised as if it had rolled down a hillside strewn with boulders and fallen trees. Then the baby kicked beneath her fingers, her son, their firstborn son, the one they would name Philip, after her esteemed and wonderful father. A sense of calmness and purpose filled her. She remembered what she was fighting for. Not just her future, or Alex's, but Philip's. Her pain didn't fade, but her resolve overpowered it.

Nodding, she accepted Drayton's outstretched hand and stepped out into the night.

24
MIDNIGHT RENDEZVOUS

The Hamilton Town House
New York, New York
September 1785

He had thought nothing could equal his private shame, but he was wrong.

He had stared down at the latest letter from Emma informing him of Eliza's illness and understood how easily his life could have slipped away from him. Marriage was like a country, he realized, a union that lasts only when all the members involved actively work for its continuation. But while Eliza worked day in and day out to make the marriage a success, he had let his attention waver, and suddenly he found himself teetering at the edge of a precipice. Would he be able to jump back in time, or would the ground collapse beneath his feet? And would there be anything waiting for him if he did manage to escape the trap he had made for himself? He had no idea.

He forced himself to go to bed but lay awake tossing and turning in misery until at last the sun was up. He roused himself groggily, washed with the frigid water in his basin, threw on the first clothes he pulled from the wardrobe. In the kitchen he went through the motions of trying to light a fire, but his shaking hands couldn't produce so much as a spark, let alone a flame, and after ten minutes of increasingly ridiculous mummery he threw aside flint and steel and staggered out into the day.

As he pulled the door open he glanced into his front parlor, and there, over the fireplace, hung Eliza's portrait, painted last year by Ralph Earl. With her white wig and lightly powdered skin she had an ageless look to her. She could have been seventeen or seventy-seven. Her bright eyes, twinkling at some private amusement, stared into the future fearlessly, as if nothing could ever go wrong. His first thought was the girl in that picture was naïve to place her trust in him, but as he continued to stare at her calm expression, he realized that it wasn't Eliza who had been naïve. It had been he. She understood that, more than anything else, marriage required steadiness, and she delivered that every day since they took their vows a mere five years ago.

Five years. Half a decade. Three years shorter than the revolution. That was all the time it took for him to lose his way. How on earth did people do it for twenty-five, or fifty?

I could do it, said the eyes in the picture. *I would do it for you.*

If only you would forgive me. Please, Eliza, forgive me.

He pulled his hat over his eyes in shame and crept out into the morning.

Outside, his feet turned habitually toward Water Street, but it wasn't long before the sign for Ruston's appeared in front of him. He whirled about as if dodging enemy fire and trotted in the direction of Fraunces Tavern, but as it came into view he remembered that this was the place where General Washington had summoned his troops to bid them adieu at the end of the war. He had no place taking so much as a bowl of gruel at an establishment where so great a man — as true to his country as he was to his wife — had taken his last meal as leader of the Continental army. He wandered about aimlessly then, at last slinking into some hole-in-the-wall inn so dingy it did not even seem to have a name, and there he forced himself to eat a few slices of bacon more fat than meat and a couple of eggs whose odor suggested the fetid coop from which they'd been gathered. The coffee tasted like — oh, who knew. Burnt acorns, half-cured leather, moldy bread. He pressed himself to drink it down.

He walked past Turkey, Nippers, and Bartleby without greeting them and shut himself in his private office. He made himself go through the stack of papers there, amending and signing documents until a little after one o'clock, when it was time for him to head to court. It was a routine day, with nothing exceptional on the docket. Or at least Alex thought until he walked into the courtroom and saw the smirking face of Aaron Burr exchanging pleasantries with the judge, who for some reason was already on his bench.

Of all the days, he thought with a silent groan.

"Counselor!" the judge said with false brightness. "So nice of you to join us."

Alex glanced at his watch and saw that it was just past one. The proceeding wasn't due to start until one thirty. But something didn't add up. He had left his office just after one, and it was a ten-minute walk here. How was it still . . . ?

With a start, Alex realized his watch must have wound down sometime last night.

Sometime while he was with Maria.

He felt his face go bright red.

"I — I'm sorry, Your Honor, Mr. Burr. It seems my watch must have wound down during the — that is, I must have forgotten to wind it this morning."

"Too busy, no doubt," Burr said with snide wink, then took his place at his table.

If it was possible for Alex's face to go redder, it did. He felt the sweat beading under his shirt, which was suddenly uncomfortably clammy. An image flashed through his mind, half-sensation, half-mental picture, of the first day he had visited Maria at Ruston's when he had removed his jacket and waistcoat and then laughed off Sally's off-color conjecturing.

If I go any redder, Alex thought, *I shall become apoplectic.*

The proceeding passed in a blur. The affair was as purely formal as a chess game, the outcome all but predetermined. Alex made his moves, Burr made his countermoves, and then the judge handed down his decision: 20 percent for Alex's client, 80 percent for Burr's. It was somewhat less than Alex had expected, but not far off.

As he was packing up his satchel, Burr came over to Alex's table. His own papers were being shuffled into an embossed leather case by a fresh-faced assistant.

"I do so enjoy beating you," he said without preamble, and with more than his usual one-upmanship.

Alex couldn't be bothered to make eye contact. "I do hope your client enjoys his thirty-two pounds. Tell him not to spend it all in one place."

"Oh, it's not the amount that matters," Burr said as a rejoinder. "It's just knowing that you are not the golden boy everyone claims you are."

The edge in Burr's voice had turned genuinely nasty, and Alex paused in his packing to regard his rival. They had sparred in the courts for the past two years, and though it was well-known that Alex thought of Burr as a dilettante and Burr thought of Alex as a poseur, their animosity had never risen above the level of competitiveness between two headstrong lads who cannot bear to be anything other than the best at what they do. But Burr was looking at Alex as though he were something unpleasant on the bottom of his shoe. Not even his shoe. His horse's shoe.

"Is there something bothering you, Mr. Burr? If you would like to retry our case, I'm sure the judge has nothing better to do with his time. Perhaps you can win that last eight pounds."

At this, Burr grinned, his small but plump lips shiny with spittle. "You'll never guess where I breakfasted this morning."

Alex sighed and turned back to his papers. "You're right. I'll never guess."

"A little place over on Water Street," Burr continued as if Alex hadn't spoken. "A little seedy for my tastes, but I had no idea just how seedy it was."

Alex froze. It took an effort of will to stand up straight and look Burr in the eye.

"If there is something you are trying to say, Aaron, just say it."

Burr shrugged. "I don't have to say it. The barman there, a fine chap named Thomas, is telling everyone who comes in."

There was no blush this time. Alex felt all the blood drain from his face as his skin turned to ice.

"Saying *what*, Mr. Burr?"

"Oh, come now, Alex, don't make me be so crass as to put it in words. I'd much rather hear your own flowery expression for stepping out on your wife."

When something like this happened in

books of chivalry, the affronted party would slap his accuser with an empty glove. For better or worse, Alex wasn't wearing gloves, and he never read books of chivalry either. His punch sent Burr hurtling backward, where he sprawled across the foremost pew.

Fortunately the judge had gone, and the bailiff as well, or Alex might have had a night in jail to add to his troubles. Although if he had been hauled off, it might have saved him from saying what he did next.

"You slander me, sir, in front of these esteemed men of my profession," he said, even as he felt his guilty heart beating as he indicated the dozen or so people who remained in the courtroom, who looked less like lawyers and clerks than spectators at a cockfight. "In front of these witnesses, I assert my rights as a gentleman. I call you out."

Burr, who had struggled a bit to stand up and was now clearly resisting the urge to touch his lip to see if it was bleeding (it was, copiously), nodded contemptuously.

"They say you rushed heedlessly to

your death at Yorktown, and it was only the poor aim of the British that allowed you to survive. I am no redcoat, sir. I won't miss."

Without another word, he whirled on his feet and, after steadying himself, marched out of the courtroom.

Alex's head was reeling as he left the courtroom, as if he had taken the punch, not Burr. It seemed to him that everyone was staring at him. But were they staring at him because he had punched Aaron Burr, or because of what the barman had charged him with?

Though the claims had some validity, he could see no way around it: He would have to return to Ruston's and inform Maria of what was being said about them. He dragged his feet as slowly as he could over the boards, but within less than half an hour he was there.

Alex did not fool himself into thinking that he was in love. He felt a kind of tenderness toward Maria, it was true, but it was a tenderness born of pity rather than affection. He wanted her to know that not every man would treat her as roughly as James Reynolds had, and who knew how many others, but he knew that in the end it would be the same. He would go back to his wife, and she would be left alone. Perhaps Eliza wouldn't take him back, for which he could hardly blame her. He had sullied her name as well as his. But that didn't change things. His marriage might very well be destroyed, however, he could not marry Maria, and would not, even if it was an option.

What he didn't realize was that Maria understood this as well as he did, if not better. Which is to say, when Alex entered the inn he found Caroline in the barroom, clearly waiting for him. After a rather formal greeting, she informed him that Mrs. Reynolds had checked out that morning and left no forwarding address. She deflected his questions coldly, yet there was something she was concealing. Alex thought it was less likely that she had sent Maria packing than that she had given her money to disappear. She handed Alex a note, then stood to take her leave.

Alex assumed it was his bill, but when

he looked down he saw only his name in Maria's handwriting.

He sighed heavily. "Very well then. If you will send me my bill at my office, I will see that you are paid immediately."

Caroline's lip curled in disgust. "There will be no question of payment, Mr. Hamilton. It is bad enough that you have associated my establishment with this kind of affair, but if people think I received compensation for it I should die of shame." She took a breath. "You have done far too much for me to allow me to denounce you openly, and as an innkeeper I am familiar enough with men's characters that I can attribute this to infantile weakness rather than pure venality of character. Nevertheless, Mr. Hamilton, you have shamed me, and shamed that woman, and your wife and child-to-be, but above all shamed yourself and your good name. You will understand when I say that you are no longer welcome at Ruston's Inn. It gives me no pleasure to say this, but whatever your virtues, you have demonstrated that you are not a man who can be trusted."

Without another word, she turned and

walked away.

For the first time in his life, Alex had no idea what to do. Dumbly, he folded open the card in his hands.

Do not judge yourself too harshly, Mr. Hamilton. You ought not to have done what you did, but I ought not to have put you in that position. Thank you for all you have done for me, and good-bye.

Maria Reynolds.

Alex didn't know if the fact that she signed the name of husband-pretender made things a little bit better or that much worse.

This being New York, and Aaron Burr being a busy man, and a contemptuous one, it took days to work out the details of the duel, which was at last set a fortnight hence, when Burr should have returned from an errand before Congress. In the meantime Alex lay low and went about his work as mechanically as he could. In many ways his life was the same as it had been before, save that

Eliza was not with him, and a series of increasingly plaintive notes from Emma and a few from John, who had moved into his dormitory at Columbia, were piling up on the table in his entryway. He couldn't bear to write to his sick wife, for writing her meant lying to her, and that he could not do in a letter. Plus, he felt wretched that he was so preoccupied with the duel, his guilt, and hiding from the public eye that he barely noticed that Eliza had been gone a whole month and was sick during most of it! How was she faring? And what of their son?

But at last the appointed day came, and he found himself sitting in a bedroom in Mount Pleasant. The room was large and elegant, with a picturesque vista of the East River from its windows, yet had an air of neglect about it, quite at odds with the elegance of the rest of the mansion. The marble top of the bureau was dusty, the curtains were sun-faded, and the bed skirt had been nibbled by moths or mice.

He held a pistol in both hands as though it were a kind of relic, not fragile or holy but filled with mystery, as if it possessed the power of life and death inside its intricate layers of burled walnut and engraved silver and tooled steel. As indeed it did.

James had installed him in the room to give him a moment to collect himself.

"It is customary to write a note to those you may leave behind," he said. "I imagine that yours will be quite long." His voice was not quite hostile, but its forced neutrality sounded somehow more alienating, as if it were only the mores of social civility that kept him from spitting in Alex's face.

"This was Major André's room," James said then. "You remember him, don't you? He was that dashing young British soldier all the girls were in love with. My father invited him to stay with us, and he repaid that hospitality by sneaking out to meet with Benedict Arnold and help him in his treasonous conspiracy against the Continental army, for which actions he was well and justly hanged." James cast his eyes around the spy's one-time chamber, then looked back at Alex. "A fitting place for you."

He stepped out then, and closed the door behind him.

Sometime after he left, Alex removed the pistol James had given him and inspected it. It was as fine a piece of craftsmanship as you would expect a Beekman to own, and could easily be mistaken for ornament rather than weapon. Still, weapon is what it was, and he took the time to familiarize himself with it. He had been to battle on three separate occasions, but always with rifle and bayonet, and had fired a pistol only a handful of times in his life.

When he was certain he could operate it, he set it back in the case with its powder bag and tamping rod and single piece of shot.

James had also provided him with pen and ink and parchment, and now he turned toward those. What an absurd custom! To have a man write his own epitaph when he did not even know if he would die. Yet what else was he to do? Among the many transgressions he had made against his wife and future son, few would be greater than if he were to depart this life without at last attempting to explain his actions.

Once again, he found himself without

words. He who had written as many as forty pages a day in General Washington's employ about every subject, from military strategy to treaty negotiations, could not even begin to think how to summarize his actions of the past month. He could look back on each and every step he had taken, from the most innocent to the most carnal, yet the person he saw in his mind's eye was as much a stranger to him as he would be to someone on the street. What had that man been thinking? What had he been feeling? Alex had no idea. It was as if something had compelled his limbs to move while his mind was elsewhere.

Yet that was too easy an explanation, and too soft on himself. No one had made those decisions except him, and if anything, his blame was only compounded by the lack of consideration he had given his deeds. The man who says he is a stranger to himself is in fact the man who refuses to know himself, because he cannot bear to see his own mortality, the weaknesses of mind and body that make him human.

He forced himself to pick up the pen

and dip it in the well.

"My dear Eliza," he wrote, and stopped.

As he looked at the words, he felt that he had no right to use them. To speak to her so intimately, from beyond the grave, when she had at least some awareness of the ways in which he had abused her and their vows. It was too audacious.

Yet how else could he address her than as he always had? His feelings toward her hadn't changed after all. They had only been . . . eclipsed for the briefest of moments, by baser, more mysterious urges.

He dipped the pen again, brought it to the page, forced himself to write without knowing what was going to come out.

"Best of wives and best of women," he scribbled at last. Tears sprang to his eyes as the pen fell from his hand. Tears of self-reproach and self-pity, neither of which he was entitled to.

"What a fool I am!" he said aloud.

Just then there was a knock on the door. Soft. Not tentative but . . . feminine.

Alex turned in his chair toward the door.

"Enter," he called.

The knob turned, the door slid inward on its hinges. The form of his wife came into view. So unexpected was it that it was as if the painting over his mantel had sprung to life and appeared at Mount Pleasant.

Alex felt a surge of energy rush through his limbs and the overwhelming desire to run to his wife's arms. But at the same time he felt a deadening paralysis and the urge to shrink beneath the desk behind him.

"Eliza," he said finally. He could think of nothing else to say.

Eliza didn't answer. She stood on the threshold of the room for a moment, then walked in. She didn't close the door behind her.

She looked around at the peeling wallpaper and the dust-coated furniture. "Jane told me that this was Major André's room, the last time I was here."

"James told me the same thing, just a few moments ago."

Eliza didn't seem to have heard him. "He was a principled man. His allegiances may have contravened ours, but his values were the same. I am told he went to his death with his head held high and did not reproach the men who hanged him, because he knew they did what justice demanded. He died for what he believed." Her eyes finally settled on him. "Can you say the same?"

Alex didn't know how to answer, and he sat in silence.

"Can you say that it is worth dying to defend yourself from an accusation which is, by all accounts, true? What is it you are dying for, then? So that you can pretend that you are an honorable man? That would seem to make you both a liar and a fool."

Alex bestirred himself to speak. "If women were admitted to the bar," he said, "men would run in fear whenever you entered the room."

"Do not!" Eliza said, a note of anger entering her voice for the first time. "Do not use your smooth words on me, Mr. Hamilton, to confess your sins while simultaneously wooing me with your wit and charm. I am *pregnant,*" she continued. "That is what matters here."

"My darling!" Alex all but wailed. He knew the endearment wasn't his to use, but he couldn't stop himself. "I am not afraid of death, but dying with you believing the worst of me would be the worst of fates."

"What! Are you going to deny it now, to me, after the base stories have been flying around New York for a month and more? Have you that much gall? If so, I wish I had saved myself the trouble of flying here!"

"I deny only what I did not do. I admit fully, openly, and shamefully to what I did."

"Oh, please," Eliza spat in a disgusted voice. "Enough of your fancy phrasings. Come, Counselor Hamilton, tell me some pretty tales about how you did not — did not —"

Eliza's voice cracked, and Alex had to grab his chair to keep himself from running to her. He knew it would only make things worse.

"In a moment of terrible weakness, I betrayed you, and I wish I could take it back, take everything back," he said desperately. How could he forget his wife? His vows? His love? He was a fool, a terrible fool who did not deserve love or mercy and forgiveness, only death.

Death would be kind. He would welcome it.

But more than death, he wanted his life. He wanted his wife. His beautiful, loving, wonderful wife. He wished he had never met Maria Reynolds. Why had he done what he did? Why?

Eliza said nothing. Alex found the silence unbearable and continued talking.

"I understand if you would forsake me. I will release you from your vows if you ask," said Alex. "If Burr's bullet finds its mark in my chest I shall consider it my due punishment. I love you and only you, my dearest darling. I am so ashamed."

Still, Eliza said nothing. Alex's fingers dug into his chair so violently that he heard the old fabric tear beneath them.

"Darling, please, say something!"

At last she turned to him.

"I want to believe you," she said. Her eyes were full of sadness and steel. "Though I am not sure what difference that makes."

Alex couldn't help himself. "Is there nothing else? Is there — is there nothing left of us?"

Eliza closed her eyes for a moment. Her breath was heavy in the quiet room.

Her eyes opened again. "When Emma told me what had befallen my marriage, and what fate awaited you, my first thought was, *the father of my child must not die.* After your story, that remains my only thought on the matter. Later, I am sure I will have other thoughts, but I do not wish even to wonder what they will be. I only know that I don't want you dead." She fixed him in the eye. "Call it off, Alex. I command it. Give Aaron whatever he wants in compensation, but do not place your life in jeopardy, or his."

He didn't speak. Just nodded.

She looked at him a moment longer, then her eyes fell to the table in front of him. She saw the paper. The letter he had been writing to her. She walked toward him slowly. He wanted to hide it from her but had not the strength.

She picked it up, squinting slightly in

the candlelight. James had not provided him with a lamp. She stared at the page for a long time. Alex wanted her to react in some way. To crumple it off or laugh in his face or burst into tears, but she merely inspected it as she would a mercer's bill, then set it back on the table and turned and left the room.

25
FORGIVENESS AND FAMILY

The Hamilton Town House
New York, New York
April 1786

"I do think it will be fair after all," Eliza said, as she stepped through her front door into the mid-morning haze. "The sky looks clear to the west. I predict sunshine by noon."

"I hope you're right," Emma answered her. "Only I should hate for baby Philip to be caught in the rain. He has been a touch colicky this week."

"Baby Philip is a Schuyler; a little rain won't faze him," Eliza answered. She leaned toward her governess and bestowed a kiss on the swaddled bundle in her arms. A pair of pale blue eyes fluttered open, focused on her blearily, then drifted closed again.

"Shall I carry him?" Eliza said. "It is but a short walk to the church."

"Oh, I shouldn't like to burden you. It is only a month since you have been anything like your old self. And the walk is longer than you think, and Philip heavier than you realize. Let me carry him to church and you can hold him once we arrive."

Eliza didn't protest. The last few months of her pregnancy had been, not onerous exactly, but less than pleasant. Her bout with pneumonia — for that was what it was — had left her with weakened lungs, and even mounting a flight of stairs, especially with the extra weight she was carrying, all but exhausted her. For the final month her doctor confined her to bedrest. She had thought a month in bed would be unbearable, but the truth was it seemed she could never get enough sleep, and even when she was awake she felt fog-headed and fragile. The doctor attributed it to the pressure the baby was putting on her internal organs — judging from the size of her womb, he was *enormous* — but Eliza sensed the source of the trouble was mental rather than physical. The emotional impact of "the incident," as she had taken to referring to the depressing events of last fall, had been greater than she realized, and lasted longer than she expected.

But she had forgiven him.

It was an impossible feat, and impossible even to think that her family — the three of them — had survived intact.

And yet, there they were. Intact, and if their love was not what it was, no longer innocent of despair, it was stronger, and sweeter for surviving such a tragedy. She loved him more than she ever would, and loved him as much as she ever did. Her love was fierce and abiding and deep enough to cushion even the deepest blow. Such a blow it was — but she had weathered it. They both had. For her son, and the many more sons and daughters to come. They were a family, and Alex would always be her husband.

"Where are our menfolk?" she said now.

"Drayton was just finishing changing out of his uniform," Emma said. "He should be right down. I'm not sure where Mr. Hamilton —"

"I'm here!" Alex's voice came down the stairs just then.

"We're both here." Drayton's voice came from behind and below them. "Sorry to keep you waiting, Mrs. Hamilton."

Eliza turned and bent over the porch's balustrade to see Drayton emerging from the door to the kitchen located beneath the steps. He had shed his footman's uniform for a handsome suit that Eliza had insisted on giving him once his engagement to Emma was official. She had gone all out on it, declaring that if Drayton was going to accompany them in society, she would not have him humiliated by dressing in livery or secondhand, shabby clothes. The suit had an emerald and ruby floral motif woven across a field of midnight blue, wide collars and cuffs in pristine white silk, double-vented tails, silver buttons, and a gleaming silver-threaded arabesque dancing around the seams. The tricorne hat was trimmed with fur, and the accompanying blouse sported yards of lace at throat and wrists as white as morning fog. The breeches were snowy white, and tucked into a pair of black leather boots so shiny she could see her face in them from one flight up. The suit had been some weeks in the making, and this was Drayton's first public outing in it. Eliza was quite pleased with the results.

"Oh, look at you!" she said. "You'd think it was *you* getting married today!"

"Mrs. Hamilton, if you please!" Emma's face had gone bright red. "You know Drayton is sensitive about that subject."

Though she and Drayton had been engaged for over half a year, Drayton had insisted on delaying the marriage until he could afford to give his fiancée a proper ceremony, with a new dress for her and a new suit for him, and in Trinity Church to boot. Emma had protested she would be happy marrying in the Hamiltons' parlor with naught but their employers for witnesses, but Drayton refused to yield. Though she was marrying a "mere footman," as he said, he would give her the day in the sun she deserved.

"I am rather more uncomfortable in this suit," Drayton said, glancing up at Alex, who had appeared on the steps above him and was similarly dressed, albeit in sea green. "I must say, I do pity gentlemen who have to dress this way every day. It took me nearly an hour to strap myself in, and I am not even wearing a wig. Oh, but you look lovely, my darling," he added, his bride coming into view as she descended the steps to street level.

As it happened, Emma was also in a new dress today, another gift from Eliza. The dress was pale blue to Drayton's midnight hue, but with similar embroidery, with full skirts and a modest square neckline, but fully exposed shoulders that Emma was covering with a translucent lace shawl that did more to accentuate the hollows of her collarbones than conceal them.

"I told the tailor I wanted them to complement each other without being all matchy-matchy," Eliza said, as Emma took her place beside her fiancé, the two of them looking the very picture of youthful beauty and vigor. "I imagined the two of you appearing in them, and I wanted everyone to know you were together. And after all the grief I put poor

Emma through last summer about John, it seemed cruel to make her go to his wedding in one of my leftover dresses."

"Your leftovers suit me well, Mrs. Hamilton," Emma said, pulling at the shawl around her shoulders. "This is much too fine for me."

"Nonsense," Eliza said. "Between my illness last fall and baby Philip, I owe you so much more than I could ever repay. This dress barely qualifies as interest on the debt. Well, are we all here?"

"All here now," Rowena's voice came from the kitchen door. She emerged in a dark brown dress with burgundy accents — a little out of style but still quite fine — she had absolutely refused a new frock from her mistress. As she locked the door with a ring of keys she dropped in her coin purse, Eliza noticed a few flecks of flour on her cook's fingers. "I just wanted to set a few loaves to rise. We shall have fresh bread for everyone right after services."

"Oh, but it will only be —" Eliza began.

"Darling, you look beautiful!" Alex's voice sang out, and his arm slipped through hers. "Come, we must be on our way or we'll be late to your brother's wedding."

Eliza felt Emma and Drayton looking at her with questioning eyes. "Indeed," she said, "look at the time!" though she did not pull out a watch. She started walking so abruptly that Alex was tugged after her like a distracted dog at the end of a leash.

"Your enthusiasm will your own undoing," Alex whispered in her ear.

"Thankfully I have you to shut me up," Eliza whispered back. "I would hate to spoil John and Betty's big surprise."

"To think that after all of Mrs. Hamilton's efforts to push Emma on Mr. Schuyler and Drayton on Miss Van Rensselaer, it was Mr. Schuyler and Miss Van Rensselaer and Emma and Drayton who ended up together," Rowena sang out. "It is so funny how things work out, isn't it?"

"Indeed it is," Alex said in a musing voice. Eliza felt his arm tighten a bit around hers, though she couldn't help but wonder if he meant John and Betty, or himself and his wife.

For it hadn't just been the pregnancy

that made the fall difficult, or the lingering effects of pneumonia. Upon their return from Mount Pleasant, after Mr. Burr withdrew the charges and the duel was called off, she had directed Alex to move into John's room across the hall, which her brother had vacated for the dormitories at Columbia. Even after baby came, three months later, Alex remained there, with Philip sleeping in a crib at the foot of her bed. Their separate sleeping arrangements had continued until just three weeks ago, when they threw their first party since the baby had come.

It was an engagement party for John and Betty, and none other than James Madison, having somehow learned of John's or Betty's fondness for his whiskey, had sent an entire *barrel* of it up from his estate in Virginia. The party had gone until three or four in the morning, and when at last the guests had been shooed home (or covered with blankets where they had passed out on couches and chairs), Alex and Eliza picked their way upstairs, leaning against each other heavily. At the top of the stairs, Alex pushed the door open to their room by habit, catching himself only after the crib came into view.

"I'm sorry," he said, his voice suddenly sober. "I'll go back to —"

"No," Eliza said, catching his arm. "Stay. Please."

She lifted her lips to his, and he took them hungrily, as a parched man to water.

"Eliza," he said, his voice hoarse and tears flowing down his cheeks. "I love you."

"I've never stopped loving you," she told him, as he buried his face in her neck and took her straight to bed, where, just as promised, they were blushing bride and eager groom once more.

In the ensuing three weeks, it felt like a burden had been lifted from Eliza's shoulders. She realized that she had been holding on to her anger at Alex, and even though she was entirely justified to do so, there was no benefit to it. Either she truly forgave her husband or she didn't. If she didn't, then there was no point in continuing the marriage. And if she did, then she must do so fully. She must remember the man she had married, and why she had married him. And to her surprise, he was right there waiting for her. He had always been waiting, and he always would. She never gave Maria Reynolds another moment's thought.

The sun burned off the last of the mist as they walked to Saint Paul's. As they turned onto Broadway, Alex glanced south at the large construction site a few blocks down.

"Work on the new church proceeds apace," he said. "Reverend Provoost thinks it will be done in but a few years' time."

Eliza glanced down at the site, which at this point looked more like an open quarry than a building. Massive blocks of brown and gray stone were piled in a huge ziggurat waiting to be laid in place.

"It will be quite large, won't it?"

"Nearly ten times the size of the old church. It is a church built for the future of a great city."

"And they couldn't have done it without you. I hope they remember that one day."

Alex didn't answer, and Eliza regretted speaking. It was salt in an open wound.

For the repercussions from the Reynolds scandal hadn't just been marital. Eliza could choose to forgive her husband, but New York society was less forgiving, or perhaps just too in love with a scandal. Invitations didn't dry up, but they certainly dwindled, as did new clients to Alex's office. But the biggest blow had come from the church whose finances Alex had saved. Reverend Provoost had called Alex in for a private meeting the week after he and Eliza returned from Mount Pleasant and the aborted duel.

The Hamilton name had been tarnished, they were told, and he could not have it associated with the church. Though he had planned to use Alex as counsel in the church's reorganization and ongoing affairs, he didn't see how that was possible any longer. He had made Alex a generous payout, enough to ease the Hamiltons' financial load for a few years, but far from the fortune he could have earned. While it was an unfortunate situation, Alex had been in no position to protest.

Now Eliza squeezed her husband's arm.

"There are more important things than money. How are your discussions with Mr. Madison going? Do you think you will be able to put together this constitutional convention you have been talking of?"

"It is slow going, but I think we shall pull it off," Alex said, the enthusiasm returning to his voice. "There are still several opponents to the idea of a cohesive central government, not the least of which is the redoubtable Mr. Jefferson. But even he is realizing that without something to hold the states together financially and militarily as well as bureaucratically, we shall either drift apart into a hodgepodge of warring kingdoms like medieval Europe, or, even worse, be picked apart by foreign powers who will find no United States army to oppose them, just a few scattered state militias."

"Yes, yes," Eliza said, patting her husband's hand. "Save the speeches for Freedom Hall. We are on the way to a wedding, not a war council. Do you think the convention will happen soon?"

"Everything takes longer than one wants it to," Alex replied, "but I think we shall be able to organize something by next year, or 1787 at the latest. General Washington has yet to throw in his support, but I have read enough of his letters to know how bored he is down there on his plantation. Once he throws his weight behind us, it will be a fait accompli."

"It is good to hear you sound so enthusiastic," Eliza said. "I know the winter was hard for you."

"I am enthusiastic about more than just politics these days," Alex said, his voice suddenly thick with emotion. "But I owe its return to my life, and everything else I possess, to you."

Eliza's voice caught in her throat, and it was a few steps before she could speak. "Papa used to say that no one could call the cows in from the field as well as I could."

"Why, Mrs. Hamilton, are you comparing me to a cow?"

"I was very fond of our cows. You should take it as a compliment."

Their conversation continued for a few

more minutes until they arrived at the church. Then there was a good twenty minutes of milling around and greeting the guests. General and Mrs. Schuyler had not been able to come down from Albany — the general had taken a nasty fall from his horse and fractured his ankle, and though the injury was not serious it precluded long-term travel, which might lead to sepsis. Angelica was in London, of course, and Peggy had written last December to announce that she was with child again and would likely be too far along to make the journey.

It turned out she was right on one count: She was certainly far along. Eliza did not recognize the enormous figure who hauled herself out of a pew and planted herself in front of her.

"Oh, excuse me, madam, I was just —"

"Madam!" a familiar voice exclaimed. "Is that any way to greet your sister?"

"What? Peggy? Is that you? Peggy!" For there, beneath a wig the size of a topiary and a ghostly gray maquillage and what looked like hundreds of yards of orange and green silk spilling around her swollen womb, was the beaming, mischievous smile of Eliza's younger sister.

"I would throw my arms around you, but I'm not sure they'll reach!" she said, laughing.

"Oh, shut up and hug me!" Peggy said, hauling her sister close and wrapping her in folds of silk and orange blossom scent.

"Darling! It is so lovely to see you!" Eliza said when at last they let go of each other.

Peggy took a step back to show off her figure. "There's certainly a lot of me to see, isn't there? I think I have inherited Mama's propensity for twins. Either that or I'm giving birth to a five-year-old."

"If it's possible, you are even more radiantly beautiful than you've been."

"And if it's possible, you are even more of a honey-tongued politician than your husband. But I'll take it," Peggy said, "because I'm pretty sure my waistline isn't bouncing back from this one."

There were sloppy kisses then from baby Cathy, who was sitting on the pew with her nanny and was desperate to greet "Aunt Wiza," and then a rather drier lip-brush from Stephen, who, though all of twenty-one years old and still as thin as ever, had acquired the middle-aged mien of an Old World prince standing on a hillside regarding his troops about to go into war. "Such brave soldiers," he murmured into Eliza's ear. "Such fine, brave soldiers."

"Goodness, Stephen, lighten up," Eliza said with a laugh. "It is a wedding, not a funeral!"

"Oh, indeed," Stephen agreed, as if he were sprinkling the first handful of dirt upon a casket. "A most joyous occasion."

"Do not mind him," Peggy said. "He got like this right before Cathy was born. He is already contemplating how he can possibly divide our minuscule estate in half to support each of our children — or, if I have twins, in thirds."

"Can't he just give them each a county and have done?" Eliza joked.

"He could, but that would still leave him with four counties left over!" Peggy would have doubled over in hysterics if her swollen waist had let her.

"Careful now," Eliza remonstrated. "I will not have you shaking out your child or children and stealing my day."

"Your day? I thought John and Betty were getting married."

"Oh, they are, they are," Eliza said. "It's just, you know, it's not every day one's little brother ties the knot."

"We've got two more," Peggy teased. "Three? I lose count . . ."

"Even so, I want everything to go off smoothly," Eliza insisted.

Peggy peered at her suspiciously. "Eliza Schuyler Hamilton, what are you cooking up?"

"Who, me?" Eliza said, pressing a hand to her chest. "I should think today's nuptials are a lesson in why I should never meddle."

"Indeed you shouldn't," Alex said, coming up behind her. "Nor, apparently, should you be left alone. Peggy, it is lovely to see you," he added, bowing at his sister-in-law.

"And you, too," Peggy added, though her bow was somewhat more perfunctory. It was the first time she had seen Alex since the "the incident," and she was clearly not ready to just brush it under the table. Alex, for his part, didn't push it.

"We are being given the order to take our seats. Stephen, if you would join me backstage, as it were?"

Stephen nodded gravely and set off for the vestry. In the absence of fathers on either side — General Schuyler being laid up, and Stephen and Betty's father having passed away when the two were still children — Alex and Stephen had happily consented to give away the bride and groom.

"My darling, I'll see you soon," Alex said, brushing a kiss on Eliza's cheek, then hurrying after his brother-in-law.

Peggy watched him go with suspicious eyes even as she and Eliza took their seats.

"So, all is well with you two?" Her voice was as doubtful as the pout on her lips.

Eliza took a moment before answering to look after her husband as he disappeared through a door at the rear of the church. Then she turned to her sister and nodded. "It is, in its way, better than it has ever been."

Peggy looked unconvinced. "I do not see how that can be, after such a —"

Eliza put up her hand, then took her sister's in her fingers and squeezed tightly. "I appreciate your concern, Peggy. I know that should something threaten me you would defend me as a lioness defends her pride. But I want you to believe me. Though I would never have wished for such an experience, and want never ever to experience anything like it again, yet there are some trials that leave you stronger. Older, perhaps, and more guarded, but more mature, and more able to see your partner for what he truly is rather than the paper-doll image of a husband you made when you were but a teenager."

Peggy sniffed. "So your hero has feet of clay."

"Angelica wrote that he flew too close to the sun," said Eliza, who wished her older sister were there to join them. "But none of us are perfect, Peggy. And I'm glad I learned it now, while there was time and strength to repair the damage." She squeezed her sister's hand once again. "Believe me when I say there is no one I would rather be married to."

Peggy stared at her as if searching for signs of duplicity. At length she blinked, and Eliza saw wetness fill her sister's eyes. "I am glad," she said fiercely. "I so would have hated having to kill him."

Eliza nodded with pretend gravity. "I'll let you know if it becomes necessary."

Just then, the musicians picked up their instruments, and the wedding party began to march in. The reverend entered first, followed by the groomsmen — some of John's Columbia friends, including DeWitt Clinton — and then Alex and John appeared at the foot of the aisle. Though Eliza thought she detected a stiffening in the room, there was no more manifest indication of last fall's scandal. Her husband walked her brother to the altar, then took his place to the side with the groomsmen. The maids of honor were next, three lovely girls whom Eliza couldn't have named to save her life. *I really am getting old,* she thought.

Then the organ swelled, melding with the strings, and Betty appeared on Stephen's arm. The audience rose as the resplendent bride made her way down the aisle, a vision in the palest of yellows and white with a dozen feet of flowered silk trailing behind her like a summer meadow come to life. Before she had reached the head of the aisle, all the women were wiping away tears of joy, and not a few of the men.

"Oh, she looks absolutely divine!" Emma said, tapping Eliza on the shoulder from the pew behind.

"Almost as beautiful as you," Eliza said, dabbing at her eyes.

Emma blushed at this unexpected compliment even as Stephen presented his sister to the reverend and stepped to the side. The majesty of the wedding ceremony began, Reverend Provoost reading the sacred words with grace and gravitas as he began to bind the two souls together for all eternity. A picture of Eliza's own wedding day flashed in her mind as the words echoed in her ears. Yes, she told herself. For eternity . . .

At last Reverend Provoost came to the part of the ceremony when he asked if anyone objected to the union about to take place. He paused rather longer than one usually does at this juncture. Long enough that the crowd began to mill slightly, and then to murmur. And then, suddenly, someone spoke.

"Well, actually, I do," John said.

"Come to think of, I do, too," Betty echoed. The two were holding hands at this point and didn't let go. Indeed, their faces were beaming with joy.

The crowd gasped, though Reverend Provoost looked suspiciously unsurprised. Eliza did her level best to keep her eyes focused on the altar, though she could hardly see through the tears that had begun streaming down her face.

"Eliza!" Peggy hissed. "What is happening? Why are you smiling like a madwoman?"

"Do you now?" Reverend Provoost said at the altar. "Please, explain."

"It's not so much that we have an objection to our own union per se," Betty said. "It's just that it seems rather unfair that we should be getting married first when there is another couple here who had to endure the indignity of a flirtation —"

"Oh, let's not a call it a flirtation," John

said. "More like a manipulation," he continued, finding Eliza's eye and winking at his sister.

"Indeed," Betty assented. "And now they have been waiting months and months to be married while we have fairly cavorted to the altar."

"Now, now, Miss Van Rensselaer," Reverend Provoost admonished with a smile. "There is no need for such saucy language. We are still in church."

The assembled guests laughed uneasily. Though they sensed that the spectacle that was taking place at the head of the church was not wholly unexpected, they still weren't sure what was going on.

"Well," Reverend Provoost said now. "If I understand you correctly, you want to cede your place here to another couple?"

"What?" Betty exclaimed. "Heavens no! This wedding cost a fortune! My brother would kill me!"

More laughter from the audience. Even Stephen, who had gone white as a sheet, managed a little chuckle.

"No," John said, "what we were hoping

is that they could join us."

"Join you?" Reverend Provoost said, playing dumb. "You mean, I would marry the four of you?"

"Well, not to *one another,*" Betty said. "I mean, to each other, but as couples. Two by two, as it were."

"Like Noah's ark," John said.

"Hmph," Reverend Provoost said. "An unusual arrangement, but not without precedent. Well, who is the happy couple? For all we know they have no desire to be wedded today."

Eliza couldn't help herself. She had to turn around to see the look on their faces.

"Mr. Drayton Pennington," Betty sang out.

"And Miss Emma Trask," John said right after.

It seemed unbelievable to Eliza, but neither Drayton nor Emma seemed to have any idea that the spectacle taking place at the front of the church was about them. One moment they were looking around with the same expression of pensive curiosity on every other guest's face. The next their jaws were dropping open.

"Mrs. Hamilton!" Emma cried, turning toward her mistress.

"Mrs. Hamilton!" Drayton echoed, grabbing his fiancée's hand.

"But I haven't anyone to give me away!" Emma said. "And Drayton's family should be here!"

In answer, Eliza nodded at the back of the church. Drayton and Emma whirled around. There, at the foot of the altar, stood Prudence Schlesinger, Emma's aunt and last remaining relative, and, behind her, a handsome, rustic couple doing their best to look stoic as the tears streamed down their cheeks.

"Mama! Papa!" Drayton said, pushing his way through down the pew and dragging Emma behind him. "Joshua, Laura, Clarissa!" he added as three more figures appeared, followed by Michael Schlesinger, Pru's husband, and their adopted son, Augustus. "You're all here!"

Applause rang out as the happy couple rushed into the arms of their loved ones. Reverend Provoost waited until hugs and kisses had been exchanged all around, then called down the aisle.

"So does this mean you consent to join Mr. Schuyler and Miss Van Rensselaer at the front of the church?"

"I've got an extra set of rings, just in case you were wondering," John threw in, to much laughter.

Emma and Drayton separated from the family members and found each other. The beaming couple joined hands and looked deep into each other's eyes. Emma nodded, and a smile split Drayton's face from ear to ear. They turned and found Eliza's eyes first, and nodded at her, and then Alex's, and then finally they faced the white-robed figure at the far end of the aisle.

"We do!"

EPILOGUE

Final Midnight Rendezvous
Hamilton Grange
New York, New York
July 12, 1804

Time doesn't heal all wounds. Some fester, some scar. A mark remains, or an ache. Sometimes it's just a memory embedded in the flesh, the fingertips drifting to an arm or a leg and rubbing at a bruise that hasn't been visible in years . . .

But the body is almost always stronger than a single wound, and so it was with Alex and Eliza. The terrible summer of 1785 exposed certain weaknesses in their relationship, yet when it was over it also showed them that their spouse had reserves of strength to make up for their

544

own follies. Such is the difference between a happy marriage and divorce. Alex and Eliza's union survived, and with it came the understanding that love does not erase one's flaws. It stands side by side with them and even sometimes obscures them, which makes vigilance that much more necessary. Though they wavered from time to time — they were human — they never again lost their focus. For the next nineteen years, they prospered as individuals, and even more so as a couple and a family.

And just as they reinvented themselves, so did their nation. Rather than drift along as thirteen separate entities linked by geography and language and the shared memory of having left the Old World behind to start a new life, the former colonies united into a single amalgam of states, stronger together than they were apart. Their enduring strength owes more than a little debt to the visionary genius of Alexander Hamilton, who, though he never again held elected office, was nevertheless regarded by most of his contemporaries, including George Washington, as the primary architect of the Union. If James Madison was the initial force behind the Constitutional Convention of 1787, it was Alex who, in his *Federalist Papers,* made the case for the new document, explaining it to the American people in terms so articulate and forceful that they would continue to be consulted by legal scholars for more than two hundred years.

And even as his work on the Constitution finally gave the country a cohesive political character, his work as Secretary of the Treasury gave it the financial stability it needed to ensure its prosperity. He had already established the Bank of New York. Now he established the Bank of the United States, formulated the plan by which the federal government was able to borrow money, and oversaw the formation of the US Mint as well. As Alex's good friend was to say years later, "At the time when our government was organized, we were without funds, though not without resources. To call them into action, and establish order in the finances, Washington sought for splendid talents, for extensive information, and, above all, he sought for sterling, incorruptible integrity — all these he found in Hamilton."

While all this was going on, the Hamilton family also grew. Following the much-anticipated birth of Philip came seven more children: Angelica; Alexander, Jr.; James; John; William; and Eliza (not Elizabeth like her mother, just Eliza), culminating in 1802 in their youngest son also named Philip, because the firstborn of that name had died the year before at the tenderest of ages, not yet a man, though no longer a boy. By then Alex had retired from public life to be closer to his family and especially his wife. He worked with architect John Mc-Comb to design a home on an estate he purchased in northern Manhattan. Hamilton Grange, as the house came to be known, was smaller than the mansions built by the likes of Thomas Jefferson at Monticello, George Washington at Mount Vernon, and James Madison at Montpelier, but it had a delicacy of feature those other houses could never match, with a unique pair of oval parlors opening onto a pair of porches that gave grand views of the Hudson and Harlem Rivers, the

Palisades of New Jersey, and the rolling hills of the Bronx.

Motherhood kept Eliza busier than she would have realized. Like so many other well-meaning society wives, her charitable work became largely financial. She gave to her church and the arts and the poor, but her plans for a permanent orphanage for New York's foundlings and parentless children did not come into fruition until 1806. Despite the delay, the Orphan Asylum Society became the first private orphanage in New York City, and, under the name Graham Windham, continues to serve them to this day.

Yet through all their successes, individually and as a couple and a family, there remained in Alex that restless drive toward mortality — the same drive that had nearly gotten him killed at the Battle of Montauk and then again at Yorktown. It was as if there were some part of himself he needed to destroy. Perhaps it was the memory of his mother and father, the one who failed him through weakness, the other through selfishness. Perhaps it was the memory of his childhood self, dependent on the kindness of strangers yet never able to depend on them. Perhaps it was his need to win no matter the cost. Eliza didn't think he knew himself. But she could always see it, behind the ever more elegant frock coats and larger and larger houses.

Even when he was at the peak of his power as Secretary of the Treasury and leader of Federalist Party, she could see that her husband wanted to do more than influence American political life: He wanted to control it as an extension of his own personality. When he couldn't do that, he withdrew from public life, at least formally. But in private he still wrote constantly about American politics (and politicians) — letters, essays, pamphlets, some running to hundreds of pages — always piercingly, sometimes scathingly, on target.

It was one such letter that led finally to his long-postponed duel with Aaron Burr. Alex had campaigned extensively against Burr when the latter attempted to succeed to the governorship of New York State. Thanks to Alex's efforts, Burr was defeated, and Morgan Lewis took over from the corrupt George Clinton. A furious Burr accused Alex of slandering his name. Alex coyly professed ignorance of the charge, yet also refused to deny it. The code of chivalry being what it was, Burr felt compelled to issue a challenge. Alex accepted eagerly.

By that point, in fact, Alex had already been involved in half a dozen previous face-offs, including with Governor George Clinton and future president James Monroe. In all of those encounters, however, he had either refused to fire his weapon or shot it into the ground. The important thing was not to kill one's opponent, but to demonstrate that one's belief in one's honor and honesty was so great that one was willing to die to protect it. It was, in other words, a boasting ritual, more about impressing others than frightening one's rival: a grouse's puffed throat; a peacock's fanned tail; the bark of a caged dog. And yet the guns were real, and loaded, and were sometimes aimed before they were fired, and so it was that fateful night of July 11, 1804.

Dueling, though popular, was illegal in New York, but not in New Jersey. In keeping with the tradition of "plausible deniability," Alex's and Aaron's seconds stood with their backs to the two principals, so that they could honestly say they never saw the two men fire at each other on that moonlit riverbank in Weehawken. All that anyone could say with certainty was that two shots were fired, one by Alex, one by Aaron. Alex's shot passed several feet above Aaron's head. But Aaron's pierced Alex's abdomen and lodged in his spine, paralyzing him instantly, and killing him within a day.

Burr insisted that Alex had fired first. He testified that he had expected his rival to shoot into the ground according to custom, and when the bullet whizzed over his head, he said he fired back instinctively as anyone under attack would do. The courts believed him — enough to dismiss the charges of murder against him anyway, but some people were never satisfied. Why, after firing into the ground in every previous duel he had been in (or even refusing to fire), had Alex now decided to risk hitting his opponent? No doubt he had come to loathe the man, whose smarmy opportunism made him persona non grata in both state and national politics, but he had not been particularly fond of his previous opponents either. It didn't add up, and there were those who insisted that in fact it was Burr who fired first, deliberately killing Alex, and Alex's shot was nothing more than the reflex of a mortally wounded man. The suspicions were enough to destroy Burr's reputation, and the one-time vice president of the United States never again played a significant role in American politics. Indeed, he narrowly missed being hanged for treason and passed his last days in relative (if well-heeled) obscurity.

Eliza knew what Alex was up to, of course, though he had pretended he was merely going south to the city for business. For all his skill with words, her husband had always been a terrible liar. She was too late to stop him this time, and even she could not save him from himself in the end.

July 11th was a hot night, but the Grange, high on its hill and cooled by western breezes blowing across the Hudson, was chilly enough that Eliza needed a shawl around her shoulders. The children were asleep; the house was quiet. She sat in a soft chair in the bay window in the west-facing parlor, with its view all the way down to the river. She was thinking back to long-ago days, when the country had not yet been a country, when the island she had called home for the past twenty years had still been a British stronghold, and when Alex had been a handsome young soldier serving at the right hand of General Washington.

But what stood out most sharply in her mind was a frigid night in November 1777. Her mother had thrown a ball that night in an effort to find husbands for her three eldest daughters. The party had gone off brilliantly, and though it would be a few years before anyone realized it, Angelica and Peggy and Eliza had all secured their futures on that single evening, Angelica with John and Peggy with Stephen and Eliza with a ginger-haired boy from the islands who, it was said, had no past but the brightest of futures.

■ ■ ■ ■

"He looks a little . . . wan," Angelica whispered, holding up her lantern to shine it more brightly on his face.

"Angie!" Eliza hissed, waving her hand at the lantern. "You're going to wake him!"

It was the middle of the night — closer to cock's crow than the witching hour. The sisters had sneaked out of bed to catch one last peek at General Washington's chief aide-de-camp, who had been banished to the hayloft for the unforgiveable sin of being the bearer of bad news. They had shed their hooped ball gowns and jeweled slippers for nightdresses and heavy robes and a layer of woolen socks, and their lithe forms clung to either side of the ladder to the hayloft, from which came the sound of wet, heavy snores.

"Oh, please," Angelica said, giggling. "Did you see the way he was hitting Papa's cider at the end? That stuff packs more of a wallop than corn whiskey. He'll be lucky if he wakes up before noon."

Alex snored blissfully through this

prognostication. Little bubbles rose from his open mouth and popped silently, leaving his lips slick and shiny in the lantern light.

"Only I wish he weren't so cute," Eliza said. "It would be easier to dislike him."

"Eliza Schuyler!" Angie whirled on her sister. "Have you got an infatuation?"

"I most certainly do not!" Eliza insisted. "He said the most horrible things to Papa! What kind of traitor do you think I am?"

"Oh, you cannot blame him for that. He was just the army's errand boy. Papa will admit as much as soon as his temper cools." Angie sneaked a sly look at her sister. "You are crushing, aren't you?"

Eliza gave Angie a little smack. "You're terrible!" she said. But she couldn't keep the smile off her face as she stared at the sleeping boy. "They say he speaks French as well as English, knows numbers like a banker and strategy like Cincinnatus. He is the very model of what Papa says we are fighting for: a country in which one's talents will determine one's fate, not one's name or the circumstances of one's birth."

Angie stared at her blankly for a moment, then clapped her hand over her mouth to suppress a snort. *"Cincinnatus?"* she said when she could speak again. "Oh my word, if you don't marry this boy I'll never let you live this down!"

Eliza's cheeks went so red she could have sworn they outshone the lantern.

"I will likely never see him again," she protested weakly. "He is a soldier. There is probably a British musket ball out there with his name on it."

Angie rolled her eyes. "He is a secretary in an office in Morristown, New Jersey. If he gets shot in war, it will only be because he went looking for the bullet."

Eliza continued to stare at the boy's sleeping face. His skin was as fair as the frost-nipped grass outside, his hair nearly indistinguishable from the straw it was half buried in. His thin, taut body was curled into a tight curve beneath the woolen blankets, and one stockinged foot stuck out at the far end. There was a hole in the sock through which poked the shiny cap of a toenail. Eliza thought she had never seen anyone so innocent in her life. Her heart melted.

"Enough!" she whispered fiercely. "Let's have some fun!"

Angie's eyes narrowed. "You shock me, little sister. I thought pranks were more Peggy's speed." Then, grinning: "So? What did you have in mind?"

In answer, Eliza slipped down the ladder, leaving Angie no choice but to clamber after her. The two girls skipped through the barn to the chicken coop. Eliza's first thought had been to grab a few eggs and slip them beneath Alex's blanket for him to roll on in the middle of the night. But then she heard a disturbed clucking from the corner and looked over to see the coop's rooster squatting atop the nesting crates.

She looked at Angie, then at the rooster, then back at Angie. Angie nodded.

There was a burlap sack hanging from a nail. It was a simple matter to toss it over the sleepy rooster's head. He fussed for just a moment, then went silent as darkness engulfed him.

Suppressing their laughter, the two girls hurried back to the ladder and hauled their booty up to the top. Eliza unrolled the burlap gingerly, and the rooster half rolled, half tottered out, and immediately bedded down in the straw. Alex snored on, blissfully unaware of the feathered and clawed surprise that awaited him in the morning.

"I only wish we could stay to watch them fight," Eliza said with a giggle.

"My money's on Attila," Angie said. (As little girls, the sisters had named their rooster Attila the Hen, not caring that his gender didn't match his title.)

"Oh, I don't know," Eliza mused. "I think Colonel Hamilton might be more resourceful than we think." She stole one more look at the sleeping boy. "There is something so innocent about him as he sleeps," she whispered. "You'd never know he was so annoying when he was awake."

Angie groaned so loud that both Alex and Attila actually started, though neither woke up. "Come on, you crazy girl. Let's get you back in bed before you wake him up and he proposes to you right here. Is that the story you'd want to tell your children?"

Eliza didn't say anything as she scampered down after her sister, but in her head she was thinking: *I don't think that's such a bad story at all.*

AUTHOR'S NOTE

As those familiar with Alexander and Elizabeth Hamilton's story know, while Philip was indeed their first son, he was born in 1782, not 1785. Aside from that, the story is very much rooted in history, as Alex was a young lawyer building his reputation in New York at the time while Eliza devoted herself to their domestic affairs and social engagements.

Maria Reynolds is all too real, of course; however, the affair, which Alex famously admitted to in "The Reynolds Pamphlet," took place in 1791–92 in Philadelphia and did not come to light until 1792. Also, it appears highly likely that Maria entered into the affair with her husband's knowledge, with the express purpose of blackmailing Alex.

Eliza was pregnant with one of their

children while Alex was having the affair; their son John Church Hamilton was born in 1792.

John Schuyler and Elizabeth (Betty) Van Rensselaer did indeed marry. John did attend Columbia College. Whether he was a dashing playboy and Betty an irrepressible flirt and unapologetic snob is up for debate, but I like to imagine they were fun and amusing to know.

The Trinity case is based on factual events.

Eliza's orphanage was (and still is) real.

To the best of anyone's knowledge, Hamilton and Burr did not almost fight a duel in 1785. However, Hamilton admitted that he and Burr had faced off in one previous duel before the fatal one of 1804, while Burr said they faced off in two. The dates of the previous contest or contests are unknown.

Emma and Drayton are both completely made up. However, Emma was inspired by Fanny Antill, a motherless child the Hamiltons took in at the age of two and raised until she was twelve.

Astounding as it is, Eliza Hamilton

forgave her husband his indiscretion. She devoted her life to his legacy and died wearing a locket with a sonnet he'd written her during their early courtship that is quoted in the epigraph in the beginning of this book.

It is her forgiveness and her love that inspired me to write a story celebrating their union after my daughter wanted to know more about them.

Thank you for reading it.

— Melissa de la Cruz
New York, New York
June 25, 2018

ACKNOWLEDGMENTS

So many heartfelt thanks to everyone at Penguin, including my amazing editor, Kate Meltzer, and the girl bosses I'm so lucky to call my friends — Putnam publisher, Jen Klonsky; Penguin Young Readers president, Jen Loja; and the entire awesome team: Emily Romero, Erin Berger, Felicia Frazier, Jocelyn Schmidt, Elyse Marshall, Shanta Newlin, and Anne Heausler. So glad we are all Hamilfans! Thank you to Richard Abate and Rachel Kim, my 3Arts family. Thank you to everyone at Spilled Ink. Thank you to all my friends and family. Thank you to Mike and Mattie. Thank you to all my loyal readers.

ABOUT THE AUTHOR

Melissa de la Cruz is the #1 *New York Times, USA Today, Wall Street Journal, Los Angeles Times,* and *Publishers Weekly* internationally bestselling author of many critically acclaimed books for readers of all ages, including the Alex & Eliza trilogy, Disney's Descendants novels, the Blue Bloods series, and the Summer on East End series. Her books have sold over eight million copies, and the Witches of East End series became an hour-long television drama on the Lifetime network. Visit her at melissa-delacruz.com

The employees of Thorndike Press hope you have enjoyed this Large Print book. All our Thorndike, Wheeler, and Kennebec Large Print titles are designed for easy reading, and all our books are made to last. Other Thorndike Press Large Print books are available at your library, through selected bookstores, or directly from us.

For information about titles, please call:
(800) 223-1244

or visit our website at:
gale.com/thorndike

To share your comments, please write:
Publisher
Thorndike Press
10 Water St., Suite 310
Waterville, ME 04901